The Mind of Oliver C. Cox

African American Intellectual Heritage Series

PAUL SPICKARD

General Editor

The *Mind*
of
OLIVER C. COX

CHRISTOPHER A. McAULEY

UNIVERSITY OF NOTRE DAME PRESS

Notre Dame, Indiana

Library of Congress Cataloging-in-Publication Data
McAuley, Christopher.
The mind of Oliver C. Cox / Christopher McAuley.
p. cm. — (African American intellectual heritage series)
Includes index.
ISBN 0-268-03472-9 (cloth : alk. paper)
ISBN 0-268-03473-7 (pbk. : alk. paper)
1. Cox, Oliver C. (Oliver Cromwell), 1901–1974.
2. Sociologists—United States—Biography.
3. African American sociologists—Biography. 4. Sociology—
United States. I. Title. II. Series.

HM479.C69 M37   2003
301'.092—dc22

2003017885

∞ *This book is printed on acid-free paper.*

Contents

Acknowledgments

Like countless other writers, I am following the convention of taking sole credit for what is always a collective project. Of course, the cost of such conceit is that I must take full responsibility for its shortcomings. Be that as it may, in addition to the many scholars whose works appear in the notes, I have many people to thank for having been sounding boards, encouraging critics, and moral supporters. Those whom I have not forgotten to mention include: Kum Kum Bhavnani, the Carter family, Steven Dalton, G. Reginald Daniel, Douglas Daniels, Nicole Della Croce, John Foran, Kofi Buenor Hadjor, Herbert M. Hunter, Patricia Rago Kelley, the McAuley family, Claudine Michel, Catherine Nesci, Beth Osterbauer, Paul Reck, Paul Spickard, and Nancy Sterlin. For research assistance and for tracking down lesser-known Cox documents, I would like to thank Suzette Harrison, a graduate of University of California, Santa Barbara, and now, I might add, a novelist; Yvette Ford and Elizabeth Wilson of the Inman E. Page Library, Lincoln University; Patricia Bartkowski of the Walter P. Reuther Library, Wayne State University; and Kevin B.

Leonard of Northwestern University Library. For release time and a travel grant, I thank respectively the Office of the Chancellor, UC Santa Barbara, and the Institute for Social, Behavioral, and Economic Research at UC Santa Barbara. Finally, I must thank my editor, Jack Kirshbaum, for having made these pages more "reader friendly."

A sketch of many of the themes addressed in this book appeared as "Cox, the Caribbean, and Comparisons," in *The Sociology of Oliver C. Cox: New Perspectives,* edited by Herbert M. Hunter (Stamford, Conn.: JAI Press, 2000). A shorter version of chapter 2 was previously published as "Oliver C. Cox's Situations of Race Relations: The Interplay of Populations and Capital," in *Black Studies: Current Issues and Enduring Questions,* edited by Jacqueline Bobo and Claudine Michel (Dubuque, Iowa: Kendall-Hunt, 2001). And most of the material in chapters 4 and 5 is drawn from my article "The World System According to Oliver C. Cox: Insights, Omissions, and Speculations," *Review* (2000): 313–408.

This, my first book, I dedicate to my mother, Pamela Silveira McAuley, to whom I owe more than words can express. Slick, be patient. The next one will be a tribute to you.

Introduction

During his lifetime and thereafter, the Trinidadian-born sociologist Oliver Cromwell Cox (1901 –74) was frequently taken for either what he never was or ever claimed to be. Some thought that he was born in the United States when, in fact, he grew up in the Caribbean;[1] many branded him a "Marxist" though he repeatedly disavowed that label;[2] and others were not aware that he was trained as a sociologist.[3] All these mistaken identities suggest, at least, one thing: Oliver Cox defies categories. His various aliases also suggest that we are in need of a detailed treatment of his life and work in order to "set the record straight."[4]

In the course of roughly a thirty-five-year academic career, Cox authored more than forty scholarly articles and five significant books in the areas of race relations theory, economic history (or world system's analysis), political economy, sociological theory, and historical sociology. The books are *Caste, Class, and Race* (1948), *The Foundations of Capitalism* (1959), *Capitalism and American Leadership* (1962), *Capitalism as a System* (1964), and *Race Relations: Elements and Social Dynamics*

(1976). Yet, in spite of his long list of academic achievements and, more important, the depth of his thought, relatively few scholars in the social sciences either know of or refer to Cox's scholarship. On the rare occasions that Cox's work is cited at all, it is usually done for one of two reasons: either for his convincing refutation of the caste interpretation of pre–civil rights movement southern race relations or for his "Marxist" interpretation of modern race relations. Certainly, Cox did address these themes (specifically, in *Caste, Class, and Race,* his best-known book), but, as will become clear as we proceed, these are only two of many. I believe that Cox's neglect is, in part, due to lack of a descriptive and analytical survey of his contributions to social theory. It is my hope that this study will serve to revive interest in the work of this important scholar.

My first approach to Cox's intellectual trajectory is shaped by the belief that his Caribbean upbringing is essential to an understanding of the development of his thought. Though this perspective is hardly remarkable, it is arguably not one shared by many of those who are familiar with his work. In the course of my research on Cox, I have been repeatedly surprised by the number of American scholars who either fail to consider, or dismiss by omission, his Caribbean background and by those Caribbean scholars who largely interpret him as an African American. It is extremely difficult to make sense of his unorthodox perspectives on race relations theory, the structure of the world capitalist system, and on movements for social change without taking into account his Caribbean past. Another way of stating this is that Cox was a "natural" social comparativist. Furthermore, I contend that Cox's Caribbean frame of reference is precisely the component of his analyses that makes his vantage point so important and timely: his is an early "Third World" perspective on the most pressing problems of our time—capitalist globalization, ethnic conflict, and the future of social relations.

My second approach to the project is based on the phases that I have detected in Cox's intellectual journey. Before his arrival in Chicago in 1919, Cox had a fairly typical, middle-class, West Indian childhood in the Caribbean; that is, his family was by no means affluent but his parents put a premium on being "respectable." His first ten years in Chicago did little to fundamentally alter his middle-class outlook on his new surroundings, but they did reveal to him that "race relations" of the American kind differed greatly from those he knew

in Trinidad. As I see it, 1929 was a critical year in Cox's intellectual formation not only because it marked the beginning of the Great Depression and the general calling into question of the viability of capitalism, but also because in that year he was stricken with polio; for
the remainder of his life he was forced to rely on crutches. It is my
contention that the upshot of these roughly simultaneous events
was to drive Cox to rethink his middle-class beliefs and aspirations
(one of which was to become a lawyer) and to recognize that one's
social situation is not always the result of one's choosing. At this juncture, Cox began both to embrace the causes of those less fortunate
than himself and to devote his intellectual energies to a comprehension of the social forces guiding the lives of poor people. Toward that end, he took a master's degree in economics and a doctorate in sociology, both at the University of Chicago. In spite of the
general reputation of the school and of its department of sociology
in particular, Cox did not find the university seminars intellectually
up to the task of grappling with the many social forces of the 1930s.
It was at this juncture that Cox turned to European (particularly
German) sociologists and economists—Max Weber, Karl Marx,
Werner Sombart, and Joseph Schumpeter—for bolder theories of
the modern social world. The influence of these thinkers on Cox's
understanding of sociological analysis is most clear in his *Caste, Class,
and Race,* written while teaching at both Wiley College and Tuskegee
Institute from 1937 to 1948. Soon thereafter, however, Cox turned
his attention to the origins and reproduction of the capitalist world
economy, due in no small part, I imagine, to the fact that the global
proletarian movement of the 1930s which he so lauded in *Caste,
Class, and Race,* had largely petered out by the 1950s. Now it was
time to come to terms with the staying power of the capitalist world
economy, which just withstood perhaps its greatest crisis to date.
The result of this new focus was his trilogy on capitalism, which appeared between 1959 and 1964. It was written during his long tenure
at Lincoln University in Jefferson City, Missouri, where he spent the
better part of his academic career (1949–70).

In the last phase of his intellectual development, Cox returned
to a middle-class cultural conservatism (all the while declaring his
commitment to socialist principles) in response to the emergence of
the Black Power movement. His objection to the movement was based
on two convictions: one, that assimilation into, not ethnic nationalism

against, mainstream American society should be the striving of black Americans, since the process of assimilation transforms American society itself; and two, that the ideologues of Black Power were little more than ghetto thugs who were now playing politics. In short, Cox was both elitist and antipluralist. These sentiments are most clearly expressed in his posthumously published *Race Relations.*

I have divided the work into four parts. The first (chapter 1) chronicles Cox's life in both Trinidad and the United States, high-lighting what he considered the most relevant social patterns and events of the twentieth century. The second part (chapters 2 and 3) provides an exposition of Cox's typology of race relations through extensive discussions of representative cases as well as analyses of his perspective on the anti-Asian movement in nineteenth-century Cali-fornia and of what he considered the social differences between black and Jewish experiences in the West. The third (chapters 4 and 5) is an exegesis of Cox's theory and history of the development of capi-talism from its origins in thirteenth-century Venice to its twentieth-century leader, the United States. The last part (chapter 6) focuses on Cox's theory of social transformation, underscoring his rejection of ethnic nationalism in favor of Soviet Union–inspired socialism.

These pages are not meant to be the final word on Cox the man and social scientist. Even if that had been my inspiration, its achieve-ment would have proven elusive. For what the dean of Cox scholars, Herbert Hunter, told me some five years ago has also been my find-ing: that Cox's personal papers and the bulk of his unpublished writ-ings are still unavailable. Apparently, his literary executor has taken their whereabouts to his grave. At best, then, the student of Cox's life and ideas must rely on his already published work, the secondary material about it, the scant pieces of information about Cox in the possession of the libraries of Northwestern, Lincoln, and Wayne State Universities and of Wiley College, and on the scholarly works that address the topics about which Cox also wrote, as the main sources of information about him. As a result of these limitations, this work can only be interpretive, not definitive.

On this matter of interpretation I might also add that while I share with other Cox scholars a profound admiration for what I think no exaggeration to call his genius, I am not one who believes that he could write no wrong. Quite the contrary. As the reader will discover, I disagree with a number of Cox's positions although I believe that

I understand the reasons why he took them. I have tried my best, nevertheless, not to allow those disagreements to color my suppositions of how he arrived at certain sociopolitical conclusions. Moreover, I have also seen fit on occasion to speak normatively or prescriptively about Cox's approaches to various themes, injecting my opinion of what I believe he should have considered or posited about the issues he tackled. This sort of endeavor runs the risk of engaging in hypothetical or, at worst, counterfactual arguments. However, my choice is made on two grounds: one, that Cox himself did not shy away from writing normatively about courses of social interpretation and action; and two, that I have tried to remain consistent with Cox's own theories and social examples when I have done so. In any event, the success or failure of my prescriptive remarks is ultimately the reader's decision.

Finally, to those readers interested in the intellectual history of the African diaspora generally and in Caribbean intellectual history specifically, I would suggest that this study and Cox's own works be read along with those by or about C. L. R. James and George Padmore (Malcolm Nurse).[5] What is remarkable about these three men is that they were all from Trinidad, were born at roughly the same time (Cox and James in 1901, Padmore in 1902 or 1903), and became key left figures in the Atlantic world from the third and fourth decades of last century until the time of their respective deaths. Read together, their lives and writings provide a representative range of the concerns and passions (e.g., racial pride, anti-imperialism, social justice, Caribbean and African history) of their intellectual forefathers—Henry Sylvester Williams and John Jacob Thomas in particular—and those that would inspire future Caribbean intellectuals from Eric Williams to Walter Rodney.

1

The Molding of a Mind

Generally speaking, modern western politics is the progeny of unlikely parents: the French Revolution and the English Industrial Revolution. Whereas the one taught the children that all are equal before the law, the other insisted that inequality is the inevitable outcome of the capitalist economic order. Almost without exception, the various political platforms, ideologies, and parties which emerged in the nineteenth and twentieth centuries have attempted to reconcile these seemingly irreconcilable principles.

As paradoxical as it may seem, it should not be forgotten that these political developments owe their beginnings to the twin revolutions: it was precisely because one revolution professed legal equality that the socioeconomic outcome of the other revolution became open to political negotiation. Accordingly, the sociopolitical philosophies to which the children adhered was so varied that it was easy to believe that they had not been raised in the same household. The conservative child (perhaps the first born), though satisfied with how the advancing economic order does not "seriously contest the social, cultural, and ideological pre-eminence of the old ruling class,"[1] looks longingly to a pre–French Revolution political arrangement. The maternal twins—the socialist and anarchist children—believe that the only way to uphold the mother's legacy is by committing patricide. The nationalist child contends that the only way to resolve the social dilemma to which his father's legacy gives rise is by appealing to an alternative social principle such as to the "nation" or to the "race." And the liberal child (perhaps the last born) maintains that the apparent contradictions in his parents' philosophies can be resolved by the effective management of the market.

Throughout most of the nineteenth century and even the first third of the twentieth century, continental European politics was dominated by conservative (frequently monarchist) personalities, with liberal and socialist political movements or parties jockeying for position in what political space they were able to create, until the contest was won by the liberals in the wake of the fascist bid for world power. The Anglo-Saxon world of politics hardly differed from the continental variant in that Amerindians, Africans, African Americans, Mexicans, Asians, most Catholics and Jews, and the bulk of working people generally were not considered full-fledged citizens by their self-proclaimed social superiors and their agents.

Thus, if people of color, Catholics, Jews, and the mass of working-class people were largely considered beyond the pale of liberal society in the domestic arena until well into the twentieth century, then it is hardly surprising that in the formal and informal Anglo-Saxon empires, conservatism, when not outright fascism, was the political philosophy guiding colonial policy. And when one considers what an imperial power demands of its colonies and neocolonies—property, labor, loyal consumers, and no hint of economic nationalism on the part of either local labor or capital—the Anglo-Saxon overseas political agenda could not have been otherwise. Of course, there have been few imperial centers that have presented their multifaceted designs to their subject populations in such crude terms; hegemony is ensured when political-economic purposes are refashioned as cultural superiority. This myth not only served to keep nationalism at bay in the colonies but also promoted nationalism in the imperial centers. If as Walter Russell Mead maintains, "history is filled with examples of . . . societies that became more democratic as their empires expanded,"[2] then working people in those centers had all the more reason to support the empire.

Clearly, then, the twin revolutions did not herald the same sociopolitical changes in Europe's and North America's colonies and neo-colonies as they did (for select populations) in Europe and North America themselves. And we would be mistaken to believe that it was the Industrial Revolution that singularly undermined the principles of the French Revolution; had it been left to either the Gironde or to Napoleon, slavery would have remained (as it did in France's other Caribbean possessions) in what would become the Republic of Haiti. "When the French Revolution was made in the name of 'Liberty, Equality, Fraternity,' commented Walter Rodney, "it did not extend to black Africans who were enslaved by France in the West Indies and the Indian Ocean. Indeed, France fought against the efforts of those people to emancipate themselves, and the leaders of their bourgeois revolution said plainly that they did not make it on behalf of black humanity."[3] Consequently, in neither revolutionary center was the protest particularly loud against the continued use of unfree labor (be it enslaved or indentured) in the colonies. Thus, in 1797, when England took Trinidad from a Spain preoccupied with France's revolutionary army, the British government's claim that this measure (and others like it) was designed to contain the menace of French Republicanism in the Caribbean could not have been more transparently self-serving; it knew that outside of the brief reign of "The Terror," there were few French revolutionaries committed to uprooting the colonial social order as they had done away with feudalism at home. In any event, the threat of the French Revolution could not justify British rule in Trinidad for the next 165 years. But to a youngster growing up in colonial Trinidad in the early decades of the twentieth century, the preceding remarks would have seemed like mere "old people's talk"—interesting perhaps, but referring to events both remote and complicated. In time, however, Oliver Cromwell Cox would devote most of his intellectual energies toward understanding and explaining the significance of these and related themes. What he came up with is the subject of this book.

Cox the Younger

Though the details of Cox's early years in Trinidad are wanting, we still have enough secondary information about the social forces then at work in the island to be able to form an idea about his life there. What we do know for certain is that he was born 24 August 1901 in Trinidad's capital, Port-of-Spain, to Virginia Blake and William Raphael Cox. He was one of his father's ten children, five of whom were born to Virginia Blake, and the other five to Oliver's stepmother, Louisa Cox. "Very little is known about either" Virginia or Louisa Cox, reports our most knowledgeable Cox scholar, Herbert Hunter, "except that they performed the traditional roles of housewives and were very supportive of the family."[4] We do know more about the public occupations of Cox's father. After having "work[ed] for a time as a captain of a revenue schooner," that is, "a government ship which sailed around the island enforcing its sea laws and regulations," he took a job as a "customs and excise officer, collecting duties and checking for contraband and pilferage for the British colonial authorities." In colonial Trinidad, this line of work solidly placed a fair-skinned person of color in the ranks of the middle class and, in this case, afforded William Raphael not only the Cox home in Port-of-Spain, but also a "small estate in Tabaquite Village in central Trinidad,"[5] which served as both the family's summer home and cocoa farm.

The extent of the emotional ties that developed between Oliver and members of his family are matters for which we have no immediate information. In light of some of the recollections on the part of Cox's relatives, though, we have reason to believe that Cox never formed intimate relationships with members of his family. This tendency toward formality in interpersonal relationships was probably less a reflection of something distinct about Cox's personality than it was of the nature of social relationships in the immediate post-Victorian era. Apparently, Cox learned to maintain a certain emotional distance from those around him from the two dominant male figures in his early life: his father and his uncle, Reginald Vidale. For his part, William Raphael was a demanding father, particularly about the academic achievement of his children: he was not above "requiring them to routinely awaken in the early hours of the morning, take cold showers and study before going to school."[6] Although it is doubtful that Reginald Vidale went to the same lengths as his brother-in-law to see to it that his and his neighbor's children excelled academically, as headmaster of St. Thomas Boys' School it is highly likely that he also was an exacting taskmaster. Nevertheless, according to Vidale's son, Aldwin, Cox relished even this tough love, if not from his father, certainly from his uncle: "He [Cox] kept telling me that his uncle was so sound, so dignified; you notice how choice his language is—and then he would laugh and say what a disciplinarian! At times, I was a bit baffled at his attitude toward his uncle. He seemed to accept his uncle's wrath without question. Whatever his uncle said was okay. Oliver appeared to me that he was focusing all along on his uncle as a guideline for his achievements."[7]

As a professor, Cox expected his students to engage in the role play between mentor and pupil that he knew in his youth. Usually unaware of both his past and of the terms of tough love (that is, admiration gained through proof of sacrifice), many of his students found him unnecessarily demanding and pedantic.

However, in spite of his best efforts to model himself after his uncle by excelling in school, Cox's academic success would only come later in the United States. The fact that he did not win a "free place" in either Queens Royal or St. Mary's College (Trinidad's top two high schools) suggests that he was not among the top graduates at St. Thomas Boys' School and therefore ineligible to sit for the "island scholarship" exam, which allowed a handful of British West Indian colonials to study at Oxford University. Instead, after graduating from St. Thomas, Cox "attended for a short time a local agricultural college and worked as a clerk in a dry goods department store, where he brought dolls and rackets home to repair and sold them back to his employer for a small profit."[8] At this rate, Cox was fast descending Trinidad's narrow social ladder. Nonetheless, Cox would spend his whole life in higher education, and so it is appropriate to address what education meant in colonial Trinidad and why it meant what it did. More specifically, why did William Raphael and Reginald Vidale insist that the young Oliver be college educated, if not in England, then in the United States?

Education in a Colonial Society

Colonial Trinidad's educational system functioned ideally to maintain the colonial social order. The same, of course, could be said of many an educational system. In the case of colonial Trinidad, it was imperative that the educational system served at least three ends: one, the structure of a colonial economy; two, an undemocratic political system; and three, a class structure that was closely correlated to skin color. Overall, England's educational designs for Trinidad fared best in the first instance, worst in the second, and somewhere in-between in the third. For what Her Majesty's imperial government learned in due course was that what it hoped to achieve through colonial education and how colonials used it were not always one and the same.

Europe's colonial world was, from its inception, designed to benefit the home economy in several ways: by mining and cultivating, as cheaply as possible, a range of commodities in high demand in Europe and elsewhere; by providing a protected market for Europe's manufactured commodities the production of which was actively discouraged in colonial areas; and by creating and maintaining the commercial institutions—e.g., shipbuilding, insurance, banking— to sustain the first two aims. Thus, like Britain's colonial peoples throughout the world, Trinidadians fulfilled their obligations to the metropole by cultivating sugar and cocoa and by drilling for oil (the island's leading export as of the 1920s) in the years of Cox's youth. Some figures are worth noting. When Cox was sixteen, Trinidad's sugar production grew more than 60 percent from its yearly average of 40,000 tons since the 1890s.[9] In that same decade, Trinidad's cocoa harvest averaged better than 56 million pounds to lead all of the island's exports. Finally, in the year that Cox left home for the United States, Trinidad's annual oil production neared the two million–barrel mark.[10] Production figures, however, do not convey even a fraction of the physical energy that various labor processes exact from workers; statistics reveal little about the lived experiences of work. Lost in these figures are the punishing labor routines, pathetic wages, the disease-ridden quarters, scant material possessions, and "widespread malnutrition."[11] Nor do they capture the fact that apart from rum-aided repartee and joke-telling, music making and dancing, religious release and Carnival, the only consolation for pressing on day after day under a relentless sun was the knowledge that one worked as a "free" person (excepting, of course, indentured Indian Trinidadians), however qualified the adjective in practice.

From this brief sketch, we can infer what subjects would be avoided in the island's primary and secondary schools: economics, politics, and sociology. The "usual Cambridge subjects—Geometry, Latin, Greek, French, History, Algebra and English Literature"[12]—did not address issues of labor, political power, or the structure of England's colonial empire.[13] Cox, C.L.R. James, George Padmore, and Eric Williams, among other Trinidadians, would devote their energies toward the chronicling of what the colonial curriculum so glaringly omitted.

This evasion in the colonial curriculum did serve well the goals of those who were fortunate enough to attend school. Of these we can name at least two (which were hardly separable): one, what it is no exaggeration to call "self-preservation"; and two, what we may call, to borrow a Barbara Ehrenreich title, the "fear of falling." Each warrants a brief elaboration.

If "self-preservation" is too strong a term, then we can substitute any phrase that captures the idea that engagement in the colonial economy was generally bad for one's health. The list of urban and particularly rural hardships listed earlier was not meant to paint an unduly damning portrait of English colonialism in Trinidad or elsewhere, but rather to begin where Eric Williams began his autobiography, *Inward Hunger*.[14] Williams included that social portrait both to describe the society into which he was born and to argue that only political independence from England could change those conditions. His autobiography—or better still, his life—bore witness to the paradox that only by securing an education could one escape being subjected to those very social conditions. Similarly, Williams's autobiography underscores another motive—the maintenance or improvement of one's social standing—for pursuing an education in colonial Trinidad. As the son of a clerk, Williams (like Cox), discovered from an early age that without a diploma, if he remained in Port-of-Spain, he would either join the ranks of the service workers, artisans, or the partially employed or, if he migrated to the countryside, the ranks of the modest cocoa farmers. Either way, the prospects for enjoying a rewarding life (both materially and psychologically) were not promising. Again, the British education system in Trinidad suited equally well those who did not want colonial realities to be examined as those who had reason to run from them.

Nevertheless, education in a colonial setting presented its own set of sociopolitical problems. Although the process of training young minds often validated and justified the colonial social order, those who had mastered the literary canon that at one time separated the culture of the colonizer from that of the colonized were fundamentally calling into question the political justification of colonial rule. The intellectual trajectory of this paradox was not difficult to discern: when the colonized had successfully mastered the same educational standards which theoretically supplied the colonizer with the "right" to rule the colonized, the central pillar of colonialism would be dislodged. One of the earliest and perhaps best-known expressions of this political tension did not take the form of a movement but rather of a book. John Jacob Thomas's *Froudacity*—a scathing critique of James Anthony Froude's *The English in the West Indies, or, The Bow of Ulysses*—was proof positive that a black Trinidadian trained in English schools could intellectually surpass one of England's own. The political implications of Thomas's successful ridicule bear repeating: if Froude was representative of the best and brightest of late-nineteenth-century Oxbridge, then by virtue of his scholarly failings as evidenced in the book, the English had, in a sense, effectively forfeited the right to rule in the West Indies in the minds of Thomas and others. This was a case of publishing to perish.

Fear of the actual and potential Thomases provides one reason why Trinidad remained a crown colony throughout its history under British rule in spite of the numerous attempts in the nineteenth and twentieth centuries to reform the island's political status. By its practice as of 1831, crown colony government meant that England's appointed representative—the governor—named "all the members of the [legislative] council" and "could enact any measure he wished by commanding the official members . . . to vote for him." "Official members" of the legislative council were the "leading officers of the local government," while unofficial members were the "private citizens nominated by the governor" from among the island's largest landowners. And as far as its mechanics were concerned, the council "was authorized to enact Ordinances, to which both the governor and the Colonial Office in London had to assent, and after 1831 this became the usual method of making laws in Trinidad, although the British government kept its right to legislate by Order in Council."[15]

Trinidad had been designated a crown colony after the island was taken from Spain in 1797 in order to deny propertied people of color the right to participate in local government—either as an

electorate or as candidates—since a property requirement for enfranchisement would not have disqualified all of them. It was only
after the English government had more or less successfully both
quarantined the Caribbean from the aspirations unleashed by the
French Revolution and facilitated the expansion of the landhold-
ings of English planters in Trinidad that it could ensure the political
neutralization of the remaining propertied Trinidadians of color on
the basis of higher property standards for entry into political life.
Apparently, however, even property requirements did not provide
in the mind of the English government sufficient insurance against
the potential political might of Trinidadians of color; no political
reform measure was offered to them until popular pressure forced
the government's hand in the course of the First World War. Before
then it would have risked little to have made minor political concessions to the island's propertied or educated people of color, for they
too shared the conviction that property requirements should serve
as the basis of enfranchisement. Why were they of that opinion? For
two ostensible reasons: one, in many cases, they were property owners themselves; and two, in most cases, they believed, like the planter
elite, that only property owners could make intelligent decisions for
the good of the entire community. Here, then is a prime example of
how an educational system (both formal and informal) could simultaneously promote political radicalism (or, better said, reformism)
and conservatism. We shall see this intellectual tension at work in
the life and ideas of Oliver Cox.

Today, even in those countries where access to primary and secondary schools has long been a right, securing an education is still
largely a privilege. Money and status continue to afford some students more educational opportunities than others as well as to enhance their academic performance. In colonial societies these tendencies were the rule. Elite opinion in both the metropolitan centers
and in the colonies maintained that those children who were inevitably going to work with their hands required little if any schooling particularly if it was generally believed that the receipt of a cer-
tificate rendered the student "too good" for manual labor. Therefore,
if any educational program was appropriate for the children of
Trinidadian agricultural workers and artisans, so the elitist argument prescribed, it was the kind that "inculcated . . . [t]he dignity of
labor" and instructed students "how to use tools."[16]

Apart from the biases of teachers and the curriculum, the best way of ensuring the association between a secondary school diploma and a student's eligibility for a white-collar job was to price such education beyond the means of Trinidadians. Thus the tuitions of Queen's Royal and St. Mary's Colleges were artificially inflated. This mechanism also ensured that the complexions of the student bodies at both high schools remained the same as those of their planter, merchant, professional, and civil servant parents—beige with a hint of tan. These tan or "colored" faces, in addition to the possibly darker handful of scholarship students, were essential to the normally smooth functioning of the educational system, for they served to obscure the social formula that education is a privilege and privilege is frequently justified by one's education. And herein lay the power of the colonial education system to maintain the social order.

There is a similar conservatism in the institutions of education: an educational system should promote the intellectual growth of the student beyond the knowledge of her or his teachers, but these instructors steadfastly insist on the conformity to traditional or accepted standards of excellence, at least before the student ventures out into the unknown. The teacher has reason (and the mechanisms) to resist this future. In a colonial society where the class structure was markedly truncated, both teachers and students had an interest in cultivating the conservative tendencies of the prevailing educational system; between the mass of struggling rural and urban workers and the club of large planters, merchants, and government officials, there was not only little room for an educated class to find its niche, but by remaining small it maintained both its privileged position (relative to those below) and the social hierarchy (managed by those above) without threatening either one by pushing to increase its numbers. In short, like other privileged Trinidadians whose parents could afford to make the necessary financial sacrifices to pay for their children's education, Cox was a passive participant in what Eric Williams aptly termed the "Anglicanisation of the colony."[17]

Given the socioeconomic structure of post-Victorian Trinidad, educated Trinidadians could not constitute a middle class in the European sense of the term—that is by virtue of its property, political weight, and income—but rather one based on "two essential criteria," according to the era's most knowledgeable scholar:

an occupation which involved no manual labor, and the command of European, or British, culture, especially the ability to speak and write correct English. . . . Members of the colored and black middle class, then, were distinguished from the black masses by their education, their familiarity with European literary culture, and their "white-collar" jobs. . . . They were not part of the ruling class, but their literacy and intellectual skills, which they valued highly, clearly marked them off from the black and East Indian masses.[18]

As both an unorthodox and relatively recently constituted class, Trinidad's middle class of color was highly conscious of the culture that should accompany their intellectual training. It included an inordinate emphasis on impeccable public presentation, exemplary hard work, speech that never resorted to vulgarity either in pronunciation or subject, unfailing religious attendance and mindfulness, conservative dress, and a tastefully decorated home. In short, a local imitation of British landed and bourgeois cultures. "They attached so much importance to culture," maintains Bridget Brereton, "because they had no other valuable and valued possessions to hold on to."[19] The hope was that through "proper" bearing, one could rise "above the mass of poverty, dirt, ignorance, and vice which surrounded the islands of black lower middle-class respectability like a sea ever threatening to engulf them." And as C. L. R. James went on to say, "Respectability was not an ideal, it was an armor."[20] Little wonder then that appearances would assume such importance in post-Victorian Trinidad.

Thus, the colonial educational system pulled those it trained in two directions: one looking forward, the other looking back; one inclined toward radicalism (loosely defined), the other toward conservatism. And this built-in dialectic or negotiation of contradictions within the schooling process was reinforced by an otherwise promising development in post-Victorian Trinidad: black and colored primary school teachers (like Reginald Vidale) were now shaping the minds of black and colored students (like Oliver Cox). Teaching, in that period of Trinidad's history, was "one of the few 'respectable' white collar jobs available to young men from humble backgrounds, who had no chance of a university education and so could not enter the more favored professions of law and medicine."[21] A promising development, yes, because these teachers were models after whom students of color could fashion themselves; a problematic one, however, because these models fashioned themselves after explicitly conservative "originals." I believe that from as early as his teenage years Cox was torn between the two ideological camps inherent in the educational process. In later years he would be able to write critically on the subject of colonial bourgeois pretensions, for example, but he would never shed some of those same preoccupations from his worldview. Though unapologetically left-leaning politically, Cox was unwilling to recognize the class bias in what he took to be "proper" behavior even when discussing and, at times, encouraging, political protest against socioeconomic exploitation. This unwillingness to purge himself of middle-class adolescent "baggage" would greatly impede his ability to respond creatively to new social forces and energies, particularly those embodied in ethnic-racial movements like the Black Power movement. Unlike either C. L. R. James, who had recourse to cricket and calypso as means of discovering "plebian habits" (as one of his biographers so aptly put it)[22] or George Padmore, who had been introduced to alternative black thought by his independent-minded father,[23] we have no indication that Cox was exposed to these perspectives as a youth in Trinidad. These social limitations would reappear in Cox's academic-cum-political positions.

Like others both before and after him, Cox framed the modern history of the Americas within the larger tableau of settler societies. These are societies reconfigured by the colonization and settlement of foreign populations wherein the indigenous and unfree populations are economically, socially, and culturally subordinated to those settlers. Thus, settler societies automatically create and are made viable by racialized divisions of labor. As we have already remarked, in colonial Trinidad this pattern of settler societies could be seen in the faces of agricultural and domestic workers and artisans, while the island's "commercial establishments were almost exclusively owned by whites in this period, and even the 'clerks' or store assistants employed in these firms tended to be young white Creoles or Britons."[24] However, unlike most other settler societies (save those in southern Africa and a few other select cases), those in the Americas gave rise to another social development: the differentiation of the progeny of foreign and indigenous populations (or the foreign and unfree populations) from either of their parents. We call or have called these people by a variety of names: *mestizos, mulattos, pardos, ladinos*. We also valorize these "new people" more than we do less visibly multiracial Amerindians or Blacks. As Cox would learn while living in the United States, the social status of these bi- or multiracial populations would vary with both the size of the population of primarily European descent as well as with the demands of a capitalist division of labor. In the United States, their social status was only negligibly better than those of their darker relations, whereas in the Caribbean their numbers dominate the middle class of color. (Of course, we must still be mindful that in both societies "[t]here are many fair-skinned persons who are not upper class, and many dark-skinned persons who are.")[25] We will detail these different "situations of race relations," as Cox called them, in a later chapter. Suffice it to say here that complexion or color distinctions particularly within the Trinidadian middle class were marked enough to evoke some vivid descriptions from Cox:

> The colored people as a whole tend to become perennially occupied with the problem of degrees of pigmentation and lament the luck of their dusky progenitors. Brothers of different color may become estranged, and dark parents may keep themselves out of the way of their lighter children. Indeed, children may implicitly disavow their darker parents, while lighter persons who have been awarded in social status for their lightness may become rigid and even fierce at any attempt of darker persons to recognize them publicly and familiarly. This constricting sense of color shame tends to be heightened when the relationship is under the surveillance of white people. Lighter persons seek to group themselves and to clique darker aspirants into oblivion. In fact, true friendship between lighter and darker young people is scarcely possible, for even schoolboys evaluate the color of their pals.[26]

Were some of these examples taken from Cox's own experiences or were they merely observations and recollections of what had happened both publicly and privately to neighbors and friends? The answer is probably a combination of the two. What is certain is that some of Cox's most impassioned and perceptive lines are devoted to the discussion of the pathologies resulting from these social distinctions and that few, if any, have been the Caribbean intellectuals whose reminiscences fail to mention the pervasiveness of color consciousness in the region. However, if we trust C. L. R. James's judgment on the subject that the "people most affected by this are people of the middle class,"[27] then we have no reason to doubt that complexion consciousness infected the Cox household. Moreover, Cox the sociologist, like Frantz Fanon the psychiatrist, would have argued that it is the rare individual who escapes unscathed from the exigencies of his or her social world.

This pattern of social stratification based on complexion has its roots in the era of the enslavement of African people whereby white men initiated sexual relationships (frequently by force, at times by consent, always by calculation) with women of some African descent, both enslaved and free. On occasion, these men saw to the education of their children or bequeathed to them some property; on rarer occasions, they even freed them if their mothers were enslaved. As a result of these practices throughout the Americas during the period of race-based slavery, the numbers of mixed-race people who were free and even property owners was substantially greater than those of more visibly black people in both categories. Even if their numbers were modest in relation either to the total number of enslaved mulattos or to the total number of enslaved people of color in colonial Trinidad, as elsewhere in the Americas, their presence fueled the association made throughout the hemisphere between complexion and class. Some eighty years after the end of racial enslavement in England's Caribbean colonies, stratification based on color was nearly as strong in Trinidad as it had been under slavery: light-skinned people of color (like Cox himself) continued to dominate the ranks of propertied and educated non-Whites.

If this pattern of social stratification had any one positive effect, it was to temper the notion that mental capacity (an important index to the racist) was determined by any strict definition of racial membership. At most, the racist could claim that the intellectual heights reached by some mixed-race people were due to the genetic contributions of their white foreparents. Yet, even this admission was an attenuation (albeit a begrudging one) of uncompromising racist thinking; for it conceded that the genes or "blood" (as many would inaccurately term it) of people of pronounced African descent did not automatically degenerate the blood or genetic structure of their progeny. Ultimately, in the Caribbean context at least, the erstwhile racial argument was gradually replaced by a cultural one in the post-emancipation era: that Europeans are culturally superior to Africans and Amerindians, who could copy only their cultural practices. Dark-skinned colonials could become culturally British, for example, though never as "authentically" as the "real" embodiment of the culture in question, that is, as English as the (white) Englishman from England. Of course, the cultural racist could not entertain the possibility that his culture would one day no longer be an object of envy but rather one of pity. Such were some of Cox's observations on the workings of race that he would take to the United States.

Impressions of the Windy City

When Cox came to the United States, he chose to settle in Chicago rather than in New York, which was the final destination of no less than half of the roughly 90,000 black immigrant aliens who officially entered the country between 1913 and 1926.[28] He may have chosen Chicago because of the counsel of his two older brothers, who had immigrated there some years before Cox's arrival.[29] For the purposes of our analysis of Cox's intellectual development, however, it matters little exactly where Cox settled; American social patterns only vary in degree in different locales. As a Caribbean immigrant, Cox would have formed similar opinions about American society had he gone to New York or Los Angeles rather than to Chicago. However, what I intend to show is that Cox's readings of a number of events and movements—from Garveyism to fascism—were, in part, formed by where he did live.

Apart perhaps from the novelty of snow and the seemingly infinite multitude of people, buildings, and cars, it is likely that Cox was quickly struck by the concentration of black people into, by and large, one area of Chicago by residential segregation. The "black belt," as it was aptly called, was a narrow strip of land that began "at the edge of an industrial and warehouse district just south of the Loop (Chicago's central business district) . . . [and] stretched southward along State Street for more than thirty blocks, remaining only a few blocks wide except at its northern end." Already home to more than three-quarters of the roughly 44,000 black Chicagoans in 1910,[30] by 1919, when Cox arrived, the black belt had to accommodate the living needs of more than twice that number.[31] Though probably unaware of the precise number of black people who, like himself, had recently arrived in Chicago, Cox would come to learn that the black belt's unyielding boundaries made its rents among the highest in the city for comparable housing[32] and its units the least spacious ("usually because black tenants paying appreciably higher rents than whites took in lodgers to compensate for the differential"). Its structures (and infrastructure) were among the most wanting in the city, a situation made worse by the fact that "[d]uring the [First World] war residential construction largely ceased in Chicago as elsewhere." Summarizing the factors that contributed to the physical deterioration of the black belt during and after the great migration, William M. Tuttle Jr. noted: "In addition to the excessive rents levied by black and white landlords alike, the migration accentuated both the overcrowding and the shabbiness of the facilities; and with lines of migrants waiting to occupy any vacancy, few landlords felt obligated to maintain their buildings in a decent state of repair."[33] Cox would note these consequences of residential segregation in *Race Relations.*[34]

Cox found that even middle-class Blacks (however loosely defined)[35] were also confined to the black belt. A half century after his initial experience with this typically American social pattern, Cox remarked that the "Negro neighborhood tends to be more *socially* heterogeneous than the various white neighborhoods,"[36] for the simple fact that racism "abhors . . . movement across a color fence which surrounds each race regardless of social position of the individuals."[37] Unlike in Port-of-Spain or in other Caribbean cities where middle-class Trinidadians of color could set themselves apart geographically from the less fortunate, middle-class black Americans were accorded no such luxury by either elite, middle-class, or working-class Whites.

Among the many factors that Cox would name in later years that contributed to residential segregation, in the final analysis he concluded that "national, state and local white real estate associations" were most responsible. "These organizations," he continued, "are highly expert, well financed, and maintain effective lobbies in national, state, and city legislatures. They have been the mainstay of racial neighborhood zoning, zoning ordinances, and restrictive covenants."[38] If there was a single Chicago organization in Cox's mind when he penned these words, it was probably the Hyde Park–Kenwood Property Owners' Association, which had formed in 1908.[39] Its purpose was to end the purchase of homes by middle-class Blacks in the community to the southeast of the black belt, and the association employed a variety of tactics toward that end: "the community newspaper, the boycott, and in the last resort, violence."[40] The preferred use of force was the bomb. As Tuttle recounts: "From July 1917 to the eruption of the Chicago race riot in late July 1919, no fewer than twenty-six bombs were exploded at isolated black residences in once all-white neighborhoods and at the offices of certain realtors who had sold to blacks. Over half of these bombs were exploded during the six months leading up to the riot . . . [S]even explosions punctuated the six sultry weeks preceding the riot."[41]

That the association was responsible for some of these bombings, there would have been little doubt in Cox's mind; in its meetings, its members openly threatened the "use of bombs and bullets" to repel what they considered a black "invasion" into "their" community.[42] It was probably the activities of real estate associations such as this one that led Cox to the conclusion that middle-class and especially elite Whites were greater perpetrators of racist practices than were working-class whites. Even if Cox was not immediately aware of the exact material interests involved in the bombings, he would not have been surprised to learn that "[a]s to motive, the association was dominated by realtors who held extensive property in Hyde Park and who affirmed unequivocally that blacks and property depreciation were synonymous. They endeavored, therefore, to preserve their interests by encouraging the blacks to move away and by discouraging any future influxes." Conversely, the activities of working-class Whites to prevent Blacks from purchasing property west of Wentworth Avenue were "unorganized and assumed no more violent form than that of warning letters."[43]

Cox may have found white American hostility toward Blacks shocking, and irrational, particularly the fact that Whites, by and large, grouped into the same "racial" category any and every person of either visible or known African ancestry regardless of lightness of skin tone or ambiguity of phenotype. In some cases, it was life-threatening. It seems unlikely, however, that Cox would have been a partisan of "New Negro" self-defense and retaliation (particularly in light of his writings in the mid-1960s and in the early 1970s).[44] He might already have interpreted this political stance as a prelude to black nationalism (particularly its Garveyist form), for which he had little sympathy. This does not mean that Cox would have automatically taken a "turn-the-other-cheek" approach to American racism and intolerance, but rather that it is likely given his social background, his unfamiliarity with the First World War experience, and possibly his Christian upbringing,[45] he would have sided with those who maintained that proof of black "respectability" was the best way to combat white prejudice. Furthermore, Cox's social education in Trinidad would have made him familiar with the criteria of respectability used in the black belt; the two sets hardly differed. In addition to a "stable income," respectability—"the badge of middle-class black status in black Chicago," as James R. Grossman aptly describes the term—"frequently depended upon property ownership, membership in the appropriate organizations, and leisure habits. Church, club, or lodge activities conferred as well as signified status; symbols of respectability could include affiliation with one of the larger Baptist or African Methodist Episcopal Churches, a YMCA membership, or a Masonic identification card."[46]

Unlike in the Caribbean, however, self-declared "respectable" black people in the United States devoted a lot of energy to the cultivation of respectability in those who they felt lacked it: the recent arrivals from the rural "Deep South."[47] This setting of standards of appropriate behavior for the newcomers was one of the explicit goals of organizations like the Urban League, the YMCA (for Blacks), the Phyllis Wheatley Association, the Frederick Douglass Center, and the Negro Fellowship League. At bottom, however, the efforts of the black administrators, donors, and staff of these institutions had little to do with the migrants themselves. "Fearful that the migrants, with their rural southern manners, would disrupt the community and embarrass the race," remarks Grossman, "middle-class black Chicago tried to protect its respectability by instructing newcomers in acceptable forms of behavior. . . . 'Respectable' black Chicagoans recognized that even if they could avoid living among migrants they would still be associated with them."[48] Accordingly, the list of social "don'ts" that the *Chicago Defender* included among other newsworthy items revealed just how much what respectable black people did was governed by the omnipresent (though largely physically absent) eyes of white observers:

> Don't use vile language in public places.
> Don't act discourteously to other people in public places.
> Don't allow yourself to be drawn into street brawls. . . .
> Don't make yourself a public nuisance. . . .
> Don't congregate in crowds on the streets to the disadvantage of others passing along. . . .
> Don't live in unsanitary houses. . . .
> Don't allow children to beg on the streets. . . .
> Don't abuse or violate the confidence of those who give you employment.
> Don't leave your job when you have a few dollars in your pocket.[49]

Respectable black Chicagoans saw themselves as crusaders against the black community's ultimate arch rival: the black "underworld." In their mind it was already bad enough that city hall and the Chicago police department connived to situate the vice district within the black belt without some black people fueling the stereotype of black criminality by participating in it. This viewpoint had its merits outside of its obvious self-interest: it was a refusal to succumb to social obstacles however daunting. Middle-class black Chicagoans saw themselves as living proof that no social hindrance was insurmountable. One of St. Clair Drake and Horace Cayton's respondents succinctly phrased this social philosophy in the following manner: "The theory that it all depends upon economic status doesn't hold water to me. There are people who are not lower-class who have less than many who are lower-class."[50] To upstanding black Chicagoans there was simply no excuse for making a living by gambling, theft, or by selling illegal intoxicants or sex. Young Cox would have agreed. Neither did they excuse the choices of those who they considered to be the likely parents of these wayward young people: commitment-averse men and libertine women partnered in short-lived common-law marriages. Eventually the man leaves, so the story goes, leaving the abandoned woman to raise and support the children, all-too-often performing both poorly.

Again, in the collective mind of self-labeled respectable black Chicagoans, lower-class home life epitomized irresponsibility and was the social incubator of many of the ills that befall the black community. Yet, what was even more revealing about black middle-class self-conception was what Cox and others saw as its source: slave and early postslavery southern society. Racism and discrimination in the twentieth century notwithstanding, middle-class and elite Blacks, by and large, explained lower-class black family life as cultural retentions from slavery and its immediate aftermath. Accordingly, Cox wrote:

> Probably the most costly aspect of the system [southern share-cropping] for its colored members has been its tendency to generate irresponsibility among them. Irresponsibility tended to become a trait of the Negro masses. It contributed to the instability of their family and to the slovenly state of its physical upkeep. It has been doubtless accountable for the disreputable community existence that followed when the group moved into towns and cities, as well as for the relatively weak incentive toward formal education.[51]

Although these remarks were penned some forty to fifty years after his initial observations, it is hard to imagine that Cox was not remembering his years in Chicago in the preceding passage; it was the only urban environment he knew well. It is also worth pointing out that, according to the same reasoning, the relative success of middle-class Blacks was due to their ability to slough off their one-time southern modes of thought and behavior and to adopt "modern" urban ones.

Yet observations made in reflective maturity do not prove that in the 1920s Cox was thinking about the roots of certain patterns of particularly the poor black family's organization, or rather, disorganization. He did discuss them in later years and he seemed to do so with his Chicago years in mind, but there is little early textual evidence on which to base judgment. Bearing in mind his middle-class Trinidadian background and the absence of strong pressures to change the inclinations of that worldview, it is unlikely that young

Cox harbored thoughts about the wanting conditions under which black Americans lived. It is for this reason that I think of this period of Cox's life as his prepolitical or precritical phase. He had yet to come to the understanding that his worldview was the product of a particular social context, not of some universal experience. Nor had he come to exchange his old ideological baggage for a new set. In the absence of Cox's own description of his old set of ideas, that which W. E. B DuBois provided is arguably comparable with some modification: "I grew up in the midst of definite ideas as to wealth and poverty, work and charity. Wealth was the result of work and saving and the rich rightly inherited the earth. The poor, on the whole, were themselves to be blamed. They were unfortunate and if so their fortunes could easily be mended with care. But chiefly, they were 'shiftless,' and 'shiftlessness' was unforgivable."[52]

Clearly, Cox took note of more than racial discrimination, ghettoization, and familial hardship during his early years in Chicago. However, I have deliberately limited myself to these topics because they are discernible without political analysis and because they are themes about which he wrote in later academic writings. For similar reasons, I have opted to introduce his understanding of both American politics and this country's labor movement in later sections because Cox only referred to those themes in the context of events in the 1930s and after. At least in some instances, what Cox wrote about is a reliable indicator of when the theme in question entered his consciousness. He wrote remarkably little about his first decade in the United States. However, before turning to the reason why Cox immigrated to the United States, I would like to address the opportunity costs of his decision to settle in Chicago rather than elsewhere.

Roads Not Taken

By his own indirect admission, Cox considered Harlem the intellectual center of the black American world. Of the twentieth-century black leaders named in his long chapter "Leadership Among Negroes in the United States,"[53] only Booker T. Washington was based outside of black New York; none hailed from Chicago. As the names alone suggest—Garvey, DuBois, Robeson—there was a great variety of political thought in Harlem. The headquarters of the NAACP and the UNIA were located there, and it was home to black socialists like A. Philip Randolph, Chandler Owens, and black communists such as Hubert Harrison, Cyril Briggs, and Ben Davis Jr. It is hard to say what ideological effect the Harlem environment would have had on Cox's early political formation or how it would have changed his subsequent career choices, but it is reasonable to assume that his process of radicalization would have occurred earlier. This political transformation would likely have been aided by the fact that fellow West Indians were frequently at the forefront of radical politics in Harlem.[54] A shared background in a foreign land might have led Cox to identify with these Caribbean radicals and their political-economic positions.

Attending school in New York, particularly during what was retrospectively labeled the "Harlem Renaissance," would have opened Cox's eyes to the possibility of earning a living as a writer—journalist, novelist, playwright, or poet—rather than as a lawyer. As mentioned earlier, in a Caribbean middle-class household, it was expected of the male children to pursue a career in one of two professions: medicine or law. The latter was Cox's intended field of study.[55] The notion that one would use (or, as popularly thought, waste) one's education on the dream of becoming a literary writer would have been entertained in few such households and we have no evidence to suggest that it would have been different in Cox's. When added to the distance from parental or fraternal supervision, the Harlem Renaissance might have changed Cox's outlook on the life of a person of letters; not only viable, that life might have proven singularly exciting, stimulating, and appealing. And even if the Harlem environment did not compel him to change significantly his career plans, it might have pushed him to consider adding an avocation to his vocation: perhaps journalism or political organizing.

Settling in Harlem, however, probably would have heightened Cox's self-awareness as a Caribbean immigrant as opposed to being a black man in America regardless of provenance. The black inhabitants of the city with the highest concentration of Caribbean immigrants in the United States were arguably more likely to draw distinctions between those of their "race" who were mainland-born and those who were island-born than in those areas where the number of Caribbean immigrants was not large enough to be a basis of division. Despite their shared position in the socio-racial structure of American society and of their frequent interaction, collaboration, and intermarriage, their different geographical origins were often a source of tension and resentment. For example, though not a Garvey defender, Cox, along with other West Indians, would probably have taken offense to the *Messenger* headline of an article on the black leader: "A Supreme Jamaican Jackass."[56] Although most Caribbean immigrants and black Americans recognized such unnecessary insults for what they were—low political potshots—they could only be effective if they played on popular sentiments. And often these were not endearing: "Resentment against Harlem's growing West Indian community was already welling up. West Indians were reputed to work harder for less, to speak and write better English than the southern migrants, and were disliked for their considerable aggressiveness in small business affairs and ward politics. The saying was already current in Harlem that a revolutionary invariably turned out to be an overeducated West Indian out of work."[57] Lacking a large Caribbean immigrant population, Chicago's black community could not fracture along mainland vs. islands lines and it seems likely that the absence of this particular social dimension facilitated Cox's assimilation into (black) American society.

Great Britain was another frequent destination of Caribbean immigrants. What effect might the British social environment have had on Cox's intellectual development had he chosen to cross the Atlantic to further his education?

At the time, black life in London, Liverpool, and Cardiff, Wales, shared many characteristics with its equivalents in New York and Chicago. Like the two American cities, these three cities of Great Britain had small but socially significant black populations, though the number of black Britons as a percentage of the total population was miniscule in comparison to the same ratio in the United States: 20,000 of 38 million in the British case, 10 million of some 90 million in the American one.[58] Still, because Great Britain's black population was concentrated in important urban centers, it appeared larger and, consequently, more threatening to its white counterparts. This perceptual magnification of the *real* number of black Britons by some white Britons goes some way to explain why London, Liverpool, and Cardiff were much like Chicago and about twenty other American cities in 1919: they, too, had their "red summer" of mass attacks on black people.[59] However, the Caribbean experience in England differed from that in the United States in, at least, one important respect: Caribbean people from English colonial possessions were legally English citizens in England, whereas in the United States they were another immigrant group seeking American citizenship. In practical terms, this official status meant that attacks on Blacks in Great Britain were not only acts of racial intolerance but also assaults by Britons on fellow British citizens. Thus, the attackers called into question not only the presence of the immigrants on "mainland" British soil, but like white American assaults on black Americans, also the supposed political status or citizenship of Caribbean people in Great Britain. It seems to me that under these circumstances, Cox's awareness and appreciation of Caribbean and even of black nationalism would have been heightened and intensified.

It is one of the great ironies of the twentieth-century political history that Anglo-Caribbean nationalism emerged in response to the British government's refusal to allow the region's 16,000 volunteers[60] to be counted among the million who died (three-quarters of a million Britons and 200,000 Indian colonials)[61] fighting for the Union Jack in World War I. Some 1,100 of the men who constituted the British West Indies Regiment did lose their lives.[62] In the collective mind of the British government and armed forces, people of African descent were not biologically suited to engage in combat (either as allies or as adversaries) with white men. If they could play any part in modern warfare, so this logic dictated, it could only be as munitions carriers or cleaners of latrines. It hardly needs to be stated that this biological argument served and camouflaged specific political-economic ends: if black colonials could prove themselves valiant soldiers in a war one of whose aims was to "fight for the smaller nationalities," then there would be little keeping them from fighting for their own smaller nationalities against the British government.

Had British military officials and rank-and-file soldiers been able to prevent the Caribbean volunteers from engaging in combat without resorting to racial insults, the British government might have been able to stave off the emergence of Caribbean nationalism for another generation. They could not. Without repeating what others have poignantly chronicled elsewhere,[63] it will suffice here to say that when word and the veterans themselves returned to the Caribbean, they transformed, almost overnight, the attitudes toward the British of even the staunchest colonized defender of the empire; what was once a mark of pride had become a badge of shame. And when the stories of racial attacks on Caribbean people in Great Britain was added to those about the war, the lit fuse of rebellion began to inch its way to the powder keg.

In few places in the British Caribbean were the combination of anti-British, anticolonial, and antiwhite sentiments running higher in the immediate postwar era than in Trinidad. The local catalyst was a week-long dock workers' strike centered in Port-of-Spain, which eventually won a 25 percent wage increase for the stevedores. The strike resuscitated the Trinidad Workingmen's Association (of which Arthur Andrew Cipriani, a white creole veteran, was designated president by the association's constituency) and reestablished it as a force to be reckoned with in crown colony politics. Also noteworthy about the strike was that many war veterans counted among its leaders.[64] Moreover, many of the strikers, if not certificate-bearing members of Marcus Garvey's United Negro Improvement Association, were sympathetic to his ideology. In fact, Garvey's spirit did not limit itself to Trinidad's main ports but, as Tony Martin chronicles, traveled far into the interior of the country: "By the early 1920s Trinidad was the most thoroughly organized UNIA stronghold in the British West Indies, and of the non-British islands only Cuba had a larger number of UNIA branches."[65]

How would all of these social developments have affected Cox's intellectual trajectory? My feeling is that if Cox had remained in Trinidad until after the December 1919 strike, he would have had reason to offer different assessments of everything from the sociopolitical roots of the Garvey movement, to the social bases of the variations in American race relations, to the role of the war experience in transforming political consciousness (particularly in giving rise to nationalism) than he did in his later academic writings. About Garvey's program generally, I believe a longer stay at home would have forced Cox to modify his later remark that the "racial situation in his native country, Jamaica, could not have been approached in this way."[66] Obviously, many Caribbean sympathizers (among whom were a large number of fellow Trinidadians) found it an appropriate one to address many of the region's social ills.

Having explored the situations that might have affected his intellectual development, we need now return to Cox's actual experiences between 1919 and 1929.

The University of Chicago

School records and letters indicate that Cox did not move to the southern edge of the black belt until 1931.[67] Before that he lived on the West side in his brother Ethelbert's home, first on Washington Boulevard and later on Walnut Street.[68] If Cox's Chicago addresses prefigured any one aspect of his future career as a sociologist, it was that his studies would not be based on participant observation. In any event, having only completed primary school in Trinidad, Cox entered Chicago's YMCA High School at the relatively older age of eighteen. How this age difference between him and his classmates may have affected Cox we cannot say. However, it is easy to imagine that in terms of maturity, discipline, and direction, not to mention the fact that he was a young immigrant having come to this country for the explicit purpose of improving his social standing at home, Cox was well ahead of his classmates in more respects than age.

A month after having graduated from Central YMCA High School in 1924,[69] Cox began his college studies at Crane Junior College, Chicago's first city college and little more than a decade old at the time. Awarded an associate's degree in 1926, Cox entered Northwestern University as a junior and took a bachelor of science in law degree there in 1928. According to Cox's "Personal Data Sheet for Teaching, Counseling, and Administrative Personnel" (dated 10 August 1970 and submitted for his last academic post at Wayne State University),[70] Cox took on some other responsibilities and pursued other interests in addition to attending classes in the 1920s. He lists working part-time at La Salle and Steven's Hotels from June 1923 to August 1927 as an "assistant engineer," which could have been a euphemism for anything from a janitor to a repairman. It appears that Cox's only other nonacademic employment was as a stenographer (assuming that this is what he meant by "stationery engineer for Chicago") for which he earned a license in 1925.[71] As a future lawyer, licensure as a stenographer would have afforded Cox the opportunity to observe (and to record) courtroom proceedings at the closest proximity for a nonprofessional save as a juror. Also, under the heading "Extra-Curricular activities," Cox named painting courses at the Chicago Art Institute.[72]

Here, then, was Oliver Cromwell Cox in the summer of 1928: college graduate, soon to be 27 years old, and well on his way to realizing his goal of becoming a barrister before returning to Trinidad. Then tragedy hit: in 1929 Cox was stricken with polio which, by his own account, "partially paralyzed" both of his legs; he would need the aid of crutches to get around for the rest of his life. Cox spent a year and a half in convalescence, during which time his brother Reginald "postponed his own education to care for [him]."[73]

Among other consequences, the disease dashed his career plans. Rather than despair, my feeling is that Cox's initial response to his illness was what we may consider an existential self-interrogation. It is easy to imagine him thinking, "I neither know nor understand why this has happened to me, but since it has, I must discover what I am supposed to learn from it. I must understand how the experience will make me a better person."[74] One lesson that I believe Cox did learn from his illness was that one's condition—physical, socioeconomic, or otherwise—is not always of one's making. If Cox's upbringing instilled in him the belief that the realization of one's personal goals requires nothing more (and nothing less) than the application of one's will toward those ends, then his initial struggle with polio must have forced him to reconsider the certainty of that proverbial formula. It compelled him to see the role of forces larger than merely individual effort to explain individual, and even group, success and failure. I do not believe that Cox knew then exactly what these "forces" were or where they came from or how they operated. Not being a devoutly religious person, Cox could not have been satisfied with explanations of personal and social events based on sayings such as "it is the Lord's will" or "the Lord works in mysterious ways." He sought rather a secular understanding of his immediate world. Now, rather than cast a disapproving eye on those who were less fortunate socioeconomically than himself though more able in body, Cox looked sympathetically on his fellow men and women. In short, I believe that through his challenge with polio Cox discovered the plight of the poor. And there was no more conducive time to do so than during the Great Depression.

In light of his circumstances, then, I do not believe that his decision to study economics after abandoning law was as fortuitous as he made it seem in his letter to Dean Wigmore of Northwestern University.

2824 Walnut St.
Jan−3−1931.

Dear Dean Wigmore,

Thanks for New Year greetings.

I am happy to tell you of my intentions. It is becoming a common thing now to see my plans for returning to some form of school go up and vanish as quickly as a bubble. But this time I have crossed the Rubicon. Although I see dark and almost insurmountable hills before me, I am going on and saying "there are no Alps," or "be thou removed and thou cast into the sea."

I must hurry on to the soul of wit: On Monday I shall start at the University of Chicago. Since I must still use canes, since no doctor will venture a prognostication of my case, and since I am convinced that I shall need two strong legs to be the kind of lawyer I dreamed of being, I have decided to take post graduate work in economics.

It is a decision beneath my aspiration, but it is the best of what is left me. I have found living quarters near to the school, and that is so vitally important that it has selected this institution. On the progress of my health depends my future course: if after I obtain the Master's degree I feel equal to the task, I shall return to law; if not I shall proceed in the study of economics with a view of the chair in some school. Wishing you a happy year. I remain

Respectfully yours
Oliver Cox [75]

There is no reason to doubt Cox's assertion that his restricted mobility rather than the reputation of the University of Chicago determined his application to department of economics. As an explanation for his choice to study economics, however, it seems somewhat inadequate given both the economic realities of the time and what would soon be the topic of his master's thesis: "Workingmen's Compensation in the U.S., with Critical Observations and Suggestions."[76] About Cox's choice of subject, Hunter offered a plausible argument: "One can surmise from this early writing that Cox's own physical disability had sensitized him to some of the issues surrounding the early attempts in this country to establish workingmen's compensation. At one point in the thesis, for instance, Cox argues that compensation for disability should be [for] life; that rehabilitation should be included to make the injured party employable; and [that] workers' compensation should cover all classes of workers."[77]

This is not to imply that Cox's academic work was always guided by what he encountered at an experiential level. (It would be equally remiss, however, to deny altogether its influence on his work.) In this instance, moreover, such a conclusion would be grossly unfair to the impressive roster of scholars assembled in the University of Chicago's department of economics, among whom were Frank Knight, Harry Millis,[78] John Nef, and Jacob Viner. "Under these teachers," reports Hunter, "Cox took such courses as the Economic History of the United States, Labor Problems, and Transportation and Communication the Winter Quarter of 1931. Among other subjects that interested Cox were courses in Economic Theory, The State in Relation to Labor, and a course on Trade Unions."[79]

The curriculum reflected the ideological bias of the university's department of economics during Cox's brief stay there. In the words of one of its best known graduates, Paul Samuelson, the "Knightian Chicago school," as he terms it "advanced use of the market, but recommended redistributive taxes and transfers to mitigate the worst inequalities of the laissez-faire system. It pragmatically favored macroeconomic policies in the areas of credit and fiscal policies to improve competition and favored utility regulation where competition was severely compromised."[80] In essence, these were standard liberal capitalist positions that maintained that any failings of the capitalist market economy can be corrected with minor adjustment. Knight, specifically, can be credited with having introduced Cox to the work of Max Weber. As translator of Weber's *General Economic History,* it is likely that in his courses Knight stressed the "value of

Weber's comparative and historical approach to study world civilization; a method . . . Cox adopted in his own works on race relations and capitalism."[81]

Ultimately, however, all these academic tools proved insufficient to Cox's intellectual needs. His expressed reason for having left the department in 1932 with only a master's degree is often cited in works about him: "I felt that if economics did not explain what I wanted to know; if economics did not explain the coming of the depression; if economics did not help me to understand that great [economic change], then I felt that I did not need it. Thus, I changed over to sociology."[82]

According to no less a mainstream economist than John Kenneth Galbraith, Cox's frustration with the University of Chicago's brand of economic reasoning was sound: "until the mid-thirties, in both England and the United States, the notion of the grave depression was not only foreign to the accepted system of economics but its admission was largely barred to analysis."[83] Why, however, Cox felt that the field of sociology held the answers to the depression riddle, he did not say. Perhaps Herbert Hunter's suggestion that Cox "thought that the problems of the Depression could be more satisfactorily explained through an understanding of modern society and human behavior, than from the standpoint of a formal economic analysis,"[84] is largely correct. The Great Depression encouraged, if not demanded, an ideological (beyond the disciplinary) shift in Cox's mind as well as in the minds of other social observers, academic and lay. In this regard, historian and University of Chicago graduate William H. McNeill's reflections on the intellectually destabilizing effects of the Great Depression effectively capture the mood of the time:

> In the back of everyone's mind lurked the recollection of old-fashioned life on the farm where all human needs were routinely met by family and neighborly action, and where, in time of business depression, subsistence farming could keep everyone going until the exchange economy recovered. That Eden had vanished from America with World War I or before. The professorate of the University of Chicago knew it had disappeared, yet still clung to moral attitudes and expectations inherited from the rural past. Such a posture was a recipe for

indecision, confusion, distress. It meant that Chicago's social scientists—and the faculty at large who shared America's rural and small-town Protestant past with them—were unsure of themselves as never before. Resulting uncertainty, in turn, created an opening among students for wielders of radical new doctrines, Thomist and Marxist alike.[85]

The ultimate lines of both Cox's and McNeill's reflections are arguably related. Once Cox recognized the inability of "classical" economics to come to terms with the Great Depression, he, like countless others, looked elsewhere for explanations.

Though hardly a hotbed of Marxist thought at the time, the university was (and arguably has always been) a liberal institution; that is, the university community was by and large open to alternative interpretations of social phenomena even if its faculty rejected the conclusions of those unorthodox viewpoints. If any single figure was most responsible for this liberalism during Cox's tenure there, it was the president of the university, Robert Maynard Hutchins. Among his accomplishments were the introduction of the "social science survey" (the precursor of the "Great Books" courses later adopted by a number of prominent American colleges and universities) on whose list of titles that all University of Chicago undergraduates were required to study was Marx and Engels' *Communist Manifesto*.[86] Cox noted in *Caste, Class, and Race* the heavy fire which the university and Hutchins drew from the drugstore millionaire, Charles Walgreen, when Walgreen alleged that the university was using its lecture halls to espouse bolshevism.[87] It was under his administration, moreover, that the university allowed both communist and socialist clubs to use university facilities for meetings and other activities in the early to mid-1930s. We do not know if Cox attended the meetings of either of these leftist clubs during the five years that he was a graduate student in the sociology department (1932–37), but it is likely that their presence made Marx's writings and Marxist literature available to those who were interested.

If, however, Cox did not find Marxism at the University of Chicago, it is likely that Marxism (or its self-proclaimed agents) found him nearby. Washington Park—the public domain that separated the black belt from southside white residential neighborhoods and the one through which Cox occasionally passed on his way to and from the university[88]—was the gathering place of multitudes of the black belt's un- and underemployed,[89] students, and soapbox orators of all persuasions. Cox must have heard effective Communist Party speakers like David Poindexter and Justin De Lemos offer their audiences compelling explanations for the Great Depression as well as new courses of action to combat its class-selective effects. One of these—organized by the Unemployed Council[90]—was to preempt tenant evictions by leading large groups of workers to the site of the attempt and obstructing police action. In the case that a family's belongings had already been put on the sidewalk before the arrival of the council's representatives and their sympathizers, they would defiantly restore them to their former unit. It was frequently from Washington Park, moreover, that these "Black Bugs" (as the council's black belt agents were popularly called) launched their antieviction attacks, making the park, in Halpern's words, a "staging ground" for popular protest. As observant and mindful of current events as Cox was, particularly during his political awakening in the Great Depression, we can be sure that these developments were not lost on him. These activities along with the Communist Party's willingness to expel members who exhibited racially discriminatory behavior,[91] to attend funeral services for slain black activists, communist and noncommunist, to support the "Don't Spend Your Money Where You Can't Work" campaign,[92] and its willingness to defend the Scottsboro boys, earned the party the respect of the black belt, Cox included.

Cox's interest in Weber's sociological writings was similarly piqued and satisfied outside of the university's sociology department.[93] Knight's introduction to Weber's *General Economic History* probably extended to some of his related essays on economic themes while Cox was still in the department of economics. These intellectual seeds would prove fruitful after Cox had lived a few years in the South in the late 1930s and throughout the 1940s, during which time he would come to question the caste characterization of southern race relations as taught by Robert Park and other sociology professors at the University of Chicago.[94] Accordingly, in his lengthy discussion of the Indian caste system in *Caste, Class, and Race,* Cox not only cites Max Weber's description of the ideology that inspires the caste system,[95] but he also models his exegesis after Weber's studies of the Hindu and other world religious systems that were posthumously assembled in *Gesammelte Aufsätze zur Religionssoziologie.*[96]

If the sources of neither Cox's Marxist nor Weberian orientation can be traced to his sociological training at the University of Chicago, it seems fair to ask just what he did learn in its department of sociology. At the risk of sounding unduly harsh, the answer appears to be not much. Certainly, like other graduate students in the department, he studied "statistics with William Ogburn, social psychology with [Ellsworth] Faris, sociological theory with [Ernest] Burgess, research methods with [Herbert] Blumer, and race relations with [Robert] Park,"[97] but judging from the contents of *Caste, Class, and Race,* their lessons did not bear the same import to Cox as did those of Marx and Weber. In fact, Cox would spend the early part of his career demonstrating precisely the failings of most of his former teachers' ideas. Instead, what Cox became conscious of in graduate school was the political economy of scholarship, that is, not only the production of scholarly works, but also to the equally if not more important issue of whose and what ideas are promoted in the academy. Cox would come to know intimately the politics of scholarship in the wake of the publication of *Caste, Class, and Race.* What Cox may have learned about the subject while in graduate school remains uncertain, but there are clues in his introduction to Nathan Hare's *The Black Anglo-Saxons.*[98] It is hard to believe that some of Cox's opinions were not first formed in graduate school:

> It was [E. Franklin] Frazier's lot to be a student at the University of Chicago when three great sociologists, Ellsworth Faris, William F. Ogburn, and Robert E. Park dominated the department. I have become convinced, from my personal association with and study of these men, that they were profound liberals in the sense in which that term is currently defined by direct-action leaders. They were men possessed of praiseworthy attitudes towards Negroes, but still strongly opposed to any definition of them as fully equal to whites; they were willing to do many things *for* Negroes but sternly opposed to Negroes taking such initiative as would move them along faster than a *proper* pace; and they would rather turn conservative than tolerate independent thinking or acting Negroes.[99]

These are provocative remarks. In approaching them, we might begin with their context: Cox agreed to write the introduction to

The Black Anglo-Saxons after having spent nearly twenty years (from the time of the publication of *Caste, Class, and Race*) in relative academic obscurity, during which time E. Franklin Frazier (the inspirer of Hare's study in Cox's opinion), was feted as the premier black sociologist since W. E. B. DuBois worked at Atlanta University. One must wonder, then, if in addition to resentment, there is a hint of annoyance with Frazier in Cox's remarks. However, there is more in them than even that.

Cox's larger charge is that Frazier's success in the academy (and perhaps that of other black graduates of the University of Chicago's department of sociology) was due to never having taken a position greatly at odds with those of his mentors. He believed that Frazier had never grown up. Accordingly, Frazier's "stunted growth," to employ lay terminology, largely explains why he enjoyed the highest praise from his "peers" (the culmination of which was his election as president of the American Sociological Association in 1948, the same year, ironically, that Cox's *Caste, Class, and Race* was published). Frazier remained in their eyes (and in those of their heirs), one "of their own," their product, their child. And, in Cox's opinion, the patent paternalism of the teachers and their protégés toward Frazier himself—that is, their insistence on assuming the roles of helper, guide, and mentor—was as far as their goodwill could go, because they could not conceive of the roles being reversed. As Cox saw himself in 1965, he may not have had two good legs to stand on, but he had stood up figuratively to his intellectual "fathers" by challenging their teachings and offering them and others alternative ways of thinking about the most pressing issues in modern social life. They characteristically rejected his offerings.

Leaving aside Cox's comments about his former teachers, his characterization of Frazier was grossly unfair on two counts: Frazier was no one's intellectual lackey, least of all Park's, according to Park himself; and although "many of his academic writings became [over time] increasingly technical and divorced from social policy," in the opinion of Anthony M. Platt, Frazier continued to "express his political persona in journalistic and popular articles."[100] On this second score, Cox should have been able to appreciate Frazier's professional strategy since he, too, followed it for a good five years after having received his doctorate: the writing of nonthreatening academic work. Of course, in 1942 Cox decided to cast caution to the wind and launched his attack on the "Chicago School" of sociology. Ultimately, what separated Cox from Frazier was that the latter chose to publish his more radical ideas in nonacademic publications, whereas the former did so in academic print and hardly ever wrote popular pieces for a wider nonacademic audience.[101] In any event, to return to Cox's budding awareness of the politics of scholarship, from the observations and sentiments that he expressed in the introduction to *The Black Anglo-Saxons,* it appears that Cox processed a great deal of information about which he remained silent for nearly thirty years.

It should also be noted that if Cox could take Frazier to task for not having broken intellectually with his University of Chicago mentors, a similar charge could be made against Cox for his steadfast defense of Franklin Delano Roosevelt. Let us now shift our focus from graduate school seminar rooms to the White House and beyond—from academic theory to the centers of power, politics, and public personalities that were greater influences on Cox's intellectual development than the University of Chicago.

Roosevelt and Popular Front Socialism

Cox's radicalism was frequently tempered by what can only be described as conservative political positions. None is perhaps more puzzling, if not outrageous, than the following claim he made about F.D.R.:

> [T]he charge of the capitalist politicians that Roosevelt was a communist is in its essence correct. His policies and actions had the potentialities of taking the economy step by step, inch by inch, out of the hands of the bourgeoisie and of turning it over to the people as a whole; and this is exactly what is meant by communistic activities. The logical conclusion of such a trend must necessarily result in the overthrow of the capitalist order. There has probably been no individual in the history of the United States who has done so much to bring about democracy and therefore communism in the United States as President Roosevelt; and there has been no individual so much beloved by the people and so much hated by the bourgeoisie as he.[102]

Cox defined democracy as the "taking over of the economic power of the State by 'the people' and the purposeful direction of urban civilization in the interest of all the people."[103] Precisely what institutions and mechanisms would ensure the "people's" administration of the economy equitably, Cox did not specify. Without having addressed these harder questions the fact that the New Deal expanded state intervention in the economy for the purpose of relieving mass poverty was sufficient for Cox to call Roosevelt both a democrat and a socialist. This was generosity above and beyond what the Comintern's "popular front" drive required. It is ironic, then, that Cox was branded a Marxist by those in the academy who read (parts of) *Caste, Class, and Race,* whereas for many on the left, his analysis of Roosevelt lost him even his "fellow traveler" credentials. The positive light in which Cox saw Roosevelt was aided by his literal reading of the latter's "socialistic" rhetoric and apologies for his conservative remarks. Thus he could assert, apparently unaware of what he was "reading into" Roosevelt's motives, that when Roosevelt declared that he "repudiate[d] the support of any advocate of Communism or of any other alien 'ism' which would by fair means or foul change our American democracy," he did so only because his critics "compelled him to deny his cause."[104]

A fair yet critical discussion of Roosevelt such as that later provided by Richard Hofstadter in his *American Political Tradition and the Men Who Made It,* gives some perspective to Cox's opinions. When one reads Hofstadter's assessment of Roosevelt, one cannot help but think that he directed many of his comments to the likes of Cox. For starters, Hofstadter called into question the very approach that Cox took to make sense of Roosevelt's political-economic objectives: "To take his statements literally, to look upon them as anything more than a rhetorical formulation of his preferences, would be a mistake; there seems no more reason to take his words as a literal guide to his projected action than there would have been to expect him to fulfill both his 1932 pledge to balance the budget and give adequate relief to the unemployed."[105]

In short, Roosevelt's "socialistic" talk was, in Hofstadter's mind, little more than necessary political (and economic) posturing during the severest economic crisis that the country had ever faced. He may have been genuinely concerned about the concentration of wealth and the growing disparity between rich and poor in 1930s

America, "[b]ut the New Deal was designed for a capitalist economy that . . . Roosevelt took as much for granted as he did his family. For success in attaining his stated goals of prosperity and distributive justice he was fundamentally dependent upon restoring the health of capitalism."[106]

Finally, as far as Roosevelt's purported championing of the cause of the working-class was concerned, Hofstadter maintained that Roosevelt only played that part when under pressure from labor itself or from threatening political opponents like Huey Long. It was not by accident that Hofstadter subtitled his chapter on Roosevelt, "The Patrician as Opportunist."

Cox was aware of this kind of criticism. "A sociologist, a colleague of the writer has criticized him for referring to Mr. Roosevelt as a communist. It seems, however, that the social scientist cannot be too much concerned about dictionary definitions for his identification of social phenomena. In so far as the social process involves the democratic tendency, there is probably no question but that the ruling class conceives of him in this way."[107] As a social scientist with explicitly leftist political commitments, it seems a curious philosophical position to accept social reality as defined by the ruling class, and not as defined by another, ideally more "objective," perspective.

It was namely what it implied about the labor movement of the 1930s that Cox's praise of Roosevelt was especially inordinate. As others have noted,[108] for a social observer with certain Marxist pretensions, it was odd that he chose to highlight the thought and policies of a socially privileged political leader, while underplaying the role of labor agitation in the shaping of that very political thought and the policies derived from it. For example, his esteem for the CIO notwithstanding,[109] Cox went so far as to say that "[I]t was President Franklin Roosevelt, in fact, and not the CIO, who initiated and won the struggle for the unionization and improvement of the economic condition of the masses of workers; and it is the National Labor Relations Act which guarantees to these masses an American right to organize into labor unions."[110]

This statement practically dismisses the activities of labor in the 1930s, in spite of the fact that most people who have studied or lived through the decade agree that the country was on the verge of, if it had not indeed passed through, a social revolution due not to Roosevelt's vision but to labor's demands. It would seem that for political purposes alone Cox would have highlighted the heroism of labor during the depression rather than that of Roosevelt, even if he honestly felt that the president was most responsible for the socially progressive programs created in the era. Finally, in looking for answers to Cox's elite perspective on the depression decade in *Caste, Class, and Race,* one cannot help but wonder to what degree his steadfast support of Roosevelt was related to the fact that they both were stricken with polio.[111]

Whatever the reason for the ties that bound Cox to Roosevelt, they were apparently stronger than those of race that bound Cox to the rest of black America, for he did not offer one word on Roosevelt's tolerance of the legion violations of the civil rights of Blacks during his tenure as president.[112] This was an extraordinary omission on Cox's part if only for one reason: "In FDR's thirteen years in the White House, a total of 109 blacks had been lynched," more than half of whom met their gruesome deaths during Roosevelt's first term.[113] That lynching, the most graphic expression of unbridled terror (and the subject to which Cox devoted half of his discussion of "The Race Problem in the United States," the last chapter of *Caste, Class, and Race*), could somehow escape official denunciation by the supposed champion of the proletariat is inexcusable.[114] However, in casting Roosevelt as he did, Cox denied himself the means to respond to this charge. If he attributed the president's silence on lynching, lower relief rates for Blacks, and their frequent exclusion from New Deal programs to the politics of pragmatism — that is, to the understanding that since "[s]outherners controlled over half the committee chairmanships and a majority of leadership positions in every New Deal Congress . . . party unity necessitated placating Democrats from Dixie on all issues of race"[115] — then either black Americans were not an important sector of the country's working class or Roosevelt was a stock-in-trade politician. And by his own indirect admission, the latter was the case. Aubrey Williams, deputy administrator of the Works Progress Administration in the mid-1930s, recalled Roosevelt as once having remarked that "[p]olitics is the art of the possible. . . . I do not believe in attempting something for the purpose of one's image. I believe you should never undertake anything unless you have evidence that you have at least a 50-50 chance of winning."[116] Protecting the lives of black Americans, among other civil guarantees, was obviously beyond the pale of the politically possible in Roosevelt's estimation and therefore not worth pursuing. Contrary, then, to what Cox would have us believe, Roosevelt himself was not responsible for any of the New Deal measures that attempted either to ensure or to promote the civil rights of black Americans. For the real heroes of those initiatives, Cox would have had to look to other figures: to Mary McLeod Bethune, director of the National Youth Administration's Office of Minority Affairs; Eleanor Roosevelt, first lady; Harold Ickes, Roosevelt's secretary of the interior; Will Alexander, director of the Farm Security Administration; Harry Hopkins, head of the Federal Emergency Relief Administration; and to the already mentioned Aubrey Williams. Cox's vision of Roosevelt, unfortunately, did not permit such latitude.

On the other hand, when it came to dissecting the propaganda put out by Roosevelt's critics, Cox was his old perceptive self. To his credit, he recognized that their appeals were based on the popular acceptance of a specious syllogism: if American society is capitalist and capitalist society is democratic, then American society is democratic. Although the second proposition is the most important of the three, as in all syllogisms, in this case, the first proposition was not taken for granted by Roosevelt's conservative critics. Quite the contrary, as Cox noted:

> Their principal device was, and still is, to identify themselves with the United States and every conceivable thing that is worth while in it—indeed, to identify themselves with God himself—so that an attack against them and their system becomes *ipso facto* an attack against God and Society. In their propaganda they take it for granted that their interests must be the interests of all good Americans; therefore, only the 'un-American' would be so treasonous as to question the basis of those interests.[117]

While this mantra may have been effective in convincing some Americans that capitalism is as American as apple pie, when the pro-capitalist sloganeers substituted "American" with "democratic," the new refrain could not enjoy the same success with the American public as the first, particularly if by "democratic" one meant more than representative government as determined by near, if not, universal suffrage. For some, like Cox, a political body had to measure up to far more demanding standards before it could earn the democratic label.[118] According to his definition of a democracy, it is a "form of government in which 'the people' participate in deciding matters of public interest."[119] Unlike the "democracies" (albeit limited) that existed in fifth-century Greece and in Republican Rome and those of the small village variety throughout the ages, modern democracy is, in Cox's opinion, a by-product of capitalism. However, the democracy that business people and their political allies were eventually able to establish in the West in the course of the nineteenth and twentieth centuries (following a gestation period of some six or more centuries) was designed to open politics and high society only to their ranks and not to the general (working) population. Thus, only proletarian democracy, the next and ultimate phase of this potentially global political process, could be the one based on and devoted to the decision-making capacity of the working class. Sounding little different from a doctrinaire Marxist, Cox explained the progression:

> Democracy . . . was made possible of achievement by the bourgeoisie, but it cannot be achieved by the bourgeoisie. In fact, the bourgeoisie is unalterably opposed to democracy. The task of establishing a democracy necessarily devolves upon the proletariat, and its final accomplishment must inevitably mean its supersession of capitalism . . . Clearly, then, accomplished democracy—democracy with its substance residing in the people—will be finally attained only when the democratic form has been fully impregnated with power to control the State and its economic resources. When the economic power of the State has been completely won from the bourgeois plutocracy by the great mass of people, the bourgeoisie will have, of course, been liquidated and capitalism will have come to an end.[120]

With these words, Cox had obviously gone beyond a mere description of "authentic" democratic politics and had outlined the economic basis of democratic society. To those already versed in Marxist theory, there was nothing extraordinary about Cox's assertion that authentic democracy requires the abolition of capitalism. What was different and certainly clever about Cox's discussion of democracy is that he insisted on calling it by that name instead of invoking socialism or communism, as I believe most leftist writers would have done. Never one to miss opportunities to score political points, he did not choose to do so here.

Cox also duly noted that when capitalist propagandists are forced to admit, in some small measure, that the political-economic system which they think sacred compromises democracy, they immediately try to shift the focus of the discussion to the merits of social freedom and individualism under capitalism. However, with regard to these supposed liberties in capitalist society, Cox did not concede anything to probusiness ideologues. For example, as far as capitalist freedom was concerned, Cox countered that the "people are not free when a relatively few masters of industry could deny them the control of their resources. Under capitalist freedom the people may not eat or shelter themselves unless, in the production of food and shelter, some individual makes a profit."[121]

Such was his opinion of the highly revered market freedom of capitalist societies; where its proponents saw "freedom," Cox could only see constraints and the unintended consequences of the profit motive. He most compellingly exposed the limited extent of capitalist freedom when he contrasted it to what he thought freedom could mean in a true democracy:

> Under capitalism a profit maker is free to exploit the human and natural resources of the people in his own interest; a slum dweller is free to live and die in filth. The new freedom of democracy is the freedom of the people so to govern themselves that they may be able to make judgements which can limit these minor freedoms. The people in a democracy may decide without hindrance both that slums should be cleared and that the individual who makes a profit from slums should give up that right. There is the loss of one kind of freedom and a gain of another; we cannot have them both.[122]

In a similar vein, Cox found little merit in the argument that praised capitalism for its encouragement of individual achievement.

In fact, as he persuasively argues in the following passage, in a capitalist society, not only is individualism ultimately elitist, but it is paradoxically a form of social control:

> As we have seen, the social system in which individualism functions is typically deaf and icy toward the welfare of individuals who cannot compel the attention of the oligarchy. In this system the individual is ordinarily presumed to be worthless until he is able to prove his worth. Therefore, paradoxically, the greater the measure of capitalist individual liberty, the greater the tendency to define the individual as having no intrinsic social worth. Capitalism seeks to atomize and segregate the individuals who constitute the masses of common people, not because of an inherent solicitude and respect for the rights and political influence of these individuals but because by means of their atomization their political influence and economic power may be nullified. Thus, the same ideal of individualism, which augments the dignity and power of the members of the ruling class, serves, when applied to the masses, as a powerful weapon of oppression and abasement. The value which individualism recognizes in the common people is 'use value.'[123]

Here we can readily detect one of the bases of Cox's advocacy of socialism: that contrary to capitalist propaganda about it, only socialism values the individual for her or his intrinsic human worth— only socialism "concerns itself with the personalization of the least privileged individuals."[124] Only in that social system does one "derive his life satisfactions through the welfare of his fellows and not by 'objectively' seeking to wring as much as he can out of them for his private enjoyment."[125] Cox never put these claims about the nature of socialist society to the test of empirical investigation. Still, it is conceivable that even this endeavor would not have changed his opinion of the promise of socialism, for as François Furet said of most American fellow travelers, their "pro-Sovietism . . . was independent of the nature of the regime in question."[126] In any event, what socialist (that is, democratic) theory provided Cox was the intellectual framework from which to conclude that the primary objective of probusiness propaganda that praises capitalist freedom and individualism is to undermine democracy:

The argument, however, is almost beside the point, for it is not particularly that the ruling class fears that the masses lack the ability to govern themselves, since it has never taken the initiative in the preparation of the people for self-government. Rather it is a self-interested objection to any relinquishment of its power to control the social system, power which this class conceives to be naturally beyond the constitutional right of the people. Democracy is thus thought of as an unjust, irrational usurpation—an unconscionable dishonesty—which the leaders of the people seek to impose upon the rightful and traditional owners of the business system. From this point of view democracy is wrong, disorderly, and larcenous—a movement which should be and ordinarily is put down by the organized might of the capitalist state.[127]

Finally, this is how Cox summarized the process and objectives of the modern democratic movement, inspired, as he thought it was, by the political-economic developments of the 1930s:

This, then, is what the modern social revolution amounts to. It involves the taking over of the businessman's society, fashioned by him in his own interest, by the masses of the people who at one time lived in that society only by suffrance—lived in it and had value only in so far as the traders and manufacturers were able to use them in the furtherance of business interests. From one point of view it may seem presumptuous that the masses of people should now declare that "democracy" demands that the material and productive wealth of the nation should be taken out of the hands of its traditional heirs, the business oligarchs, and utilized in the interest and welfare of all the people—that within the same urban, capitalist milieu the descendants of the totally non-political common people should today ask that their voice be given equal weight in the control of available economic resources. This, however, is exactly what modern democracy means, and it is with reference to its achievement that we logically use the phrase, "the coming new world."[128]

It would be hard to find in *Caste, Class, and Race* a more forthright declaration of Cox's political position in the 1930s. Tempting though it might be to claim that Cox came to assume this worldview by and large on his own (with the aid, of course, of reputable leftist litera-ture), this notion would require the removal of Cox from his larger social context. Even Cox himself would have rejected such a self-assessment. There is another intellectual current that helped carry Cox toward specific political conclusions.

The Popular Front

By and large, the popular front was the Comintern's response to Hitler's attacks on Germany's left and liberal parties upon his be-coming chancellor in January 1933. Before this time, the Soviet Union's official foreign policy had been to brook no compromises with capitalist states. However, as François Furet explained, the men-ace of Nazism demanded a change of policy:

> Nazism made no distinction between adversaries. With one sweep, Hitler liquidated the German Communist Party and the Weimar Republic. He had put the Communists and Democrats, all the various parties in the same bag. Consigning German mili-tant Communists to the first internment camps, he offered the Comintern a strategic and ideological advantage by simplify-ing the combat into two camps: fascism and anti-fascism. The identification of liberal democracy and Marxism, so familiar to German thought and so basic to Nazi ideology, was confirmed in one sense by what happened in 1933, even to the minds of those who thought it incoherent or absurd. In the end, Hitler imposed that identity even upon his enemies by forcing them to unite against him. If Marxists could be persecuted along with liberal democrats, must they not share something more impor-tant than their disagreements? Surely this indicated that they ought to unite against the common enemy.[129]

I mentioned earlier that Cox's perspective on Roosevelt was more generous than what even the "popular front" called for. The popu-lar front provided Cox with the lens through which he viewed not only Roosevelt's New Deal, but, more important, fascism and com-munism. Furet's remarks underscore a couple of the interrelated political developments that grew out of the popular front movement and which are key to Cox's understanding of both Franklin D. Roosevelt and the Soviet Union: one, that the union of communists and liberals under the antifascist popular front banner made the latter appear more politically radical than they actually were; and two, that the same collaboration made communists appear more parliamentarian than they actually were. The first case explains Cox's radicalization of Roosevelt's politics; the second makes comprehensible his ranking of the Soviet Union as first among the "three great nations of the world" (the United States and England were the other two) as far as exhibiting "degrees of development of democracy."[130] About this refashioning of the former Soviet Union (thanks to Nazism), Furet commented:

> Anti-Fascism, however, diverted attention away from the USSR toward Nazi Germany, which since January 1933 had been rife with causes for indignation on the part of friends of freedom, an indignation stimulated less by factual observation than by ideological tradition: Hitler won glory by crushing democracy, thereby furnishing his adversaries with a cause. Stalin was quick to exploit this situation. . . . Through anti-Fascism, the Communists had recovered the trophy of democracy without renouncing any of their basic convictions. During the Great Terror, Bolshevism reinvented itself as a freedom by default. Even while drawing strength from what it despised—the homage of vice to virtue—it was intimidating its adversaries by spreading the rumor that anti-Sovietism was the prelude to Fascism. Not only was Hitler useful in reviving the idea of democratic Communism, but he also provided a pretext to incriminate democratic anti-Communism. The Comintern's great shift of 1934–35 orchestrated in its own key the reorientation of the Soviet Union's foreign policy.[131]

In dividing categorically the Western world into fascist and antifascist camps, the popular front lent itself to the interpretation of fascism as one form of capitalist governance,[132] and of antifascism as anticapitalist and hence proletarian (as opposed to bourgeois) democratic. Thus, like the other popular front followers, Cox conceived both world and domestic politics as being framed by the poles of nazism and communism. Accordingly, if the dictatorship of the proletariat as achieved and practiced in the former Soviet Union was repressive, in Cox's mind it was only so against those who sought to reestablish capitalism (ultimately, fascism) in the then "worker's state." By this logic, Cox along with numerous fellow travelers, rationalized Stalin's actions as harsh, yet necessary, steps to protect the Bolshevik Revolution.[133] (It should be noted that Cox never singled Stalin out by name as he did Hitler.) As Cox saw it, and it was apparently a perspective that he took to his grave, any other interpretation of the former Soviet Union was merely procapitalist propaganda.

With the Soviet Union thus protected, Cox doubly condemned fascism. Cox's popular front Marxism led him to the conclusion that the inspirers of fascism are the "cream of . . . capitalist society." He went on to add that these would "ordinarily include the majority of men who have achieved great business success, of politicians of upper chambers, professional men of the highest order, distinguished scholars, eminent bishops and cardinals, the most powerful newspaper owners and editors, learned judges, the valiant upper crust of the military forces and so on." According to this schema, then, though most visibly active, middle-class, petty-bourgeois, and working-class fascists merely do the capitalist elite's bidding to strengthen, of all things, antidemocratic capitalism, in the name of nation and race.[134]

One of the more nagging problems, however, with this type of analysis of fascism is that it fails to explain why two of the three most infamous fascist leaders had such modest backgrounds: Mussolini was the son of a blacksmith who "worked only intermittently;"[135] Hitler's father, Alois Shicklgruber-cum-Hitler, was a customs official.[136] Only Franco could boast of a semielite pedigree of naval officers going back six generations.[137] It seems that Cox overlooked these complicating biographical facts by relying too heavily on Hitler's elitist rantings in *Mein Kampf,* undoubtedly a good source of fascist ideology, but not a reliable sociological analysis. For as much as Hitler railed against communism, parliamentarian government, Jews, and human equality, he repeatedly declared that he was fighting to improve the lives of (racially pure) poor Germans. And given the trying socioeconomic conditions that reigned particularly in Germany in the decade of the 1920s (on top of the then unprecedented number of human sacrifices that the First World War ex-

acted on all nations involved in the horror), it is doubtful that Hitler
was merely paying lip-service to the German public to gain adherents or sympathizers to the Nazi cause. For it should not be forgotten, as Cox himself recognized,[138] that the fascist movements were
mass movements, ones that relied on the participation of the popu-
lace in political rallies if not in policymaking. "Fascism," notes Eric
Hobsbawm, "gloried in the mobilization of the masses, and maintained it symbolically in the form of public theatre—the Nurem-
burg rallies, the masses on the Piazza Venezia looking up to Mussolini's gestures on his balcony—even when it came to power."[139]

Therefore, in the case of German fascism, while the Nazi movement undoubtedly aided German capitalists by both "eliminat[ing]
labour unions and other limitations on the rights of management to
manage its workforce"[140] and by expanding exponentially the German military-industrial complex and other related industries, it
did so not because, as Cox's position suggests, Hitler was the hand-
picked patsy of German Big Business, but rather because his social
aims made use of German industry.[141] This interpretation of Hitler's relationship with German industry indicates another problem
with the theory of the capitalist orchestration of fascism either to
deepen or to save monopoly capitalism: it minimizes the extent to
which fascist ideology is not procapitalist, but, ironically, aristocratic.
When the components of the two ideologies are juxtaposed, one
cannot help but be struck by the parallels between them: antiliber-
alism, anticommunism, elitism, militarism, and racism are common
to the two.[142] One way of thinking about fascism, then, as oxymoronic
as it may sound, is as the democratization or nationalization of aristocratic thought. Because Cox was prone to overlook the sociopolitical impact of the First World War, it is not surprising that he chose
not to highlight this aspect of fascism.

The popular front worldview was essential to Cox's political position. This worldview was more prevalent in intellectual circles in the
mid- and late-1930s than it was after the Hitler-Stalin Pact. Cox was
not a youngster during the period in question. It is more than likely
that he had well-formed political ideas by, say, 1936, and that he
probably deepened but did not fundamentally change them in the
course of the decade separating his departure from the University
of Chicago and the publication of *Caste, Class, and Race*. Let us now
turn to that period.

Cox's Southern Sojourn and the Making of
Caste, Class, and Race

Cox was awarded his doctorate in sociology from the University of Chicago in the summer of 1938. His dissertation topic in no way foreshadowed the massive undertaking that would be *Caste, Class, and Race* ten years later. If, nevertheless, my understanding of both the timing and content of Cox's political coming of age is correct, then "Factors Affecting the Marital Status of Negroes in the United States" was a safe topic which avoided controversial interpretations. Accordingly, although it reflected an aspect of his study of the social conditions in which black Americans lived in the 1930s and the effect that those conditions had on formal partnerships in black communities, Cox's dissertation was devoid of any politics or social commentary; it seemed hardly the work we would come to know and expect of Cox.[143] In this regard, I think it useful to consider his dissertations as Cox's academic initiation into black American life.

Cox's southern sojourn began in 1938, when he accepted a position at Wiley College in Marshall, Texas.[144] At this small, Methodist black college, Cox taught and codirected with V. E. Daniels the Bureau of Social Research for six years. During his stay at Wiley, Cox set himself the task of publishing a number of articles drawn from his dissertation. By early 1941 Cox had had published five articles dealing with the marital status of black Americans and one article calling for the expansion of facilities and resources in the South for the training of black graduate students in the social sciences and in the humanities.[145] It was in the following year, however, that Cox established himself as an academic iconoclast with the publication of his seminal article, "The Modern Caste School of Race Relations."[146] I will discuss Cox's critique of the "caste school" of particularly southern race relations in a later chapter, but here I would simply like to highlight three contextual points about the article. First, Cox waited until he was already professionally established before challenging the race relations theory to which many of his University of Chicago teachers subscribed. Second his contestation of the caste school of race relations was based on four years of residence in the South, that is, on four years of indirect fieldwork. Finally, the basis of his critique was that the caste school posited that the economic structure of the South was an outgrowth of the region's "culture" rather than the inverse.

Just as I find it hard to believe that Cox's political positions took shape only after his stay at the University of Chicago, I similarly find it difficult to believe that his reservations about the caste school of race relations awaited his residence in the South.[147] Rather, I believe that Cox "sat on" certain controversial ideas until he felt that the time and circumstances were right; that conjuncture only came when he was both professionally safe (and literally at a great distance from the University of Chicago) and had spent some time in the region, so that his ideas about its social relations were based on more than just books. Not that Cox scorned the reputable sources on southern society. On the contrary, he would underscore in the preface of *Caste, Class, and Race* that a number of previous studies on the South were nothing less than indispensable to any serious thinking on the region.[148] His issue with some of the authors that he named was not the information that they provided but with their interpretations. Simply put, Cox recognized that these scholars were employing terms and using indices drawn from a noncapitalist society—Hindu India—to describe erroneously, in his opinion, social relations in a capitalist society, those of the United States. Racism is, in Cox's estimation a necessary component of capitalist society, not of non- or precapitalist society.

Cox also critiqued the caste school of race relations on the basis of its related political repercussions, not least of which was its implicit suggestion that those who engaged in visible racist acts were most responsible for shaping public opinion on racial matters and, even more important, for maintaining racist institutions and structures. This interpretation of the bases of southern racism served the interests of black-belt planters by shifting attention away from their typical behind-the-scene maneuvers and focusing, instead, on the activities of poor, bigoted Whites. On the error of this perspective, Cox could not have agreed more with the opinion of V. O. Key Jr:

> If the interpretation is correct—and there are many deviations in detail—the political prowess of the black belts must be rated high. The thesis, however, runs counter to the idea that many top-drawer southerners firmly believe, viz., that the poor white is at the bottom of all the trouble about the Negro. The planter

may often be kind, even benevolent, towards his Negroes, and the upcountryman may be, as the Negroes say, "mean"; yet when the political chips are down, the whites of the black belts by their voting demonstrate that they are most ardent in the faith of white supremacy as, indeed, would naturally be expected. The whites of the regions with few Negroes have a less direct concern over the maintenance of white rule, whereas the whites of the black belts operate an economic and social system based on subordinate, black labor.[149]

It would be in Alabama, however, not in Texas, where Cox would come to know, firsthand, about black-belt politics.[150] He relocated there in 1944 after having accepted an offer from Tuskegee Normal and Industrial Institute to teach courses in economics and sociology as well as to head the social studies (later, science) division at the school. Bearing in mind Cox's leftist politics and his low opinion of the institute's founder, Booker T. Washington (sentiments that he expressed both in the classroom and in print),[151] Cox's salary must have been as low and his "prospects for faculty advancement" as unlikely at Wiley as Herbert Hunter claims for him to have taken a position at Tuskegee. On the other hand, Cox may well have been curious to see the vocational, liberal arts school that Washington and corporate "philanthropy" built in the heart of Alabama's black belt.[152]

And a black-belt institution is what Tuskegee was. Similar to the political-economic structure of most southern black-belt counties, Tuskegee was ultimately governed by a board of directors comprised of white corporate elites despite the composition of the student body. Here lay the reason why Cox labeled Washington a collaborationist: he catered to the economic needs of his benefactors by preparing both technically and ideologically ambitious young Blacks to work for their firms and asked of these same students that they accept political disenfranchisement as the fair cost of this bogus program of black economic development. "[A]lthough he is fundamentally antagonistic to the people's cause," Cox said of the perverse genius of collaborators in general but of Washington in particular, "he must appear to be their champion."[153] If the Tuskegee of the mid- to late 1940s differed little from the Tuskegee of the early to mid-1930s, then, as Horace Cayton observed during the earlier period, what really made matters worse for an outsider like Cox was the realization that at least some of his colleagues and university administrators were on some level aware that they were promoting a myth the hollowness of which they hid behind the façade of moral obligation.[154] It was probably this discrepancy between theory and practice more than anything else that guaranteed that Cox's stay at Tuskegee (1944–49) would be shorter than the one at Wiley.

Yet, in spite of the ideological and intellectual limitations of Tuskegee,[155] Cox made his five years there some of the most productive years of his life. These academic feats were rather typical of Cox; his internal drive was such that even when working largely by himself and well away from the nation's urban academic centers, he wrote constantly. A glance at the list of Cox's published articles written during his tenure at Tuskegee reveal that he wrote the bulk of *Caste, Class, and Race* while at the Alabama school.[156] Among the most noteworthy are: "Racial Theories of Robert E. Park, et al.," "Caste and Class," "Race Prejudice and Intolerance," "Race and Caste: A Definition and a Distinction," "Lynchings and the Status Quo," "An American Dilemma," "Estates, Social Classes, and Political Classes," "The Nature of the Anti-Asiatic Movement on the Pacific Coast," "The Nature of Race Relations: A Critique," and "Modern Democracy and the Class Struggle."[157] To borrow the words from the title of a recent biography of Ralph Waldo Emerson, Cox's mind was on fire in these years.

It should be borne in mind as well that Cox completed this impressive body of work without a reduction in his teaching load or the aid of research assistants. The best that Cox could do under such circumstances was to offer courses that were related to his research interests. He ostensibly designed two courses to serve those needs: Race and Culture and Socio-Economic Problems of the Southern Region. His other course offerings—Principles of Economics, Labor Problems, Consumer Economics, and American Economic Order—were, in the words of Hunter, "reminiscent of his earlier training at the University of Chicago."[158]

Cox's efforts proved to be a mixed blessing. On the one hand, *Caste, Class, and Race,* the culmination of his thought on a variety of sociological and political themes, earned him the George Washington Carver award from his publisher, Doubleday, in 1948. On the other hand, the publication of that very work ensured his fall from grace with the American sociological establishment whose center was Cox's alma mater. "Ensured" for two reasons: one, because he pursued a Marx-inspired line of reasoning in his approach to race relations and other sociopolitical matters precisely at the moment that the House Committee on Un-American Activities (HUAC) was launching its post–Second World War offensive;[159] and two, because he was bold enough not only to call into question the social theories of some of the country's leading sociologists and social anthropologists but also to take them to task by name. Cox's infractions were, of course, compounded by his blackness. He represented a population whose historic victimization on the basis of its economic and subsequent racial designation made it theoretically "more decidedly potentially communists than whites."[160] It undermined the supposed intellectual superiority of white people, a belief to which many Whites subscribe regardless of professed political affiliations. Little wonder, then, that Doubleday did not agree to a second printing of the book after the stock of the first one sold out in 1949. No matter how strong his perseverance and his belief in the soundness of his reasoning, it must have been a blow to Cox to see the product of so much of his intellectual energy vanish, of sorts, in the span of a year.

On some level, though, he must have expected or entertained the possibility that his work would be "received" in the manner that it was. He had spent roughly a decade sharpening his vision to see through the many illusions of particularly American society and had now committed his observations to paper. Cox would not have had any illusions about how the powers-that-be, academic or otherwise, would respond to a direct challenge to the bases of their authority, no matter how compelling the author's arguments. It is likely, therefore, that Cox interpreted the reviews of *Caste, Class, and Race* in which he was called a Marxist as so much ideological name-calling hardly worthy either of a response or of being considered scholarly.[161] They were merely signs of the times.

The Truman Paradox

We have seen that Cox believed Franklin Delano Roosevelt to be a heroic figure. A positive opinion of such conviction demands its opposite: a negative opinion of equal conviction. Enter Harry S. Truman. That Cox's characterization of Truman was as unduly critical as his sketch of Roosevelt inordinately laudatory is fairly certain, but the political logic that guided his assessment of Truman is persuasive.

At first glance, it appears that Cox indicted the former vice-president for not having followed to the letter his former boss's policies when he became president. This perspective is only partially true. What Cox objected to was Truman's simultaneous pursuit of an anti-communist foreign policy and a domestic policy for the "little man."[162] Put into political constituency terms, the first platform was generally supported by Republicans and the conservative wing (primarily southern) of the Democratic party, whereas the second was typically promoted by the remaining Democratic congressmen. Cox maintained, furthermore, that Truman was remarkably unaware of how opponents of the "Fair Deal" at home could use the philosophy informing the Truman Doctrine abroad to undermine his very domestic policy objectives. In Cox's opinion, Truman's critics were politically consistent, but the president was ideologically confused. Here Cox effectively demonstrates the manner in which foreign policy impacts domestic policy:

> We cannot, of course, imply that Mr. Truman should not have formulated policies according to his own vision and system of values. What seems significant was his ability to convince the electorate, at least temporarily, that those policies were in reality his predecessor's. On his assumption of office in April 1945, he solemnly promised to follow closely in Roosevelt's footsteps . . . Nevertheless, in foreign relations . . . Mr. Truman took the very position which he opposed at home. He seemed hardly to have grasped the implication that an anti-big-business campaign, such as the one which he waged so successfully in the United States, must certainly have resulted in a transformation of the society had it been conducted in almost any South American or Asian country. . . . [T]he very objectives sought would inevitably have brought about some form of socialism or outright communism . . . The incongruity thus became complete: accuse the capitalist system of counteracting "every decent reform" in the world toward the accomplishment of democratically desirable social goals—goals toward which socialism implicitly plans to work; and then, when the latter comes into being and begins to do the job in a non-capitalist way, charge it

with "depriving the individual of his freedom" and proceed, even with the aid of the old capitalist and fascist leaders, to stamp it out. This was, no doubt, inconsistent leadership.[163]

Cox's simplification of socialist theory and practice notwithstanding (not to mention his belief in the sincerity of Truman's anticorporate rhetoric), the basis of his criticism of Truman's politics was not unreasonable. In essence, he felt it inconsistent to give the same political program one name at home and another abroad. Moreover, it is disingenuous to say that reform elsewhere (labeled "communism" by Truman and like-minded people) infringes on the freedom of the individual while, at home, it merely seeks to curtail the prerogative of corporations to compromise that same freedom. In either case the freedom of certain individuals to exploit other individuals will have to be either checked or eradicated if some degree of socioeconomic justice and equality is the political goal. Yet, as is wont in capitalist society, by conflating freedom and capitalism, Truman provided American capitalists a slogan with which to advertise their overseas enterprises (to promote freedom rather than to increase profits) and to fight against any political measures designed to constrain their domestic operations. Their Republican and southern Democratic representatives (for their own related reasons) duly attacked the Truman administration (as they did Roosevelt's) for harboring "Reds" in federal offices. In order to, in David Caute's words, "steal the Republicans' thunder . . . Truman signed Executive Order 9835, which launched a purge of the federal civil service and inspired imitative purges at every level of American working life."[164] Here, then, was how Truman's foreign policy undermined his domestic program or, to be more specific, how the anticommunist Truman doctrine overseas became the anti–civil liberties "red scare" at home.[165] Little wonder, then, that Cox feared being called to appear before the House Committee on Un-American Activities[166] and worried about what would become of his academic career.

Lincoln University

If Cox was in any way demoralized by the immediate fate of *Caste, Class, and Race*,[167] it was only temporary. With the continuing challenge of polio, there were probably few things that could disturb Cox's mental equilibrium. His move to Lincoln University in Jefferson City, Missouri, in 1949 most likely improved his outlook. Less conservative politically and more willing to support a talented scholar than Tuskegee, Lincoln was a welcome change. Cox must have enjoyed the school's atmosphere; he remained there for the next twenty-one years, until his retirement in 1970. And he chose to remain in spite of having received numerous offers from prestigious predominantly white institutions to join their faculties.[168] Cox may have been an enemy of black nationalism, but he most certainly was a supporter of black institutions.[169]

Yet, in spite of his apparent comfort at Lincoln, his public good humor, and his impressive productivity while there, the reviewer of Cox's life cannot help but wonder if Cox ever knew sustained happiness there or anywhere else. In the opinion of one of his former students, though occasionally humorous, Cox was generally "aloof, strictly scholarly, and theoretical."[170] In that of another, he was "brilliant but very private."[171] In many respects, this dimension of Cox's personality is not surprising; as suggested earlier, by rearing, class status, the era in which he was born, and by profession, the erection of emotional walls around his person would have come naturally to Cox. This predilection was reinforced by the fact that "[h]is meals were brought to him from the cafeteria, and books and other materials were brought to him from the library at his request." For this reason it is curious that Cox first agreed and continued to live for some twenty years in a two-room "apartment" in Allen Hall, "the men's athletic dormitory, the rowdiest and noisiest dorm on [Lincoln's] campus."[172] Its proximity to the library was the rationale for residing there, but it could also indicate Cox's need for the social opposite of his own inclinations—companionship—in order to counterbalance the feeling of isolation that prolonged solitude produces.[173] If true, it was a companionship that he could control by the simple act of opening or closing his door.

Whatever the actual state of Cox's psyche over the course of his twenty years at Lincoln, behind the closed doors of his apartment he completed a remarkable amount of work. After his feverish productivity in the 1940s, Cox's writings of the 1950s seem sparse. Apart from pairs of essays on black leadership, civil rights organizations, and the medieval city, Cox published very little at first.[174] However, the appearance of *The Foundations of Capitalism* in 1959, the first volume of what would become his trilogy on the history and structure of the capitalist world economy, made it clear that he was hard at work in that decade.[175] Unlike the years approaching the publication of *Caste, Class, and Race*, when Cox consistently published articles that would become chapters of that work, Cox did not preview portions of *The Foundations of Capitalism* in article form. It seems fair to assume that, as an "accomplished" scholar, Cox no longer felt the pressure of having to publish pieces of his current book-length projects for either tenure or scholarly recognition. As to the subject matter, we have few clues why Cox undertook the daunting project of telling capitalism's story from thirteenth-century Venice to nineteenth-century England (the terminus of *The Foundations of Capitalism*) in a single volume.[176] I can only surmise that after having declared in *Caste, Class, and Race* that the proletarian movement would soon make great strides but having witnessed capitalism's survival of both the Great Depression and the Second World War, he felt it necessary to unearth the secret of that system's staying power. The result was *The Foundations of Capitalism, Capitalism and American Leadership* (1962), and *Capitalism as a System* (1964). In all, it was more than 1,000 pages worth of historical reconstructions, propositions, and analysis—a remarkable achievement to say the least and one that unequivocally established Cox as one of the "founding father[s]" of world systems analysis.[177]

In both the classroom and in Allen Hall, Cox was a tough task-master. In light of Cox's upbringing and age, it is not surprising to learn that he felt entitled to correct not only the scholastic performance of his students but even their behavior in dormitory corridors. From the recollections of some of his students, he clearly had set ideas about what he thought to be behavior becoming of educated young men and women.[178] Consequently, his complaints to both students and administrators were frequent, and their sources ranged from slouching in chairs to the use of profanity outside of the classroom. Cox's assessment of his students' assignments was equally strict. Recollecting the severity of Cox's grading, one of his former students told Herbert Hunter about a one-time Lincoln University saying: "If it is not bleeding, you have something to sell."[179] The figurative bleeding was a reference to Cox's notorious red pen. Elmer P. Martin recounts that "so many students received Cs in Dr. Cox's classes that the joke on campus was that C stands for 'Cox.' "[180] Apart from his notoriety as a hard grader, Cox also discouraged many students from taking his courses by his "slow and ponderous pace. Sometimes he would take an entire semester to cover two or three chapters in an assigned text, which he would go over in great detail—almost demanding that students know the chapters verbatim."[181] Unfortunately, the combination of Cox's teaching methods and his encyclopedic knowledge were not conducive to much classroom discussion and left many students intimidated. It was left, then, to the more mature of Lincoln's students to provide an alternative portrait of Cox as professor. They took Cox's seriousness to be indicative of his dedication (to teaching as well as to his own research interests), care (for their intellectual growth and development), and meticulousness, however tedious. [182]

As we shall discuss later, Cox also felt himself entitled to apply the same intellectual and behavioral standards by which he judged his students at Lincoln to the population of young black Americans at large. The paternalistic posture that he characteristically assumed when addressing himself to those younger in age surfaced most visibly in his remarks on black nationalism. Rather than seek to explore it as an understandable response to distinct sociohistorical inequities based on race, he chose to call it into question on cultural grounds. Of itself, this approach to black nationalism was not troublesome, but even appropriate.[183] What was problematic, however, was that Cox saw black nationalism as little more than ghetto behavior posing as a political movement. And ghetto behavior, so his reasoning went, is the urban retention of the worst characteristics of slave culture: irresponsibility, deviance, irrationality, and alienation. Cox's remarks about black nationalists suggest more than his classism and ageism. Also evident is his unwillingness to recognize in black nationalism the culture of resistance that has been part and parcel of black American culture since the time of that population's "forced migration" to these shores. It was arguably this inextinguishable force on which he himself drew that in part inspired him to be the defiant scholar that he was.[184] This is not to suggest that Cox's ideas require an analysis of his cultural milieu to be understood, but rather to say that because of historical facts and contemporary practices peculiar to and affecting black people in the West, it is virtually impossible to remove "culture" from the sociology of the black experience.

Most of Cox's writings on the sociopolitical ideologies of black Americans in the 1960s were published in the early 1970s before his death in 1974. Among his most noteworthy articles of the period are "The Question of Pluralism" and "Jewish Self-interest in 'Black Pluralism,'" to which we should also add his introduction to Nathan Hare's *The Black Anglo-Saxons*.[185] Cox also covered similar ground in the second half of what became *Race Relations: Elements and Social Dynamics*, the posthumously published version of his incomplete, final project (two-thirds of which, claims Elmer P. Martin, were discarded by the editors at Wayne State University Press).[186] From the title of one of the aforementioned articles, it comes as no surprise to learn that the charge of anti-Semitism was leveled at Cox by more than one of its readers.[187] Suffice it to say here that it is possible to read many of Cox's anti-Semitic remarks more as claims of how the collective black experience in the West differs from the Jewish equivalent than as expressions of some visceral hatred of Jews. From allegedly "Jewish" patterns of socioeconomic and sociopolitical behavior, Cox sought to show black nationalists in particular that neither ethnic nationalism (of the type they espoused) nor ethnic pluralism (of the type that Cox claimed Jewish Americans embraced) are feasible models for black Americans to follow on practical or political grounds. In spite of what he may have understood as pragmatic intentions, it is unfortunate that Cox felt it necessary to resort to stereotypes in order to make a political point.

In *Race Relations*, Cox also restated his belief in the principles of socialism and in its eventual global triumph. His convictions were not derived from extensive analyses of self-proclaimed socialist societies, but rather were based on the theoretical outlines of socialist practice. In this regard, Cox was much like Marx. Though extremely critical of "utopian" socialism, his vision of socialist society, despite being based on "scientific" reasoning, was never more than idealistic. In his final years, however, Cox disavowed one central tenet of Marxism: the primacy of the class struggle in the movement from one mode of production to another. In this evolutionary vision of the advent of socialist society, Cox maintained that conflict between the economic elite and the working class acting would not act as the harbinger of this new society, but rather social imitation will achieve that end. Cox did not elaborate on the precise mechanisms of this process, but what he did offer as a general statement on the theory was that "in the very process" of seeking to live like their social "betters," working people would "transform" the capitalist system itself.[188]

It was also Cox's contention that while the aspiration to be wealthy on the part of many members of the working class aids capitalist development in the short term, the adoption of typically bourgeois attitudes—thriftiness, reliability, and managerial savvy, among others—will be utilized in the process of realizing and maintaining socialist society. Here, then, was Cox's ultimate reason for counseling black Americans to renounce racial nationalism and to embrace a generic American nationalism that would gradually become a (race) neutral expression with the increasing adoption of socialist practices. Cox, like other socialists, was convinced that only socialism (of the sort that he believed was achieved in the former Soviet Union) could resolve the racial and ethnic conflicts inherent in capitalism. What Cox would say today, we can only imagine.

An overriding concern with the scale of population and natural resources led Cox to question the feasibility of socialism in smaller nations. Although he never specified precise thresholds for either of the two variables, Cox stated on more than one occasion his belief that the adoption of socialism required a critical mass of people and sufficient natural resources with which to supply the basic needs of the society in question. Although perhaps not entirely false, it is nonetheless true (according, at least, to the most reputable students of the economy of the former Soviet Union) that too great a population spread out over a vast territory throughout which are similarly distributed a variety of natural resources are the things of which socialist planners' nightmares are made.[189] Given Cox's theoretical rather than empirical thoughts on socialist society, I belive that Cox intentionally avoided this exploration so as not to shatter the ideal by which he measured capitalist society.

The Final Years

At the time of his first retirement from teaching in 1970, Cox's two main intellectual, political concerns were how to promote the entry of larger numbers of black Americans into mainstream American society and how this process would aid in the transformation of American society from capitalism to socialism. This retirement did not last for long; within the year he had accepted an invitation from the chairperson of Wayne State University's department of sociology, Alvin M. Rose, to be Distinguished Visiting Professor in that department. We do not know for how long Cox had originally intended to remain at Wayne State, but after a year of what he considered assembly line education and intense debates with "Black Marxist students who disagreed with [his] interpretation of capitalism,"[190] he decided to retire once again, this time for good.

In that same year the American Sociological Association honored him with the DuBois-Johnson-Frazier Award. Considering Cox's low opinion of Frazier, he may have had mixed feelings about the honor, but he probably looked on it as token recognition of what he long felt his work merited. At any rate, Cox remained in Detroit—at 5440 Cass Ave. to be precise—and continued to labor on the work that we know as *Race Relations*. Unfortunately, he would never see it completed. He died on 4 September 1974, ten days after having celebrated his seventy-third birthday.

For any one of us, life is a series of challenges, some of our making, many more not. Oliver C. Cox had his share of both. Among those for which he volunteered, we would have to include his immigration to the United States and his pursuit of a professional degree. Among those that were visited on him, polio certainly ranks first on the list, followed by the Great Depression. Though it may seem inappropriate to suggest, I believe that one of the positive results of these two events was to have rendered him more compassionate toward those less materially fortunate than himself. It was at this juncture, too, that Cox became politically conscious. Thus, national and world events throughout the 1930s—the New Deal, fascism, racial injustice—began to hold his interest as much as his sociology lectures at the University of Chicago. This transformation is evident in the contents of *Caste, Class, and Race*. Despite its impressive scholarliness, because it openly drew on Marxist thought to criticize some of this country's leading social scientists as well as capitalism generally, *Caste, Class, and Race* earned Cox the "red" badge in a red scare era and was allowed to go out of print for over a decade. Apparently undaunted by this setback, Cox, for reasons only partially understood, took on another challenge and devoted roughly fifteen years to a three-volume chronicle of the capitalist world economy. Finally, in the last decade of his life, Cox returned to his original concern—race relations—catalyzed no doubt by the civil rights and Black Power movements. All told, Cox's was a life devoted to scholarship, politics, and the politics of scholarship.

With that said, let us begin this study with the issue that first confronted Cox on his arrival in the United States.

A Typology of Race Relations

In *Caste, Class, and Race,* Cox named seven "situations of race relations": the stranger, original-contact, slavery, ruling-class, bipartite, amalgamative, and the nationalistic.[1] Each situation warrants an individual discussion in its own right, as do the relationships among the situations.[2] For our purposes here, though, descriptions of the ruling-class and bipartite situations of race relations will be most instructive. Later in this chapter I will discuss an amalgamative situation of race relations in order to show that it may be considered a composite of the ruling-class and bipartite situations of race relations. First, however, it is important to establish what Cox precisely meant by "race relations."

Terms and Definitions

At their most basic level, Cox defined race relations as that "behavior which develops among peoples who are aware of each other's actual or imputed physical differences." Accordingly, a simple definition of race sufficed for Cox: "any group of people that is generally believed to be, and generally accepted as, a race in any given area of ethnic competition."[3] That this definition of race is highly subjective and variable is entirely consistent with Cox's view of the role of the sociologist (as opposed to that of the biologist or the physical anthropologist):

> The sociologist is interested in what meanings and definitions a society gives to certain social phenomena and situations. It would probably be as revealing of interracial attitudes to deliberate upon the variations in the skeletal remains of some people as it would to question an on-going society's definition of race because, anthropometrically speaking, the assumed race is not a *real* race. What we are interested in is the social definition of the term "race." To call that which a group has been pleased to designate a race by some other name does not affect the nature of the social problem to be investigated.[4]

Thus, each of the situations of race relations that we named above has its own definition of "race."

Finally, unlike some current theories of social stratification that situate "ethnicity" within larger racial categories, Cox considered race a subcategory of ethnicity. Thus he concluded that "[w]hen the ethnics are of the same race—that is to say, when there is no significant physical characteristics accepted by the ethnics as marks of distinction—their process of adjustment is usually designated nationality or "minority-group" problems. When, on the other hand, the ethnics recognize each other physically and use their physical distinction as a basis for the rationale of their interrelationships, their process of adjustment is usually termed race relations or race problems." Cox defined an "ethnic" as a "people living competitively in relationships of superordination or subordination with respect to some other people or peoples within one state, country, or economic area."[5] From this definition of an ethnic, we can infer that Cox held that physical or cultural differences between distinct populations will not give rise to social confrontations when those populations share political-economic equality in a given society. Cox believed that the Soviet Union had achieved such equality.

Trinidad and the Ruling-Class Situation of Race Relations

The system of racial stratification that Cox labeled the ruling-class situation of race relations was undoubtedly based on his reflections on his native Trinidad some twenty-five years after having left. According to Cox, a ruling-class situation of race relations is established when a small[6] and foreign[7] settler population (European in the Atlantic cases) "adopts a policy of 'cooperation'" with the indigenous population (or in those cases where that population has been the victim of genocide or near-genocide, the imported population) whereby "favors are distributed to the mixed-bloods on the apparent degree of admixture."[8] In the American ruling-class situation of race relations, the children of European and Amerindian and European and African parents are conceptualized as biologically and socially distinct people (from either of their parents) who require novel racial labels—e.g., mestizo, ladino, pardo, mulatto, quadroon—by settler elites and subsequently by their social subordinates as well. These social labels, moreover, are active determinants of socioeconomic position: color and class ideally work in unison. "Degrees of color," Cox commented, "tend to become a determinant of status in a continuous social-class gradient, with whites at its upper reaches. Thus, assuming cultural parity among the group, the lighter the complexion, the greater the economic and social opportunities." Moreover, "[t]he cultural *rapprochement* of the ruling-class whites and the upper-class colored people facilitates the use of the latter as a cultural cushion and an instrument of exploitation of the masses."[9]

The Trinidad of Cox's youth was comprised of roughly 325,000 people of whom the largest number—about 175,000—were of predominantly African descent. Second were the 110,000 Trinidadians who traced their ancestry to the Indian subcontinent. They were followed by about 40,000 Trinidadians whose heritage was both African and European, and the remainder of Trinidad's population was comprised of those of predominantly European ancestry.

Thus in 1910 Trinidad had all of the characteristics of a ruling-class situation of race relations. Yet, this situation was then only a recent development. Unlike most of the other islands of the English-speaking Caribbean in which the demographic and economic characteristics of ruling-class situations had appeared as early as the eighteenth century, it was only in the aftermath of slavery that Trinidad followed suit. In 1808, for example, a year after the British government outlawed slave imports into its colonial possessions, British officials recorded 31,500 Trinidadians of whom 22,000 were enslaved Africans, 5,500 free people of color, 2,500 Europeans ("of whom less than half were British, nearly one-third French, and nearly one-fifth Spaniards"), and some 1,500 were Amerindians.[10]

In comparison to the demographic composition of other Caribbean islands at earlier periods, Trinidad's nineteenth-century figures hardly seem the human material out of which ruling-class situations of race relations were made. For example, according to one estimate, Barbados's population in 1700 was comprised of 12,000 Europeans and 42,000 people of African and African-European ancestry.[11] A century later, their numbers had climbed to roughly 16,000 and 64,000 respectively, with the population of free people of color advancing above the 2,000 mark.[12] The contrast between Trinidad's 1808 population figures with those of Jamaica a century earlier is even more stark. In 1700, Jamaica's total population amounted to 53,000 of whom 8,000 were white and 45,000 were enslaved.[13] By 1800, the number of slaves had grown more than sixfold, attaining the staggering figure of 300,000; the island's white population increased nearly four times to 30,000, while the population of free people of color stood at 10,000.[14] Of course, the archetypal plantation society of the late eighteenth century, San Domingue (Haiti), also fulfilled all of the requirements for a ruling-class situation: more than 450,000 enslaved sugar producers, 40,000 people of primarily European ancestry, and 28,000 free people of color and free blacks.[15] Trinidad may have been a "model British slave colony,"[16] in the period between its annexation by Britain from Spain in 1797 to the official termination of enslavement in English colonial possessions in 1834, but a model plantation society it was not.[17]

One way of estimating what kind of race relations (according to Cox's categories) operate in a given slave society is to determine the size and social standing of the population of free people of color. When we compare, for example, Trinidad's population ratio of free people of color to people of primarily European descent with those of Barbados and Jamaica at the end of the eighteenth century, what immediately calls our attention is that whereas Trinidad's is more than 2 to 1, Barbados' is 1 to 8 and Jamaica's 1 to 3. This atypical demographic development had significant sociopolitical repercussions. In fact, it largely explains why, until 1961, Trinidad was a "crown colony" (that is, one "with all essential powers reserved to the British Government through the Governor") rather than one with a "self-governing constitution like Jamaica or Barbados."[18] For not only did this population numerically dominate white Trinidadians, but it was also in possession of a considerable amount of property. Therefore, if property requirements were the means by which the vast majority of Trinidadians were legally disqualified from either holding public office or from voting for local representatives, then they had little effect on the majority of free people of color. To avoid that likely, yet unimaginable, possibility, the British crown opted to govern the island itself.

The size and wealth of Trinidad's free population of color were remarkable for the region. Though the majority of its members were artisans,[19] a sizable minority were landowners. In fact, it was precisely the promise of land in exchange for the promise to settle and work it that brought many of them to Trinidad. So desperate was the Spanish Crown to populate the island in the last quarter of the eighteenth century that it extended to free people of color the same inducements to relocate as it did to potential white settlers, albeit in reduced amount: "Blacks and people of colour, being free men and proprietors, received half of the proportion allotted to whites, the allotment to be increased if they brought slaves with them."[20] For their part, free people of color (particularly those from the French Caribbean) were only too happy to find a safe haven amid the revolutionary upheavals reverberating throughout the Caribbean as a result of both the Haitian and French Revolutions. Ironically, however, this same population that fled revolutionary changes elsewhere to protect both person and property, was suspected, in Trinidad, of encouraging social rebellion. Ironic, as James Millette explains, because "[I]t was completely forgotten that of all West Indian free coloured communities the Trinidad community had least reason to be revolutionary. The free coloureds were prosperous and they were, by current standards, privileged."[21] In other words, Trinidad's free population of color may have been "revolutionary" with regard to racial matters, but with regard to the sanctity of property rights, they were partial to the Caribbean's *ancien régime.*

Given that in a ruling-class situation of race relations "a premium is put upon degrees of whiteness among the people of color,"[22] it stands to reason that color consciousness (as opposed to race consciousness) is a major obsession in this type of society. For Cox, however, a graver consequence than even the psychological effects of the ruling-class situation on its members is the confusion it creates around the actual source of color consciousness itself:

> In an ideal [ruling-class] situation the position of the white ruling class is impregnable. Its members are envied, admired, and imitated religiously, but they are never questioned. The rest of the population is too absorbed with the immediate business of achieving increments of whiteness or their equivalent to give much attention to the inciting social force in the system. The system tends to be self-regulating. The colored people as a whole do not look upon whites as a people particularly prone to race prejudice, but rather each aspiring color stratum grapples with the problem of holding its own and of whittling away the distance attitudes from the stratum above. Therefore, to any given color group, the persons who are most exasperatingly color prejudiced are not necessarily white people, but rather the cold-shouldering, snubbing, lighter-color group immediately above.[23]

Of course, the relatively insignificant number of resident whites in ruling-class situations of race relations only serves to further veil the origins of color consciousness.[24]

Yet, an intended though paradoxical consequence of the preoccupation with skin color is the collective belief that individual perseverance can overcome color prejudice, at least the kind that is manifest in ruling-class situations of race relations:

> In the ruling-class situation colored people are not hopelessly depressed; for them the ceiling of opportunity is high, but attainable. Although the color ranks are practically checkmated by color cliques, color is never explicitly accepted by the group as a whole as a consideration limiting success. There are ordinarily sufficient instances of brilliant victories over color barriers to warrant sanguine illusions that they do not exist. Exem-

plifying cases of colored persons holding positions of enviable dignity are always available.[25]

A related ideological consequence of a ruling-class situation is the tendency to rate class over race. This predilection is easily explained: those living within the social structures of a ruling-class situation recognize consciously or unconsciously that within the wide racial designations of "black" or "brown" there are representatives of a relatively wide range of class positions. Otherwise stated, the range of color-class pairings which typify ruling-class situations defies either neat or categorical associations between "race" and class which characterize other societies, namely those in bipartite situations of race relations.

For Cox, the ideological culmination of the beliefs characteristic of this situation is the generalized respect there for civic institutions. In spite of the fact that the state responds first and foremost to the socioeconomic needs of white nationals with property, the demographic constitution of these societies makes citizenship (both formal and unofficial), at least, a far more democratic and popular claim than one might imagine.

> Although in the ruling-class situation the colored people are ruled by whites, the masses are never deprived of the sense of having a country. Here the colored people know that they have a permanent home and, if pressed, they will readily become conscious of the fact that the whites are foreigners. Therefore, these people can develop a genuine patriotism; and, in spite of their exploitation, their lives are more frequently planned; they are securely anchored in the social system. . . . Out of these attitudes defensive nationalism among the colored people tends to have a comparatively easy growth.[26]

These ideological characteristics of ruling-class situations of race relations should be borne in mind since they served as Cox's point of comparison with the next situation of race relations up for discussion, the bipartite one.

First, however, it may be useful to point out two key variables in Cox's theory of racial dynamics: demographic pressures[27] and the division of labor. According to Cox, the factor that most shapes

socio-racial stratification in a given Atlantic arena society is the numerical strength or weakness of the European settler population in
relation to the Amerindian or African populations as they are structured in a capitalist economy. As we just outlined, in the ruling-class
situation of race relations a small European settler population makes
use of an intermediate biracial population by which to order that
society socio-racially.[28] Conversely, in the bipartite situation of race
relations—the marker of which is a substantial, or, numerically dominant, European settler population—the total population is nearly
categorically divided by uncompromising definitions of racial membership, leaving color or skin-tone distinctions relatively inconsequential. In other words, the dominant European community is
generally indifferent to shades or grades of brown.

The United States and the Bipartite Situation of Race Relations

Cox's reflections on the bipartite situation of race relations were
based on his then nearly thirty years in the United States, which
was a decade longer than he had lived in his native Trinidad. Like
other Americans of color reared outside of the United States, Cox
immediately recognized that the American system of race relations
differed from the Trinidadian one, and as an outsider-insider he
set out to determine the material bases of the distinction. He concluded that:

> Where whites are in numbers large enough to fill all preferred
> occupations or where there is possible competition with a large
> colored population along the whole cultural hierarchy, defi-
> nite racial attitudes are developed. Here the tendency is to di-
> chotomize the society into color groups, for any system of in-
> creasing acceptability according to degrees of lightness of color
> will quickly threaten white dominance. We do not have, in this
> case, merely a white ruling class, but a white population; there-
> fore, anything short of dichotomy will leave masses of white
> persons subordinated to numbers of enterprising colored per-
> sons, a situation extremely favorable for rapid amalgamation
> and consequent depreciation of color per se as a social value.[29]

Cox did not specify the exact number of European settlers required in a particular society for it to be designated a bipartite one. If we take colonial Algeria as an example, particularly the Algeria of the 1950s about which Frantz Fanon wrote in *The Wretched of the Earth,* it appears that the critical mass of white settlers could be as low as 10 percent of the total population. However, Pierre van den Berghe offered a figure of "more than 20 or 25 per cent" for the socially dominant population in what he termed the *competitive* type of race relations, the equivalent apparently of Cox's bipartite situation of race relations. Whatever the minimum number of European settlers necessary to establish a bipartite situation in a given society, the roots of the American one, like those of the ruling-class situation in Trinidad, can be traced to the time of the nation's founding.

The English settlement of the thirteen colonies in the seventeenth century bore a certain resemblance to the Portuguese colonization of Brazil in the sixteenth. The most obvious similarity was that in both areas European settlement was first confined to the coast before it spread into the immense hinterland, unlike, for example, Spain's colonization of what is today northern Mexico and the western territories of the United States, which proceeded as much overland as it did from the littoral. There were obvious reasons for the development of this pattern of settlement not least of which was that the coast was the site of both landfall after the long voyage from Europe and the point of cultural and commercial contact with home. Yet, the most important factor in restricting to the coast both English and Portuguese settlement in the Americas was a human one: the undeniable presence of sizable Amerindian populations. Informed estimates of the "pre-contact" indigenous populations of the areas that would become the thirteen colonies, put their numbers between a quarter and half a million.[30] Under these demographic circumstances, "[b]y and large . . . colonials preferred not to provoke beyond the patience of surrounding Indians. . . . It was not the part of wisdom to stir up so great a potential enemy."[31] However, there were other practical reasons that served European settlers to respect, at least at the outset, their Amerindian hosts: the native peoples were the providers of food, procurers of desired commodities (pelts in the thirteen colonies, "Brazil" wood in coastal Brazil), and potential agents of imperialist designs. For their part, the coastal indigenous populations accommodated (or rather, tolerated) these lost souls from across the seas only to the degree that their settlements did not violate the territorial sovereignty of a particular nation and that they had valuable items with which to trade. Thus, whatever disputes that arose between Amerindians and European settlers within the first decades of contact were easily offset by indigenous codes of hospitality, the exchange of goods, and the belief on the part of probably most indigenous populations that the newcomers would soon make their way back from whence they came. In Brazil, the introduction of sugar cane indefinitely forestalled the fruition of Amerindian expectations, while in the thirteen colonies, the sheer force of European numbers had the same effect.

Had the average rates of European immigration to and mortality in the thirteen colonies remained at their pre-1650 levels throughout the colonial era, a ruling-class situation of race relations would have undoubtedly developed there as in the other European colonies in the Americas. Instead, after 1650 Europeans poured into the thirteen colonies at a staggering rate, and once there, they lived longer than those who immigrated before 1650. From barely viable settlements in Massachusetts and Virginia, whose respective populations did not total more than 1,500 in the 1620s, the number of non-Amerindian inhabitants of British North America had grown to 55,000 by mid-century.[32] By 1700 their numbers had increased more than five-fold from their 1650 totals, surpassing in less than a century the estimated number of indigenous peoples who had inhabited the areas before the British arrival. In short, "[d]uring the seventeenth century, European colonials grew to outnumber the constantly diminishing Indians along the eastern seaboard, and as colonial numbers increased, colonial cockiness inflated."[33]

The next three-quarters of a century proved decisive both in wholly undermining the territorial basis of Amerindian sovereignty in eastern North America and in preempting the development of a ruling-class situation of race relations in colonial America. The nonindigenous population of the thirteen colonies surpassed the 1,200,000 mark by 1750.[34] Yet, the truly extraordinary demographic leap was this population's addition of over a million people in the next twenty years. While some of this growth can certainly be attributed to "natural increase" (a higher birth rate coupled with a declining mortality rate), much of it was stimulated by the arrival of nearly a quarter of a million Europeans and Africans in the fifteen years between 1760 and 1775.[35]

For the Amerindians of eastern North America, this vast and seemingly unending stream of settlers could only mean more territorial concessions and ultimately more relocations into temporarily safer havens. "Sooner or later," remarks Francis Jennings, "as colonial populations grew, newcoming European immigrants established farms and towns of their own . . . and pushed the Indians farther west or north: or north or south, but away."[36] However, in all fairness to European settlers, the retreat of indigenous populations was sometimes less the direct than indirect effect of European population growth. Larger number of settlers increased Amerindian susceptibility to diseases for which they lacked the necessary antibodies, deepened Amerindian entanglements in European imperial power struggles,[37] intensified the enslavement of Amerindians, and increased the availability of alcohol which "while serving as a painkiller for the eroded quality of life . . . contributed further to the Indians' demise."[38] In short, for the original inhabitants of eastern North America, the arrival of Europeans in their lands initiated an exercise in social coexistence that soon became an Amerindian struggle for physical survival.

The population that largely came to replace Amerindians as the social Other in the thirteen colonies beginning in the latter part of the seventeenth century was an African one. Of course, this was especially true of the southern colonies, where the concentration of Africans was greatest.[39] Southern planters imported Africans to labor in the tobacco plantations of the greater Chesapeake, in the marshes of South Carolina to cultivate rice, and in the Republican era, in the cotton plantations of the Deep South. Though the African population of colonial and early Republican North America was never more than a fraction of the European one, its rate of growth was higher. As we already intimated, the twenty representatives of Africa who were purchased by Virginia Company agents from a Dutch man-of-war in 1619, grew to over half a million by the time the Republic was won. Of this number, over 200,000 were slaves in Virginia,[40] the provenance, curiously, of more than one "Founding Father" of the Republic. It is equally disturbing to contemplate that something as humanly beneficial as a decline in the mortality rates of indentured

servants probably played a significant role in moving Virginia planters to gradually replace their servants with African captives in the
latter half of the seventeenth century. As Edmund S. Morgan argues,
as long as mortality rates were high across races as they were in early-
seventeenth-century colonial Virginia, for example, "there could
be no great advantage in owning a man for a lifetime rather than a
period of years, especially since a slave cost roughly twice as much as
an indentured servant. If the chances of a man's dying during his
first five years in Virginia were better than fifty-fifty—and it seems
apparent that they were—and if English servants could be made to
work as hard as slaves, English servants for a five-year term were the
better buy."[41]

The mortality rates of Virginia's black population apparently declined in the 1680s, for it was then that the "first major slave codes"
were written and they were "placed squarely on a racial foundation."[42] The gradual substitution of black slaves for white indentured servants on the part of Virginia's planters was reinforced by
three other contemporaneous developments. First, "[a] decline in
English birthrates during the second third of the seventeenth century, combined with rising real wages, had by the 1680s substantially
reduced the number of men at risk to come to the New World." Second, "a severe depression in the tobacco economy at the end of the
seventeenth century decreased relative opportunities in the Chesapeake colonies." As a result, the "proportion of British immigrants
who came to the Chesapeake colonies . . . declined from a high of over
two-fifths in the 1670s to just over a third by the 1690s."[43] Finally,
yet perhaps most important, the partnership in crime of enslaved
Blacks and indentured Whites played a key role in the increasing
preference for enslaved over indentured labor by colonial planters
in the latter half of the seventeenth century. Of course, to call their
actions "crimes" is to speak relatively; petty theft, flight, and revolt
in a society that legally justified social inequality were forms of
social protest against the social order that the Law served. In any
event, more troubling than the crimes themselves to colonial elites
was the fact that, despite the racial differences that should have
divided them, enslaved Blacks and indentured (and formerly indentured) Whites were too frequently making common cause based on
their shared class position. Colonial elites shrewdly responded to
what they considered troublesome collusion between their social in-

feriors by upgrading the status of indentured and poor Whites in
relation to enslaved Blacks. Accordingly, "[p]lantation owners attempted to enlist the support of lower-class whites in the control of
the Black workforce . . . hiring them in positions as overseers, super-
visors, guards, slave patrollers, and police."[44] In ruling-class situation
of race relations terms, poor whites in colonial America were encouraged by their social superiors to assume the role of mulattos
and mestizos, or, of the "social buffer between the ruling classes and
the most exploited laborers."[45] When these social trends were combined with the physical distinctiveness, cultural foreignness, and
legal vulnerability of Africans in Virginia as in the rest of eastern
North America after 1680, the Republic inherited more than sufficient material out of which to establish a bipartite situation of race
relations.

In bipartite situations the "social advantage of lightness of color
within the colored group,"[46] is less than that which it commands in
ruling-class situations of race relations. It is not surprising, then,
that one consequence of such simultaneously strict and loose criteria for racial identification in bipartite situations (strict on granting
the label "white," while loose in defining one as "black") is the tendency on the part of all its members, irrespective of racial categorization or identification, to privilege racial solidarity over class consciousness. Among Blacks in a bipartite situation, "Here people of
color tend to be humbled, not only by the engrossing importance of
their color but also by the fact that the color interest is inevitably
common to them all. Here the colored person of the lowest class
has an intuitive way of quickly establishing rapport with the most
advanced colored gentleman, for the basis of their sympathy is ele-
mental. It tends to keep the social-class hierarchy among them quite
obtuse."[47] For Whites the psychological effects and, arguably, psychological necessities of this type of econo-racial regime, demand
that the proof of white superiority be rendered visible by material
disparities between Whites and Blacks:

> In the situation under discussion . . . colored persons may ac-
> quire marks of cultural distinction only by sufferance. Moreover,
> the cultural degradation of the colored people as a whole is be-
> lieved to be an asset to the whites, and they strive to achieve it. . . .
> In the United States a relatively illiterate, criminal, diseased,

base, poor, and prostituted colored people serves by comparison as proof to the world that Negroes do not deserve the social
opportunities available to whites. . . . It is, of course, in the interest of the ruling-class whites . . . to make the colored person, as
a human being, ashamed of his very existence.[48]

Given such forces committed to the preemption of black social
advancement, black people have little or no faith in most institutions
in the American bipartite situation of race relations. From this perspective, Cox felt that black Americans could rarely, if ever, feel
themselves fully part of the national body politic:

But civic pride is denied colored people in the bipartite situation, and this fact is in no small measure responsible for their
social instability. It keeps them spiritually on the move; it
denies them the right to call their country home; it limits patri-
otism severely, thus making a genuine love of one's country virtually impossible. . . . Restrictions upon cooperative efforts of
colored people in communal life tend to determine their pattern of community organization. Here their effort becomes
tentative, they establish impermanently, and their impaired
sense of ownership in their country tends to be reflected in
their comparatively disreputable communal life. In America
especially, fanatical gambling and the emergence of wealthy
messiahs register somewhat the mental atmosphere of the colored community.[49]

Two other social mechanisms served to reinforce the differences
in quality of life between the races: segregation and unpunished
racial violence. About the first, Cox remarked that "[s]egregation
obviously limits the opportunity for communication and inter-racial
understanding and makes possible an easy exploitation of antagonistic stereotypes. . . . If the races live in protected residential zones
and are kept apart in schools, in churches, in cemeteries, on the
playgrounds, in hotels and restaurants, on transportation vehicles,
and so on, they will tend to believe in a disparity of every possible
group interest and purpose, a social fact which is basically anti-
pathetic to assimilation." As for unchecked racial violence, Cox focused on what he thought to be its most graphic expression: lynch-

ing. He broadened the traditional definition of lynching, a practice meant to keep Blacks "in their place, that is to say, kept as a great, easily exploitable, common-labor reservoir."[50]

> Specifically, we may think of a lynching situation as one in which one Negro or several encounter one white or more and in which they find themselves exposed to coercion, insult, or violence, their rightful reaction to which, as normal citizens, threatens to lead either to their being beaten or killed by one white or by a mob of white persons; and, for this impending exercise of arbitrary violence, there is a consciousness on both sides that the law will not punish and that the organized ruling class in the community will show condonement.[51]

According to this definition of a lynching, many instances, past and present, of the unjustifiable use of force by police officers on black people constitute lynchings. This is not surprising in light of the fact that law enforcement has historically either participated or connived in unambiguous lynchings for which only a miniscule number have ever been indicted.

Cox also added the following unconventional assertion on the actual and potential sites of lynchings in the United States: "Lynchings occur mostly in those areas where the laws discriminate against Negroes; sometimes in these areas, the administrative judicial machinery may even facilitate the act. However, the lynching attitude is to be found everywhere among whites in the United States." Although lynching is "[n]owhere [in the United States] . . . advocated on the statute books . . . there is a prepotent sanction . . . that whites may use force against any Negro who becomes overbearing."[52]

Yet, in spite of these seemingly relentless and desperate efforts on the part of some Whites to contravene the attempts of Blacks to become part of "mainstream" American life, Cox emphatically repeated that the sociopolitical orientation of the majority of black Americans is assimilationist, not nationalistic. "The solidarity of American Negroes," he asserted, "is neither nationalistic nor nativistic. The group strives for neither a forty-ninth state leading to an independent nation nor a back-to-Africa movement; its social drive is toward assimilation."[53] On this issue as on others, it is hard to determine to what degree Cox's statements reflected his analysis or his prognosis

or a combination of both. In any event, either by reporting or declaring that black nationalism is neither a desirable nor a feasible
response to white racism (though, by his own admission, "[I]n the
United States white foreigners are ordinarily encouraged to assimilate, but peoples of color are not"), Cox was necessarily counseling
black Americans to remain Job-like in the faith that the liberal creed
would eventually carry the day. Furthermore, as a scholar with Marxist leanings, Cox maintained that the American working-class movement would be the instrument of first the liberal triumph and then
of the socialist one, at which point race prejudice and its basis
"human exploitation . . . will . . . cease to exist."[54] We will address
Cox's thoughts on the transition to socialism in chapter 6, but for
now, let us turn our attention to what he called the amalgamative
situation of race relations.

On Amalgamation

The amalgamative situation of race relations was Cox's attempt to
account for Latin American race relations or race relations in those
societies where "amalgamation between the white and black population is far advanced." In those instances, not only is it "practically
impossible to make lightness of complexion a definite mark of status," but "the group cannot attain a white 'universe of discourse'
and consensus sufficiently strong to achieve clear-cut white dominance." Thus, intermarriage "becomes a matter of personal tastes"
and "[I]ndividual cultural achievements tend to be estimated on
their merits."[55] Clearly, Cox, like other Americans of color, believed
that Brazilians and other Latin Americans had by and large rid themselves of race, though perhaps not, color prejudice.

Of greater concern to us than the "truth" or falsehood of Cox's
claims is how he explained their development. Rather than apply
the econo-demographic model that he used to determine situations
of race relations in the ruling-class and bipartite cases, here he
introduced three intervening variables: the level of nationalism in
the society in question; the historical motives that shaped a (settler)
society's founding; and the type of organization or institution that
managed its establishment. Cox asserted that the more intensely nationalism is felt, "the more inflated will be the individual's concep-

tion of himself, and the greater his unwillingness to intermarry with other peoples." He defined nationalism as "an exploitative, socio-psychological instrument of actual or potential ruling classes" in a capitalist society. It is, he added, an "integral part of the non-material cultural imperatives of capitalism, and it has developed as a func-tion of the rise of capitalism." From these declarations we can infer that in those societies where capitalism and its progeny, national-ism, are least developed, so too is race or ethnic consciousness on the part of the dominant ethnic group. Cox believed this to be true of the "Europeans of Mediterranean stock" who "settled" in Latin America.[56]

Cox defined exploitation colonies as those where the "commer-cial exploitation of native resources" was the primary impulse be-hind colonization, and settlement colonies as those where the colo-nizers "came . . . as settlers with the avowed purpose of taking over and of making the country their home." In settlement colonies (the most noteworthy of which is, of course, North America), "amalga-mation has not been accepted as a policy," whereas in the exploita-tion colonies, "amalgamation with the colored peoples was advo-cated as a salutary colonial policy."[57]

Finally, as far as the type of organization or institution that super-vised a colony's establishment was concerned, Cox maintained that those colonies which owed their founding "mainly" to the initiative of "private enterprise . . . facilitated the maneuvering of the colored people into positions which seemed most suitable to their contin-ued segregation," and those that were established "under the aegis of a monarch" were more inclined to uphold the "old religious cri-terion of equality"[58] and to promote, ostensibly, integration. Accord-ing to this formula, those colonies founded by northern Europeans fit into the first category; those established by Mediterranean Euro-peans fulfilled the criterion of the second.

If we feel somewhat confused by and unconvinced of Cox's map-ping of the interplay of the above variables in creating amalgama-tive situations of race relations, we have reason to be. For one, the correlation that he tried to establish between the extent of capital-ist development and the level of nationalist sentiment is dubious at best. It invites the question of what empirical measurements can prove, for example, that English nationalism was greater than its Span-ish equivalent in say the eighteenth century apart from economic indicators. Questionable, too, is the claim that exploitation colonies indulged cross-ethnic intermarriage to a greater extent than did settlement colonies, since the "commercial exploitation of native resources" lends itself to ethnic/racial exclusivity equal to that in settlement colonies.[59] Finally, Cox's claim that colonies founded and governed by monarchs yielded greater social equality than those established by colonial companies is similarly unconvincing since it presumes that the economic motives for colonization were less pronounced in the minds of monarchs than they were in those of the men in the field.

In the final analysis, there was little reason for Cox to have felt it necessary to depart from his earlier model of race relations in order to explain the apparent peculiarities of what he termed the amalgamative situation. An alternative hypothesis was at hand; one, moreover, that was consistent with his original model. As we shall see in the amalgamative situation of Brazilian race relations, this type of society may simply be one which has oscillated between ruling-class and bipartite situations of race relations throughout its history. This reformulation adequately explains why, for example, European-Brazilians continue to constitute the vast majority of the economic and political elites of their country and why "a preponderance of dark-colored people are in the lower economic strata [though] the population is necessarily marbled with color."[60]

Brazil as a Test Case

With a total population of between 7 and 8 million, sixteenth century Spain could only spare 1,000–1,500 settlers annually with which to populate its American possessions.[61] Contemporary Portugal with a mere million nationals and a world empire, could hardly supply Brazil with more.[62] In fact, until the Portuguese crown decided to formally underwrite "nothing less than the colonisation of the entire 2500 miles of coastline east of the Line of Tordesillas" by granting hereditary land titles to fourteen select citizens (*donatarios*) in the 1530s,[63] it seemed as if the French were in a better position to make claims on the future Brazil. Like their Portuguese counterparts, French explorer-merchants were interested in the wood found there (from which the land mass would derive its name), principally for its use in textile dye. Ironically, from 1500 to roughly 1535, the conflicts between French and Portuguese interests were greater than those that existed between either European power and the Tupi-speaking inhabitants of coastal Brazil. There were at least three factors that tended to mitigate abusive relations between Europeans and Amerindians in this early period of Brazil's history: first was the numerical disparity between the relatively few colonies of French and Portuguese sailors and the hundreds of Tupinamba, Temimino, and Tupinikin villages, each with 400 to 800 kinspeople;[64] second was the common Amerindian practice of offering kinswomen to the European newcomers as a means by which to ensure that contracts between the two parties were not violated;[65] and third was the general recognition on the part of the European traders that the supply of both brazil wood and foodstuffs depended on Amerindian labor. This last reason grew in importance as the depletion of coastal woodlands required that felling move into the interior. In short, the stage was set for the emergence of a ruling-class situation of race relations in Brazil.

The French crown failed to come to the aid of its subjects, who persistently challenged Portuguese claims on Brazil until the 1530s, and so Brazil was lost to the Portuguese. Of course, had the French crown known then of the gold and diamond deposits in the future Brazilian states of Minas Gerais, Mato Grosso, and Goias, Brazil might now be a part of the francophone world. The Portuguese, who would not learn of these precious metal deposits for another century and a half, decided to cultivate the crop that made fortunes for both landlords and the crown in the Atlantic islands: sugar cane.

With the shift to a plantation economy after 1535, social relations between Portuguese sailors-cum-settlers and indigenous Amerindians went from a state of peaceful coexistence to low-intensity warfare. In addition to the social effects of fatal alliances, slave raids, cruel punishment, Jesuit indoctrination (as of 1540), and forced labor, European diseases ravaged Brazil's indigenous populations particularly in the mid-sixteenth century, the very period of substantial plantation expansion. The toll on the lives of indigenous Brazilians was of the same horrific order as in the Atlantic islands, though of greater magnitude in terms of numbers. Within a century of initial contact with Portuguese adventurers, the indigenous populations of Brazil had dwindled from a million and a half people to a mere 35,000.[66]

Yet, as the Portuguese population of Brazil was on the verge of equaling the remaining number of Brazilian Amerindians in 1600, the "50,000 Africans [who had] arrived in the colony up to that time"[67] foreshadowed the human terms of racial negotiation in the centuries to come. In Cox's terms, Brazil's race relations were moving from those characteristic of a ruling-class situation to those suggestive of a bipartite situation.

However, in few social formations is it the case that the ethnic composition of the total population uniformly defines the situations of race relations operating everywhere within its borders; the geographic distribution of the population's principal racial groupings is an equally important determinant. For what the Brazilian case suggests is that both bipartite and ruling-class situations may operate simultaneously in different regions of a single social formation, though it may be common for the situation of race relations which characterizes the dominant economic or political region to influence other regions considerably. The principal reason for the oscillation of Brazilian race relations is that as the country's major export crops or minerals have changed since the sixteenth century, so too have the sites of the extractive industries as well as the geographic concentrations of Brazil's African labor force. For example, from the mid-sixteenth century to the latter half of the seventeenth century, the sugar industry in Pernambuco and Bahia largely shaped race relations throughout Brazil; in the eighteenth century, the gold and diamond industries of Minas Gerais, Mato Grosso, and Goias assumed that responsibility; and in the nineteenth century, the coffee industry of the states of São Paulo and Rio de Janeiro set the terms of racial stratification in those states and beyond. Some local examples further illustrate the point.

By the beginning of the eighteenth century, both the African and European populations of Brazil had increased threefold from their numbers just a century earlier. These raw population figures suggest that a bipartite situation of race relations then obtained in all of Brazil. The ecclesiastical census of Bahia taken "between 1718 and 1724"[68] also appears, at first sight, to confirm this conclusion. Of the roughly 80,000 inhabitants of the state, roughly 45,500 were enslaved and 36,000 were designated "free" people. Unfortunately, the census in question did not further divide the free population by race or color. However, if we suppose that at least half of the unenslaved population was comprised of people of color, then the demographic distribution of black and white Brazilians which initially appeared to constitute a bipartite situation of race relations now resembles a ruling-class one.

By the end of the eighteenth century, Brazilian population statistics required no such scrutiny in order for one to conclude that a ruling-class situation of race relations then characterized the entire colony. Of the approximately 2.3 million Brazilians in 1789,[69] only 300,000 were of predominantly European descent,[70] a ratio calling to mind the mid-sixteenth century one between Portuguese settlers and indigenous Brazilians. The demographic pattern of Minas Gerais—then Brazil's most economically dynamic state and the one in which 15 percent of all Brazilians lived—perhaps best reflected the national one. According to one estimate of Minas Gerais's population in 1786, the white Brazilian population of 66,000 was only a fifth of the total number of people of color in the state.[71] In addition, there was a comparatively large number of free multiracial or *colored* people. The number of free coloreds was twice that of the free black population of Minas Gerais (80,000 vs. 43,000), and enslaved colored people made up less than 15 percent of the total of enslaved people of African descent (20,000 vs. 154,000).[72] In short, the colored population of Minas Gerais at the end of the eighteenth century was the intermediate population par excellence of a ruling-class situation of race relations in terms both of color and condition.

Yet, the racial distribution of Brazil's population did not remain this way for long. Within forty years the European component of Brazil's population climbed to just over a million.[73] In the main, the increase was due to the arrival of between 300,000 and 500,000 European immigrants, of which the largest concentration apparently entered Brazil between the years of 1790 and 1820.[74] Though not nearly as large as the influx of European immigrants later in the century, this earlier migration to Brazil did foreshadow the shape of race relations to come.

A remarkable development in the course of Brazil's coffee era was the significant rise in the number of free people of African descent (roughly 75 percent of whom were multiracial),[75] whose ranks eventually eclipsed that of Brazil's enslaved population by a multiple greater than two. By the third quarter of the nineteenth century, the free colored constituted more than 30 percent of Brazil's total population of about ten million,[76] and when the roughly one million free Brazilians of predominantly African descent are added to the population of free coloreds, Brazil's total free population of African extraction was larger than the approximately 4 million Brazilians of predominantly European descent. Thus, even excluding the 1.5 to 2 million colored and black slaves, in the third quarter of the nineteenth-century Brazil once again exhibited the demographic characteristics of a bipartite situation of race relations.

At least four forces contributed to the extraordinary growth of Brazil's free population of African descent in the nineteenth century. First, many Brazilian slaves were able to purchase their freedom through formal and extra-legal means during the precious metals and gems boom which literally put the price of freedom in their hands. Second, slaveholders from regions that were now past their economic prime and who could only profit marginally from the internal slave trade, were now more inclined to manumit their slaves, particularly their children by enslaved women. Third, slaves abandoned the plantations in large numbers, particularly in the years just before the formal abolition of Brazilian slavery in 1888. Finally, the "legal procedural reform of 1841, which replaced locally elected justices of the peace with professional magistrates appointed by the Ministry of Justice,"[77] emboldened Brazilian slaves to seek redress against slaveholders and overseers in the courts. "Now, instead of running away," adds George Reid Andrews, "slaves were increasingly likely to turn themselves over to the police, confess their crimes, and demand the opportunity to have their cases heard in court."[78]

Like their counterparts elsewhere in the hemisphere, however, paulista (that is, from São Paulo State) planters would not submit to the impending abolition of Brazilian slavery without attempting to undermine the meaning of freedom. Toward this end, they took two courses of action, one political, the other politico-economic. Paulista planters spearheaded the republican movement (they had formed the nation's Republican Party in 1870), which drove the monarchy out of Brazil a mere eighteen months after Princess Regent Isabel signed the emancipation decree. Then, they subsidized the immigration of more than two million southern Europeans (primarily Italians) between 1880 and 1930, over half of whom settled in the state of São Paulo. The first measure ensured that former slaves would neither receive compensatory aid nor legal protection from the Brazilian state in the postemancipation era. The second was multipurpose: it kept labor costs down; it racially split the paulista labor market; it squelched the political momentum of the collaboration between former slaves and their free allies that precipitated emancipation; it preempted the possible "darkening" of the Brazilian population that it was feared emancipation would engender; and, most important, it "restore[d] landowner control over the labor force."[79] In short, the planters had reintroduced a bipartite situation of race relations in their state, and as the most important Brazilian state economically, its demographic development greatly affected race relations throughout the country in the twentieth century.

Cox did not offer any comments on the sociopsychological or sociopolitical effects of the amalgamative situation of race relations on its members. However, if the amalgamative situation is a cross between ruling-class and bipartite situations of race relations in which at any given point in time the characteristics of one are socially dominant, then we should expect a corresponding mix of attitudes about race throughout the population. Recent studies on the sociology of race in Brazil appear to confirm our hypothesis.

As one might expect, the long history of race mixture notwithstanding, the physical and social traits associated with the European portion of the Brazilian population are held in highest esteem by virtually all Brazilians. These characteristics include everything from notions of the ideal skin tone, nose shape, and hair type to how and with whom one should conduct oneself in public. Yet, more than merely defining who or what is beautiful and to which lifestyle one should aspire, middle-class and elite Euro-Brazilians also establish the patterns of formal household relationships between men and women for the entire society. For example, to the degree that most Euro-Brazilians, regardless of class standing,[80] object to formal interracial relationships, most Brazilians of some visible African or Amerindian descent similarly refuse to enter into public relationships with people darker than themselves. This is a tendency that the amalgamative situation of race relations shares with its ruling-class and bipartite kin. Nevertheless, in spite of the general objection to interracial relationships among Euro-Brazilians, there are significant variations in that populations' racial attitudes based on class. Whereas middle-class and elite Euro-Brazilians "use a binary classification system that places light- and dark-skinned Afro-Brazilians squarely in

the same racial box in terms of their undesirability as marital partners," working-class and poor Euro-Brazilians "rarely, if ever, self-
identified as white but typically described themselves as moreno."
France Winddance Twine adds that "[I]n contrast to their working-
class counterparts in the United States, they usually emphasized
what they shared with Afro-Brazilians."[81] Thus, elite and middle-class
Euro-Brazilians expressed attitudes most typical of whites in bipartite
situations of race relations; working-class and poor Euro-Brazilians
expressed racial sentiments most atypical of whites in that same situation. These attitudes account for both the "lack of generalized white
terrorism and hostility of working-class Euro-Brazilians toward the
Afro-Brazilian community" and for the "occasional" murder by elite
Euro-Brazilian men of Afro-Brazilian men who consummated relationships with elite Euro-Brazilian women.[82]

Given that Afro-Brazilians largely accept and perpetuate the socio-
racial order as designed by elite Euro-Brazilians, it is not surprising to learn that, generally speaking, they define racism narrowly:
only "formal, legal, and state-sanctioned prohibitions" against them
qualify as racism. Consequently, Afro-Brazilians, like Euro-Brazilians,
"fail to consider institutional racism, occupational segregation, elec-
toral representation, media representations of blacks, and the distribution of power in their definitions of racism."[83] Otherwise put,
Brazilians generally approach racial issues in their country like text-
book liberals; that is, as they see it, if all Brazilians are juridically
equal, then all Brazilians, regardless of color, have more or less the
same opportunities to either succeed or to fail socioeconomically.
And given the many instances in the nation's 500-year history when
the ruling-class situation of race relations predominated, Brazilian
liberalism on race matters is entirely understandable. Nevertheless,
though fewer in number, Brazil has also known periods of bipartite
situation of race relations hegemony, particularly at the beginning
of the twentieth century in the city and state of São Paulo. Therefore, if modern-day Brazilians apply liberal logic to issues of race
relations, they do so at the expense of their bipartite situation of
race relations past and present. Having both made this interpreta-
tive choice and having been politically encouraged to do so, most
Brazilians find it difficult either to define or to combat racism in
ways that seem adequate to those most familiar with bipartite situations of race relations.

Before concluding this chapter, it would be useful to compare Cox's typology of race relations with the variables and analytical tools that his contemporaries were isolating and employing to comprehend race matters in a variety of settings. As we shall see, Cox's approach to these questions was decades ahead of his colleagues.

Cox's Situations of Race Relations and Contemporary Race Theory

Cox's variables for the operationalization of racial stratification hardly seem remarkable today, but fifty years ago they were quite unorthodox. If we bear in mind that Frank Tannenbaum's *Slave and Citizen,* for example, appeared only two years before the publication of *Caste, Class, and Race,* we can recognize the intellectual distance between Cox and then-current thinking on race relations. Although it is undoubtedly true that he had not entirely disavowed cultural arguments in favor of sociological data to explain different situations of race relations,[84] Cox rejected, by omission, Tannenbaum's thesis that official Iberian codes of master-slave conduct, *Las Siete Partidas,* lent themselves to the practice of more tolerant race relations in Latin America than those which exist in Anglo-Saxon America. For could it not be said (and this may have been Cox's reasoning) that the laws guiding master-slave interaction in Anglo-Saxon America, like *Las Siete Partidas,* were also "framed within . . . Christian doctrine" and even upheld the view that "[t]he master had, in fact, no greater moral status than the slave, and spiritually the slave might be a better man than his master"[85] without this apparent contradiction necessarily encouraging slaveholders to act more humanely toward their human property? Similarly, his belief that race relations in capitalist societies are determined by the numerical strength or weakness of the different racial groupings in a particular social formation, may have relieved Cox of feeling the obligation to engage in comparative slavery studies (of which there were a spate in the late 1960s and early 1970s)[86] to explain different situations of race relations in the Americas. However, if there was one significant drawback to Cox's theory of the determinants of race relations, it was his slighting of the condition of the "free" black under the slave regime whose social position was frequently a reliable indicator of whether a bipartite or a ruling-class situation obtained in a given society.[87]

Cox's determinants also called into question another culture-based explanation of different situations of race relations, this one the obverse of the supposed Iberian predilection to indulge in race mixture: the supposed uncompromising Anglo-Saxon stance against it. Echoing what some Caribbean scholars observed before him,[88] and anticipating what others would later conclude,[89] Cox implied that Anglo-Saxon settlers have been just as willing as their Iberian counterparts to engage in sexual relations with Amerindian and African women given similar demographic forces, divisions of labor, and similar power relations. If race relations in colonial (and in many cases, postcolonial) Surinam, Martinique, and Jamaica resembled those in colonial Brazil and Mexico, the likeness suggests that similar social forces were at work in what were formally nationally (and hence, culturally) distinct colonies. In the final analysis, it appears that the myth of Anglo-Saxon insistence on racial purity relies on the exclusion of Caribbean examples.[90]

More significant still was Cox's departure from the race relations theories to which he was introduced at the University of Chicago. Of these, "the most comprehensive and systematic" and bearing the "greatest influence on American sociology" were those of Robert E. Park.[91] Park's best-known social theory was what he termed the "race relations cycle" according to which the social relations between distinct populations (as established by differences in language, religion, ritual, and physical traits and not necessarily by "race" since the theory was derived from Park's observations of "white" ethnic immigrants in the United States) followed five self-explanatory phases of undisclosed length: contact, competition, conflict, accommodation, and assimilation. Unlike earlier theorists of race relations, however, Park did not subscribe to the view that only immigrants were transformed by the social processes which culminated in assimilation. Instead, he maintained that "mainstream" society is also altered by the processes through which newcomers are assimilated. In spite of the challenges that Cox posed to Park's race relations cycle theory, throughout his life he never wavered in his adherence to two of Park's positions: the eventuality of the assimilation of even black Americans into mainstream American society, and the simultaneous transformation of American society as black Americans are assimilated into it.

Cox's retreat from the logical conclusions of his situations of race relations notwithstanding, he did call into question Park's theory in a number of ways. The most obvious was in his designation of race relations as situations or types rather than as phases which imply an evolution toward a resolved end. Among other implications, Cox's theory of race relations suggests that these situations can continue indefinitely without the inevitable amelioration of interaction between the ethnics in question. Yet, even more fundamental was Cox's assertion that racial prejudice arose with the advent of capitalism (unlike Park who posited that the "beginnings of modern race prejudice may be traced back to the immemorial periods of human associations").[92] Cox was at pains to repeat throughout *Caste, Class, and Race,* that race relations are grounded in the economic exploitation of some populations by others, not in either "instinctual" antipathy between groups or in clashes of ethnocentrism.

As Pierre Van den Berghe said with regard to his own typology of race relations, Cox's too are "[a]t best only approximations, and given instances typically show varying mixtures of the characteristics of both ideal types."[93] We have also seen that a given society may pass through multiple situations of race relations over time. To his credit, Cox recognized that a society's division of labor combined with an account of the size of its various ethnic/racial populations provide a more useful profile of race relations in that society than other, nonmaterial variables. In a way, he could not but recognize this; as a Caribbean immigrant in the United States he was a "natural" race relations comparativist. And despite the inevitable shortcomings of his typology, through the effort of systematizing the situations of race relations, Cox became one of the early scholars to explain convincingly why, in the words of Norman Girvan, it is the case that "in the . . . Americas generally, there remains a high correlation between income, occupational status, ownership of property and socioeconomic power on the one hand, and 'physical' and 'social' race on the other hand."[94] Let us now turn to how Cox handled the social interaction of a variety of ethnic/racial populations in the American bipartite situation of race relations.

3

Outcasting the Caste School of Race Relations

If Cox is known for any one contribution, it is for having made a convincing case against the once dominant caste interpretation of race relations in the American South. In his 1942 article "The Modern Caste School of Race Relations" (a slightly modified version of which reappeared in *Caste, Class, and Race*), Cox contested the position of W. Lloyd Warner and Allison Davis, among others, that the lines of social separation between whites and blacks in the American South, though not "exactly the same" as the caste society of India, "are of the same kind of social phenomena and, therefore, for the comparative sociologists and social anthropologists they are forms of behavior which must have the same term applied to them."[1] In their characterization of southern race relations, Warner and Davis maintained that whites and blacks belonged to separate superordinate and subordinate castes within each of whose boundaries operated racially specific class relations. They defined the two systems of stratification in the following manner:

> Briefly, caste may be defined as a rank order of superior-superordinate orders with inferior-subordinate orders which practice endogamy, prevent vertical mobility, and unequally distribute the desirable and undesirable social symbols. Class may be defined as a rank order of superior and inferior orders which allows both exogamy and endogamy, permits movement either up or down the system, or allows an individual to remain in the status to which he was born; it also unequally distributes the lower and higher evaluated symbols.[2]

Yet, almost in anticipation of Cox's later objections to their position, Warner and Davis were quick to add that "even in the most conservative of castes in India as well as elsewhere a few cases of marriage out of the group can always be found and a few cases of upward mobility usually are discoverable. The well-known phenomenon of East Indian hypergamy is an example of both of these variations from the caste ideal."[3]

The manner in which Cox critiqued the caste school's interpretation of endogamy characterized his approach to all of the social variables that the school believed indicative of a caste system. He began by cautioning, "We should probably be grossly misled if we were to think of endogamy, rather than that which its prohibition is intended to protect, as of primary significance."[4] To illustrate his point, Cox proceeded to describe the many possible interests that endogamy may serve:

> The interests may be political, as in the case of conquerors desiring to maintain ruling status . . . Or the interest may be nationalistic as, for example, the German Nazi laws against intermarriage with Jews and Poles. The interest may be religious, as that between sect and sect. . . . Among some groups such as the Jews, it is a religio-cultural interest which is to be preserved. . . . The interest may be mainly economic as, for example, that protected by social-class sanctions against marriage between persons of different classes, or between persons of different estates. It may be racial, in an immediate or proximate sense,

as in the case of blacks and whites in South Africa. Finally, it may
be a composite of cultural factors, as in the case of marriage restrictions between caste and caste in India, or of the ethnocen-
tric isolation of certain foreign groups in the United States.[5]

In light, then, of the myriad purposes of endogamy, Cox concluded that "[m]arriage restriction . . . is a dependent social phenomenon having as its determinants some primary interest, which
interest may vary with the situation. . . . Therefore, we cannot know
whether caste exists until we have studied and identified the form of
social organization isolated."[6]
Yet, despite having made these compelling observations, Cox himself shied away from offering a single comprehensive definition of
the Indian caste system on the curious grounds that "definitions are
seriously limited as means of describing societies." Nevertheless, in
the more than one hundred pages he devoted to the subject, Cox
did provide what he believed to be the essential components of the
Indian caste system. At its most basic level, Cox described the caste
system as "constituting a multiplicity of hierarchies determined by
custom within various geographical areas of organization." To this
he added that the "basis of status differentiation among castes appears to be caste dharma, or the way of life of the caste, estimated finally by the expressed or assumed opinion of Brahmans [priests].
Each caste has a presumptive inherited dharma in which vocation
plays a major role." Finally, Cox maintained that the "caste member
is a person consciously participating in an in-group with common
expectations of reciprocal service. The destiny of the individual is
bound up with that of caste. . . . Denied caste affiliation, the individual becomes a rudderless ship."[7]
These, however, were only the human components of the caste
system's structure; just as important to Cox were the ideological un-
derpinnings of the system. About these he noted, "There is a fundamental creed or presumption in Hindu society that persons are
born unequal in status according to the caste to which they belong;
this is the antithesis of the Stoic doctrine of human equality, adopted in Western democracies." According to Hindu doctrine, Cox
added, "[n]ot by accident are men . . . unequal, not by luck or by
variations in personal effort, not because of differences in race or
defeat in war, but because of the Divine Plan in the creation of the

social order." In other words, the social order or order of castes in Hindu society is collectively perceived as "God-given and sacred."[8]

Finally, although idyllic, the following passage summarizes how Cox envisioned the Indian caste system, particularly in contrast to southern race relations:

> The caste system does not represent a social order in unstable equilibrium; it represents rather a powerful norm toward which social variations tend to gravitate; it is capable of perpetuating itself indefinitely. Its practice and theory are in complete synchronism; it does not rationalize its position; its scriptures are outspoken on the point of man's inequality to man; it has no shortcomings; it does not excuse itself; it is totally excellent. The caste system is in the mores of all caste Hindus, not in those of Brahmans only; hence a man's caste is normal and natural for him. It is sufficient for the realization of his spiritual and social ideals; there is no individual striving or aspiration to move beyond its bounds. . . . Resting securely upon universal consensus, the system is taken for granted, and it cannot be legislated out of existence or defeated on the battlefield.[9]

Cox's hyperbole notwithstanding, no student of southern race relations in the decades before the civil rights movement could have made the claim that her or his observations approximated the above description of the Indian caste system. Even Warner and Davis themselves remarked, "Since all Negroes know . . . that according to the white society's Christian dogma of the brotherhood of man and the American democratic dogma of the equality of citizens, they are unjustly treated, and since it is they who are on the receiving end of the most violent caste sanctions, it is to be expected that basic frustrations around caste position, and expressions of hostility to the opposite caste would be relatively more frequent within the Negro than within the white group."[10] And if southern Blacks were frustrated by and felt hostility toward those white southerners who insisted on refusing to accord them their rights as citizens, and if these sentiments were based on a collective awareness that local "legal" practices defied, rather than, applied, the law of the land to black people, then it was a confirmation of Cox's conviction that southern society could not be understood as the American variant of the Indian caste system. For in that society, as he understood it, there exists little or no discrepancy between religious theory and social practice. Yet, without having "made anything approaching a careful study of the caste system,"[11] as Cox himself had undertaken, the caste theorists were incapable of realizing that the ethnographic data that they had compiled fundamentally called into question their caste model of southern race relations. Here is what Cox said about these limitations:

> The caste interpretation of race relations in the South cannot see that the intermarriage restriction laws are a social affront to Negroes; it cannot perceive that Negroes are smarting under the Jim Crow laws; it may not recognize the overwhelming aspiration among Negroes for equality of social opportunity; it could never realize that the superiority of the white race is due principally to the fact that it has developed the necessary devices for maintaining incontestable control over the shooting iron; and it will not know that 'race hatred' may be reckoned in terms of the interests of the white ruling class. Hence, it is possible for the school to imagine the anomaly of Negroes fully assimilated culturally and yet living symbiotically apart from whites on the basis of some unexplained understanding that their colors should never be mixed. In other words, the races will, as Warner and Davis believe 'isolate themselves to prevent intermarriage'! When this static approach is given up, the caste belief must also be given up.[12]

That moment came, of course, when southern Blacks refused to endure racist assaults with their characteristic self-restraint and turned instead to the collective and public forms of protest we know as the civil rights movement. At that moment, the caste interpretation of southern race relations was summarily out-casted.

Contrary, then, to how the caste theorists described pre–civil rights movement southern society, Cox viewed it as a "quasi or tentative society developed to meet certain needs resulting from their [Blacks'] retarded assimilation." He went on to say that "[u]nlike the permanence of caste, it is a temporary society intended to continue only so long as whites are able to maintain the barriers against their assimilation." These "certain needs" were predictably economic in nature and, in Cox's opinion, were served by race prejudice. This last he defined as the "socio-attitudinal matrix supporting a calculated and determined effort of a white ruling class to keep some people or peoples of color and their resources exploitable."[13] Therefore, in Cox's view of southern race relations, endogamy did not reflect a shared desire on the part of both black and white southerners to maintain racial purity, but rather the success of the southern ruling class's racial propaganda campaign to divide the populations which it exploits economically. Cox's general perspective on the social characteristics that the caste school of southern race relations interpreted as indicators of a caste system—endogamy, socioeconomic stasis, and status inequality—is best understood when it is situated within his larger cycle of "racial antagonism."

> The following seem to be characteristic of the cycle of racial antagonism which includes ethnocentrism: first, a capitalist need to exploit some people and their resources; then the more or less purposeful development among the masses, the public, of derogatory social attitudes toward that particular group or groups whose exploitation is desired—here the strategy of the capitalists will depend upon the nature of the ethnic situation; a consequent public estrangement of sympathetic feeling for and loss of social identification with the exploited group— that is to say, a development of race prejudice; the crystallization of a 'we feeling' and of social solidarity on the part of the propagandized group against the exploited group and a reaction of the latter; and, finally, the continual appeal to this 'we feeling,' consciousness of solidarity, or ethnocentrism as a means of intensifying race prejudice so that the exploitative purpose might be increasingly facilitated.[14]

Finally, the ultimate proof for Cox of the illogic of grouping together southern race relations and the Indian caste system was that it required the trivialization of perhaps the most significant difference between the two societies: that in the former case, social order was maintained by the threat and use of violence; while in the latter, the collective submission to sacred and customary law achieved the same end. About the South's reliance on violence as a means of maintaining the region's socio-racial order, Cox said:

Nothing is more discussed, nothing more provocative of heat, indeed, nothing more unstable than race relations in the South. The dominant attitudes supporting race relations are inconsistent with the fundamental democratic mores of the nation, and they are becoming increasingly so. The white ruling class is, to be sure, determined to keep the Negro exploitable, but it dares not rely upon 'the mores' to do this. It must exercise 'eternal vigilance' in maintaining an ever-present threat of interracial violence if it is to continue its exploitative social order. The Southern racial system 'lives, moves, and has its being' in a thick matrix of organized and unorganized violence.[15]

In short, if white southerners had to resort to violence in order to keep black southerners in their "place," then the South was not a caste society, since it lacked the foundational element of that system: the self-acceptance by the subordinate group of its social inferiority.

Cox's relentless logic and biting sarcasm in *Caste, Class, and Race* made the caste theorists of southern race relations appear decidedly unscholarly and plainly unconvincing. Put on the defensive, the immediate targets of Cox's criticisms[16] dismissed him in all-powerful silence, while one of their students, Everett C. Hughes, went on the offensive with a public dismissal of Cox's efforts.[17] That Hughes's review of *Caste, Class, and Race* was meant as a personal attack and not as a scholarly engagement with Cox's scholarship is not terribly hard to discern. Rather than assess Cox's attempt to refine the meaning of the term "caste" such that one could then decide upon the appropriateness of its use in the context of American race relations, Hughes took issue with Cox's assumption that it was to the Indian caste system that Warner, Davis, and others referred. Expectedly, Hughes neither suggested in the review an alternative caste society to defend his mentors' position nor detected any errors in the study to prove that Cox's work was anything less than in his own words, a "careful comparative analysis." In short, Hughes's review (or non-review as Cox thought of it) of *Caste, Class, and Race,* bolstered Cox's position that the "caste theory is invalid and how it is of the nature of a fad in the social sciences."[18]

However, Cox did not single out for attack only those scholars who thought southern race relations akin to the Indian caste system; he generously criticized anyone who attributed the rise and reproduction

of American or southern race relations to what he considered the
wrong social forces. Thus, in addition to W. Lloyd Warner, Allison
Davis, Robert Park, John Dollard, and Gunnar Myrdal, Cox also
took to task a reputable scholar who did not subscribe to the caste
model of southern race relations, Ruth Benedict, for having paid
"no attention to the materialistic source"[19] of race relations. Nevertheless, Cox's criticism of these scholars' social theories should not
be confused with a dismissal of their scholarship—quite the contrary. As he stated in the preface of *Caste, Class, and Race:*

> In our discussion of previous contributions in this field . . . we
> have been concerned only with showing how the approach of
> certain leading authorities has apparently limited their chances
> of developing a convincing theory. However, no study of race
> relations could be considered adequate without a knowledge of
> the contributions made by such works as Ray Stannard Baker,
> *Following the Color Line;* John Dollard, *Caste and Class in a South-
> ern Town;* Hortense Powdermaker, *After Freedom;* Gunnar Myrdal,
> *An American Dilemma;* St. Clair Drake and Horace R. Cayton,
> *Black Metropolis;* W. E. B. DuBois, *The Souls of Black Folk;* and
> Stetson Kennedy, *Southern Exposure.*[20]

Still, in spite of their scholarly contributions and progressive political intentions, Cox was deeply troubled by two (un)intended
consequences of the adoption of the caste model of southern race
relations by some of the country's most prominent social scientists:
one, the political implications (particularly in the South) of the academic endorsement of the caste interpretation; and two, its effects
on western academic approaches to Indian history and society, both
ancient and modern. Let us take each matter in turn.

A close reading of Cox's assessment of the caste school of southern race relations reveals that he was always mindful of the potential
or current political uses and abuses of academic social theory. That
is, in addition to his analyses of both social phenomena and of the
competing social theories seeking to make sense of those phenomena, Cox always wrote about the matters at hand with the political
or policy uses of his position(s) in mind. Thus, in the case of his critique of the caste school of southern race relations, Cox called that
perspective into question not only on academic grounds, but on

political grounds as well. This he did for, at least, two reasons. In the first instance, Cox concluded that the caste model discouraged political protest against racial injustice. Here was Cox's logic: if, as the caste school argued, southern race relations correspond to a race-determined caste system, then no amount of legislation can alter or influence a social order based on the "unchangeableness of physical inheritance." Taken to its logical conclusion, the caste model of southern race relations necessarily supported the view that the "white caste and the black caste [would] remain indefinitely intact,"[21] or, in more aggressive terms, that "nothing, nothing will ever change the South."

As Cox saw it, this type of reasoning necessarily limited the range of political responses to then current southern race relations to, at best, moral appeals to invite change (á la Myrdal) or, at worst, to a silent resignation (á la Park et al.) to the "mores" of southern society. In short, the adherents of the caste school could "see only the accommodation aspect of the [southern] interracial situation." Cox's summation of his assessment of the caste school was particularly damning: "By using the caste hypothesis, then, the school seeks to explain a 'normal society' in the South. In short, it has made peace for the hybrid society that has not secured harmony for itself; and insofar as this is true, its work is fictitious."[22]

Cox's second political objection to the caste model of southern race relations was that it lent support to the illusion that the rank-and-file perpetrators of blatantly racist acts—working-class and poor Whites—were the makers and shapers of the region's race relations. The caste model promoted this perspective by stressing racial solidarity within the South's racial "castes" at the expense of a thorough analysis of the intra- and cross-racial class conflicts in that society, particularly those between white and black labor and white capital. As a result of this bias, the reader of caste school literature is led to believe that working-class and ruling class Whites profited equally from racist practices in the pre–civil rights movement South. As the following passage indicates, in Cox's estimation, the caste school's position on both the reason and primary locus of racism could not have been farther from the truth.

It should be emphasized that the guardians of the economic and social order in the South are not poor whites; indeed, it is

sheer nonsense to think that the poor whites are the perpetrators of the social system in the South. The fierce filibustering in
the national Congress against the passage of an anti-lynching
bill, or against the abolition of the poll tax; the hurried con-
ferences of governors to devise means of emasculating a Supreme Court decision for equal educational opportunities;
the meeting of attorneys general for the purpose of sidetrack-
ing an anti-Jim Crow decision for railroads; the attitude of
Southern judges toward Negroes in courtrooms—these are
obviously the real controlling factors in the Southern order.
The poor whites are not only incapable but evidently also have
no immediate interest in the doing of such things.[23]

Nevertheless, in light of the caste school's tendency to treat racial attitudes as the independent variable(s) of race relations, poor
Whites, from its perspective, were largely to blame for southern
racism. "Those who rely upon the mores for their interpretation of
racial antagonism," Cox noted about this perspective, "always seek
to define their problem as an irrational up-thrust of primitive folk
attitudes; as having its roots in some instinctual drive toward repugnance between all biologically distinguishable peoples, a repugnance
beyond the reach of cultural variations."[24] From remarks such as
these, we gain some insight into the philosophical basis of Cox's
general refusal to place the onus of American racism on the shoulders of working-class Whites.

Another unintended consequence of the imprecise use of the
term caste in American sociological theory for more than a generation, was the subsequent racialization of early Indian history on the
part of western scholars such that the Indian caste system was recon-
ceived as based on racial distinctions. Referring to the process by
which present preoccupations inform reinterpretations of the past,
Cox made the following astute epistemological observations:

With respect to the question of identifying race relations in
other parts of the world with the origin of caste, we may observe an interesting cycle in thinking. The theorists usually
begin by comparing the origin of caste with the modern white-
black pattern of race relationships. An identification of the
phenomena having been made, they proceed to establish their

racial theory of caste; they return forthwith to identify present-day race relationship with caste. In the meantime, they remain oblivious of the ongoing caste system as we know it in India. Therefore, their origin of caste, and not that of caste in action, becomes the standard. In other words, they must assume race relations today to be caste relations only as they conceive of the latter in their origination.[25]

These last remarks explain why Cox's discussion of the Indian caste system in *Caste, Class, and Race* was so thorough and lengthy. Moreover, the fruits of his research led him to the conclusion that racial distinctions could not have been the foundation of the Indian caste system since more than a millennium of intermixture between Aryans and Dravidians had already occurred before Brahmans began to promulgate caste laws circa 200 B.C. Rather than as the result of a "conflict situation between Aryans and Dravidians," Cox believed that the caste system "had its incipience in rivalry between Brahmans and Kshatriyas [the king and nobility] for primacy in the social order." Over time, the Brahmans won the contest. Their most valuable spoils were the authority to "giv[e] a religious interpretation to all questions of moment" and to codify the doctrine that held that the "greatest blessing which could come to man is inspired by the performance of his hereditary duty without murmur or envy of another." Therefore, Cox reasoned, "Retardation of complete amalgamation was evidently a by-product rather than a main purpose of caste."[26]

Cox's critique of the caste school of southern race relations earned him the praise of, at least, one renowned student of the Indian caste system. In 1961, Louis Dumont wrote that the "criticism of the 'Caste School of Race Relations' has been remarkably carried out by Oliver C. Cox" and that he "strikes on important and incontrovertible points whenever he wishes to emphasize the difference between India and America."[27] Nevertheless, on the merits of Cox's discussion of the Indian caste system independent of what that system revealed about western race relations, Dumont voiced some reservations. "It is true," he remarked, "that one cannot everywhere agree with Cox, but we must remember that he was working at second and even at third hand (for instance from Bougle)."[28] The second part of Dumont's commentary requires two qualifications, however: one, it fails to take into account that the Trinidad of Cox's youth was already home to over 100,000 East Indians, over half of whom had been born in India;[29] and two, in the preface of *Caste, Class, and Race,* Cox stated that "[m]any persons among the white, colored, and East Indian people of Trinidad have made my interviews not only a pleasure but also a source of certain germinal ideas on race relations."[30] Although neither of these two addenda denies the thrust of Dumont's charge—that Cox did not conduct fieldwork in India—taken together, they do suggest that Cox was closer to the Indian caste system (or, at least, to a Caribbean variant of it)[31] than Dumont's remarks lead one to believe.

In order to refute the caste school of southern race relations, Cox had to undertake a detailed analysis of the Indian caste system. What he found in this endeavor is that unlike race relations, which are secular, caste relations are sacred. Moreover, caste relations are noncapitalist social relations, whereas race relations are a product of capitalist social relations. Though surely imperfect, these ideal types enabled Cox to demonstrate the perversion of the implicit claim of the caste school that black southerners believed their social subordination to southern whites divinely ordained. Similarly, the caste school could not account for the fact that some southern Whites had to resort to violence to convince Blacks what they should have already known if indeed theirs was a caste society. In short, race relations, according to Cox, are a dimension of class relations, and it is to these that we now turn.

Classes and Marx

Those scholars who have read *Caste, Class, and Race* as a Marxist interpretation of race relations (a claim, incidentally, which Cox himself never made), have typically expressed their disappointment with the work on two grounds: either because of its basis in precisely the "orthodox Marxist theory of capitalist exploitation"[32] or, ironically, because of its deviation from orthodox Marxism.[33] One possible response to these objections of Cox's work is simply to ignore them on the grounds that their authors judge him according to intentions which were not his own. However, given the current use and distribution of his work, to fail to comment on the remarks of his critics would relinquish to them, by default, the final word on Cox. That would be an even greater injustice than the misreading of his work.

In my reading of Cox's critics, it appears that their fault lies in what we may generously call lazy readings of his work. That is to say that more than one scholar has based his or her assessment of Cox's theory of race relations on, at most, a chapter or two, or, at least, a couple of sentences of *Caste, Class, and Race.* I believe, for example, that the following lines were taken as ample proof of either Cox's Marxist approach to race relations or of his economic reductionism: "modern race relations [are] . . . a practical exploitative relationship with its socio-attitudinal facilitation" and that they are "labor-capital-profits relationships; therefore race relations are proletarian bourgeois relations and hence political-class relations."[34]

However, it should be clear from the preceding section that Cox's position on the interrelation of race formation and capitalism is far more sophisticated and nuanced than these isolated passages suggest. For if Cox saw fit to borrow certain concepts from what he would have understood as "orthodox" Marxism, he was also inclined to modify other aspects of Marx's theory because of both the variations he observed in the molding of racial identities in distinct capitalist settings and of two contemporary social problems of horrific magnitude: the intensity of racism in the United States and the fascist explosion in Europe. Like others, Cox did not feel that a strict class analysis adequately explained these phenomena. Moreover, he reasoned that the reality of these social mobilizations should compel the social observer to recognize the difference between class membership and class action.

E. P. Thompson, the late English social historian, placed scholars like Cox in the camp of those who "den[y] that class has happened at all." He continued on the likes of Cox that "[s]ince the crude notion of class attributed to Marx can be faulted without difficulty, it is assumed that any notion of class is a pejorative construct, imposed upon the evidence."[35] In Cox's defense, it was not only Marx's definition of class that he found wanting, but also those of Spann, Weber, MacIver, Kornhauser, and others.[36] Still, the following passage seems to corroborate Thompson's assessment of Cox et al.: "There is no such thing as an objective social class amenable to physical circumscription; neither is there in fact a recognizable social class hierarchy in class systems of advanced societies. In other words, the class system is not stratified; stratification is only an idea."[37] Yet, Cox would have agreed with Thompson's conclusion that "class happens when some men, as a result of common experiences (inherited or shared), feel and articulate the identity of their interests as between themselves, and as against other men whose interests are different from (as usually opposed to) theirs."[38] How, then, do we explain Cox's apparently contradictory position on the subject of class?

Cox distinguished social classes from political classes. Following Werner Sombart's lead,[39] Cox considered social class a conceptual tool or "heuristic construct"[40] to hypothesize about "social stratification and differentiation" but that ultimately its definition "var[ies] in meaning and position with the status of the person seeking to estimate [it]."[41] Cox spoke here both as a historical sociologist and as an astute observer of contemporary current affairs. Taken together, Cox reasoned that unlike feudal society in which the individual was legally bound to self-identify as a member of one of the three principal estates for which there was a specific legal code, the post–French Revolution capitalist system recognizes the individual as such to whom a single, national legal code applies. In other words, individualism is the "crucial characteristic" of the modern capitalist era. It is precisely this absence of legal or organizational obligations to larger social bodies through and with which individuals were formerly identified that suggested to Cox that all social scientific attempts to fix individuals into particular aggregate groupings based on supposedly shared characteristics and experiences are necessarily theoretical or merely intellectual framings of social reality. For "[a]lthough it is still true that we explain poverty or wealth by stereotyping large groups with certain attributes," Cox stated as an illustration of his point, "individuals are nonetheless assumed to have willingly chosen the course leading to their station in life."[42]

Cox felt, moreover, that under the influence of this legal definition of his or her person in capitalist society, the individual is encouraged to think less about those conditions which unite her or him with his fellow men and women and more about those personal characteristics which distinguish him or her from them: income level, political party affiliation, consumption habits, religious beliefs, ethnic/racial identification, age, level of formal education, gender, special skills or talents, and aspirations for children. In Cox's estimation, some, or even all, of these status distinctions in combination make absolute definitions of social class membership difficult, if not largely artificial.

To illustrate his perspective, Cox used a familiar example: the typical improvement of what Michel-Rolph Trouillot calls one's "social direction" or the "path that an individual is perceived to be taking up or down the social ladder"[43] when an individual is asked to locate his or her class position. What Cox observed was that "persons like to claim membership in . . . [and] to represent themselves as belonging to that class which is their immediate aspiration. . . . Consequently, not infrequently that class to which they assign themselves will differ from the class to which they are assigned by their neighbors."[44] Under "normal" conditions "[m]embers of a class are constantly striving upward and away from their fellows, a situation which leads to their individuation."[45] Therefore, in light of legal individualism and its encouragement of "invidious comparisons" between people regardless of their respective social class positions, however defined, Cox could state that in a capitalist regime "[I]nstead of well marked-off estates or social ranks, we have in our social-class system a constant milling of social-status atoms—that is to say, a circulation of individuals or families as bearers of status."[46]

Before we turn our attention to what Cox meant by political class, a few words on Cox's conception of social class and its relationship to Marxist theory on the subject are in order. His epistemological musings notwithstanding, Cox did not underestimate the "social significance of classes." Moreover, as the following passages suggest, Cox largely subscribed to Marx's definitions of the principal social classes in the capitalist mode of production: "The proletariat, to mention again the well-known fact, is a class of freed workers, freed from the land and freed from the ownership of the means of production. It sells its services in a "free" market to entrepreneurs, and its product becomes a commodity." Entrepreneurs or capitalists are, conversely, the "owners of capital goods, who produce for profit."[47] In the capitalists' collective opinion, the worker's "place in the system [is] primarily related to production, and he [is] regarded as an item of cost—that is to say, as both a necessary and important factor of production and as an impediment to the entrepreneur in his basic urge to undersell his competitors."[48] It was over the issue of what we may call the "natural" sentiments of the proletariat toward the bourgeoisie, however, that Cox parted company with Marx. Where Marx, for example, underscored the virtually spontaneous enmity of the proletariat for the bourgeoisie, Cox put equal, if not, more, emphasis on the proletariat's emulation of the bourgeoisie or its aspiration to one day take its place with the capitalist system intact.

Yet, of greater significance for our immediate purposes than even this departure from orthodox Marxism was Cox's objection to the argument espoused by some interpreters of Marx (and by most liberals) that as proletarianization proceeds, the types of social distinctions that we named earlier will dissolve into a collective working class identity.[49] This position is contrary to Cox's on two counts: it contradicts his opinion that feudal society cultivated greater social cohesiveness between and within estates than its successor promotes between members of social classes; and it denies the historical staying power of ethnic/racial divisions within and between social classes in the capitalist mode of production—the very basis of Cox's theory of race relations. It was for, at least, these reasons that Cox could remark simultaneously and without contradiction that whereas the "current class struggle is an inherent attribute of capitalism," the working class is either a "potential or active political class."[50]

In Cox's estimation, for a political class to be just what its name suggests, it must exhibit not only "social solidarity" of the type to which class consciousness gives rise, but it must also be "explicitly revolutionary," that is, it must seek "control of the state for the purpose of reorganizing the economic order."[51] These twin goals of the political class are precisely what make this class political; and this is why and how Cox would have qualified Thompson's conception of class with which we began this section. Measured by such rigorous standards, many of the organizations and institutions which we are accustomed to consider "political" ones not only do not merit the label, but should rather be thought of as mere "political factions"[52] or "special-purpose groups":

> A gang, sect, denomination, social club, or lodge need not represent a political class. These are intraclass institutional groups, and they may have problems which they seek to solve politically; yet their end is ordinarily the fostering of their own limited interests. . . . Institutional groups of this kind may be called special-purpose groups; their outlook is circumscribed,

specialized, and exclusive. . . . Their limits of possible social activity are those of political and social reform; they are, at most, interested in a more propitious operation of the status quo.[53]

Under the heading of political factions, Cox included not only most "political" parties[54] but also most labor unions, albeit the "ordinary opportunistic" ones.[55] Class consciousness, then, (and even most forms of class-based protest) is a necessary but insufficient condition for entrance into Cox's political class.

Like the authors of *The Communist Manifesto*, Cox also asserted that political class consciousness is not the prerogative of the working class alone. "The idealism of political classes," he remarked, "may override individual differences. . . . It is, therefore, practically impossible to define the membership of a political class in terms of objective criteria only. The correlation between the material position of a person and his social attitudes may not be perfect."[56] For illustrations, one need only recall the inordinate number of revolutionary leaders, theoreticians, and participants who were not working class in background, but rather were raised in middle-class households.[57] With this social pattern in mind, Cox concluded:

> Although the political class is ordinarily weighted with persons from a special sector of the social-status gradient, it may include persons from every position. Hence we do not speak of political classes as forming a hierarchy; they may conceivably split the social hierarchy vertically; therefore, there is here no primary conception of social stratification. In other words, members of the political class ordinarily do not have a common social status. These classes, therefore, are not thought of as social-class strata but as organizations arrayed face to face against each other.

Thus, "[o]ne may put it briefly that a political-class member is one who believes in and is willing to follow the ideals of that class."[58]

One's social class position, then, does not predispose one to political class consciousness in Cox's point of view (though he was quick to admit that "it is obvious . . . that no great part of one class [viz., the bourgeoisie] will desert and enter the ranks of the other [viz., the proletariat]"). Therefore, in order for those with political class consciousness to achieve their twin objectives of political-economic transformation of the existing capitalist order, they must make of their organizational instruments "propaganda machine[s]." "A political class," posited Cox, "becomes conscious of itself only through successful propaganda; the objective position of the class and its aims must be focused by its leaders. That is, as a function of the economic order, the class has potential existence, but as a result of agitation, it becomes organized for conflict."[59]

It may come as a surprise to find that one of Cox's sources on the subject of political class propaganda was none other than that "pastmaster in the art of manipulating ideas for a purpose," Adolf Hitler. However, if we bear in mind that Cox described fascists as the "capitalists and their sympathizers who have achieved political-class consciousness" and consequently "have become organized for action against the proletariat,"[60] then Hitler's movement certainly satisfied Cox's requirements of a political class, albeit a reactionary one.

The fascist movements in both Germany and in Spain (to which Cox also frequently referred in *Caste, Class, and Race*) also illustrated another of Cox's more obvious contentions about political classes: violence "is a necessary consequence of political-class action." Furthermore, in light of the fact that "it cannot be shown that in the past any political class has yielded without a conflict . . . violence is particularly the effective instrument of the attacking class."[61] In yet other terms, if political-economic reform is not the objective of the political class out of office, it is due to the fact that political-economic reform was not the inclination of the political class in office. Violence between political classes is also inevitable because the "law itself," Cox maintained, echoing Marx, "is the instrument of the ruling class; hence it is a logical impossibility for another class to assume power legally. . . . The political postulates of the opposing classes are inevitably antagonistic; as a consequence there can be no common judicial procedure."[62] Here, then, is Cox's detailed portrait of the political class struggle:

> The aim of the attacking class is not cooperation; it does not want law and order, since law and order means perpetuation of the old order. It does not want to discuss or to negotiate problems in a conciliatory manner with the old rulers, for such a procedure tends to continue the latter's prestige. Indeed, the two

groups do not have the same but contrary problems. The end of the attacking class is the vanquishing not only of the old leaders but also of the old system itself—a problem which the ruling class cannot be expected to discuss. Therefore, the struggle for power tends to be involved with a succession of conspiracies, imprisonments, and summatory conflicts, while compromise and appeasement may postpone but not settle the basic antagonism. Moreover, very much of the sanctimonious abhorrence displayed by the ruling class and its apologists against the use of violence in the class struggle is rooted in the desire to maintain the integrity of its class monopoly of violence.[63]

With regard to the proximate social conditions which give rise to political class ferment, Cox drew his propositions from the two great political revolutions of the modern era—the French (bourgeois) and Russian (proletariat) Revolutions—and from the British-led economic "revolution" of the nineteenth century, the Industrial Revolution. From the first of these, Cox arrived at the following Marxian conclusion: "A political-class movement will develop when, because of new methods of production or maturation of old methods, economic power has been shifted to some section of the population without at the same time shifting the political power." Yet, as should be clear from his treatment of social and political classes, Cox was never one to rely on solely "economic" explanations of social phenomena; he believed ideology to be of equal importance to social transformation as socioeconomic change. He added accordingly to his first proposition that "it is only when a class comes to feel that it has power to insist upon superior rights that it thinks of revolt." Thus, the social philosophy which inspired, for example, the Declaration of Rights of Man and Citizens, was just as much the result of the growing importance of merchant's capital to France's wealth as it was its cause. Referring in generic terms to Europe's bourgeois revolutions but with the example of the French Revolution foremost in mind, Cox maintained that "[t]he bourgeoisie who instigated and fought the capitalist revolutions were clearly not the most degraded and miserable part of the population; they were simply the most dissatisfied and the most powerful subordinate class. Their wails of misery, oppression, tyranny, and suffering were largely a function of their own inflated conception of themselves." In sum, "[t]he [social] situation is ripe for revolution when some minority or majority of the population feels that it is being unjustly 'oppressed' and that it can command the *power* to bring the government to terms."[64]

Where the French Revolution provided Cox with an example of political class consciousness arising from the social ascendance of the "aggressor" class, the bourgeoisie, the Industrial Revolution supplied him with one based on the degradation of the very class upon whose existence the bourgeoisie depended. "Indeed," Cox remarked on this ironic symbiosis, "the capitalists and the proletariat are twin-born of the same economic matrix, capitalism; therefore, the challenging proletariat is not the offspring of a distinct change in the mode of production as was the case with the rise of the European 'middle class.'" However, as we just noted, if anyone was of the opinion that dehumanization alone does not produce revolutions, it was Cox: "We may state broadly that social misery of itself never breeds revolution; in fact, it is not improbable that the greater the misery of a social class the less the likelihood of its revolting."[65]

When, then, in Cox's estimation, does proletarian discontent transform itself into political class consciousness? Primarily during economic depressions, or as Cox referred to them, "business cycle troughs." As one who lived through the Great Depression, Cox saw firsthand the two aspects of economic downturns which make them politically costly to the capitalist order: they are generally "recognized as inevitable consequences of capitalism"; and they are proof of the tragic fact that "[u]nder capitalism, the more economic goods we have, the greater the likelihood of famine among the masses."[66] Cox's elaboration on this last point is worth quoting at length:

A depression is the opposite of a famine. During a famine there are practically no goods, but during a depression there is a plethora of goods. It is the abundance of goods which jams the profit system and causes the entrepreneur to shut down his machinery and turn out the workers to starve. Thus there is a double cause for irritation among the workers. They suffer privation and degeneracy at a time when the markets are glutted with goods. . . . The workers must wait until the large stocks of goods work themselves down either by gradual consumption, decay, and waste, or by their purposeful destruction. Then and only then can the owners of the means of production again give the word to rehire labor and start producing. Thus the process of building up stocks to another glut is on its way.[67]

It is during a depression, moreover, that workers are most prone to recognize in greatest measure the injustice of the material disparities between themselves and their employers; the "economic uncertainty of the profit system;" the fact that "unemployment is a function of the profit motive;" the absurdity of a social system which "offers only war as a solution" to its inherent contradictions; and that the "burden of producing a social revolution devolves upon the base of the population."[68]

Finally, Cox, like most scholars writing in a Marxist vein after the Russian Revolution, felt that the Soviet example acted as a catalyst of political class consciousness throughout the world. As he saw it, the Soviet Union provided the political class in the capitalist world with living proof for its recruiting efforts that "an economic order which admits of planning in the interest of the people is an immediate possibility."[69] Again, as noted earlier, Cox never closely scrutinized the details of Stalin's activities "in the interest of the people."

Political Class Action or Racism?
Cox on the Anti-Asian Movement in California

In spite of his insistence that a political class is, by definition, revolutionary, from his treatment of the anti-Asian movement in California in the latter half of the nineteenth century, Cox was apparently willing, on occasion, to relax that standard. The result of the compromise was one of Cox's least convincing analyses, to put it diplomatically. It led him to distort facts for the sake of a political (not a sociological) position which was neither tenable nor ultimately worth it. Precisely why Cox chose to "venture West" so to speak and tackle this important, ugly episode of American social history, is yet another question for which we may never have a definitive answer. It is possible, nevertheless, that one of his passing remarks tells most of the story behind the article:[70] "A remarkable fact about the Californian anti-Oriental movements is that they have been mainly initiated by white workers instead of exploiters of labor, the class which we have attempted to show is responsible for all modern racial antagonism. In this respect the California situation appears to be the very opposite of the Negro-white relationship in the South."[71]

Cox was undoubtedly correct to situate the modern Asian presence in the Americas in the context of the "decline of the Negro slave trade—after 1845 especially,"[72] but for obvious reasons this frame of reference had little bearing on mid- and late-nineteenth-century Chinese immigration to California. For unlike their brethren in Cuba and Peru or fellow Asians in Trinidad and Guyana who were brought to these lands as indentured servants to perform what former slaves then refused to do, most Chinese voyagers who came to California did so of their own volition even if in the process they incurred debts to those "returned emigrants, Chinese merchants, Western labor recruiters, and ship captains"[73] who advanced them the cost of their expensive passage from Canton to San Francisco. "Though contemporary observers saw little difference between Chinese shipped abroad in the coolie traffic and semifree emigrants," remarks Sucheng Chan on a social distinction which Cox failed to make, "the Chinese themselves, as well as British and American consuls stationed in China in the 1850s and 1860s, distinguished between the two groups: free emigrants to California and Australia . . . were usually referred to as 'passengers,' while those taken to Latin America were called 'coolies.'"[74] What drew passengers to California was the same magnet that drew 100,000 others to the state between 1849 and 1854: gold.[75] "That gold—everywhere it was found—was the most powerful lodestone attracting large numbers of free and semifree Chinese voyagers," contends Chan, "is clearly shown by the fact that Chinese miners were among the first on the scene in all the major gold rushes of the second half of the nineteenth century. . . . Only after all hopes of striking it rich in gold mining had faded did Chinese succumb to the necessity of laboring for wages." And even this arguably inevitable condition Chinese Californians postponed far longer than did their white counterparts: a mere two years before the passage of the Chinese Exclusion Act of 1882, "there were still about 15,000 miners, one-fifth of the Chinese population in the state. In comparison, only about 7 percent of the gainfully employed non-Chinese still mined for a living." Chan adds fittingly that "[s]o far as the Chinese were concerned, the gold rush was not yet over."[76]

In spite of their perseverance, however, most Chinese prospectors were literally forced by their white counterparts to content themselves with secondhand sites. "In the 1850s," reports Chan, "Chinese had been frequently robbed, beaten, driven away from their diggings, or even killed."[77] Much of this abuse tragically took place after Chinese miners had already paid the exorbitant foreign miners' tax (1850) which, theoretically, should have shielded them from harassment. Though the following account chronicles what frequently happened to Mexican, Chilean, and even to Californio miners at the hands of white prospectors, we can well imagine that Chinese miners suffered similar injustices:

> Even those who paid the extortionate $20 found that it brought very little protection, for if the collector neglected his monthly rounds their certificates lapsed, and if the Americans of one county refused to honor permits bought in another, the Spanish-speaking had little recourse but to leave. They knew that they alone of all foreign miners were being subjected to the tax: when they taunted the collectors to tax Irishmen, Frenchmen, and other Europeans they received no satisfactory reply. Masqueraders posing as collectors came into Mexican camps, solemnly tore up valid permits, and demanded money for new ones; when rebuffed, they auctioned off the victim's dirt and installed in his claim a "loyal citizen."[78]

While Chinese miners were remarkably able to turn a profit on "low-yield or worked over sites,"[79] the limited number of these sites in relation to the potential number of Chinese prospectors forced many of them into mining's service industries. "In the major mining camps," recounts Chan, "a small number of Chinese merchants, grocers, truck gardeners, cooks, servants, laundrymen, barbers, herbalists, prostitutes, professional gamblers, and even a fortune-teller or two served the subsistence and recreational needs of their fellow countrymen."[80] In plainest terms, the Chinese, like so many other people of color in the United States, were forced to "make do" with what Whites did not want to do. Apparently, the "democratic" spirit of civility and equality of opportunity that supposedly animated the American frontier did not extend to the Chinese.[81]

For this very reason white railway workers did not object to the Chinese presence on the Central Pacific's rail lines. As one scholar aptly described the then-current attitude, "No man who had any choice would have chosen to be a common laborer on the Central Pacific during the crossing of the High Sierra." The railroad company found willing workers in the more than 10,000 Chinese nationals (excluding job-site casualties) it hired between 1866 and 1869, many of whom, it should be noted, were drawn from the mining industry when it was "at last giving out." Furthermore, far from competing with white railway workers, Chinese track layers boosted the occupational status of their white counterparts. "To the unskilled white railroad laborer of 1865," remarks Alexander Saxton, "the coming of the Chinese meant his own advancement into that elite one-fifth of the labor force which was composed of strawbosses, foremen, teamsters, skilled craftsmen. This in itself was no small bonanza."[82]

The racial order that reigned in rural California set the social precedent for what was to follow in the urban West. Accordingly, San Francisco's industrial division of labor was similarly racialized in the 1870s and 1880s. Whereas Chinese piece and wage workers[83] were relegated to the city's mass production industries—cigar rolling, textiles, and shoe manufacturing—whose owners justified their minimal wage offerings on the grounds that it was the only way to make their products competitive with low-priced east coast goods, white workers dominated the higher prestige, trade jobs—construction and carpentry—in the Bay Area. Of course, in San Francisco, too, extra-market forces ensured the racialization of that city's industrial division of labor:

> The moment of decision in this respect seems to have occurred during the winter of 1867 when some four hundred white workingmen attacked a group of Chinese who were excavating for a street railway. The crowd stoned the Chinese, maimed several, and burned their shanties. Afterward, alleged leaders of the riot were jailed and the Chinese resumed work under armed guard. But the demonstration had made its point. Throughout the long record of anti-Oriental agitation which

followed, there appears little if any reference to Chinese as construction laborers in San Francisco. . . . Thus in the national market industry—cigar making—Chinese took over both skilled
and unskilled operation; on the local market industry—
building—they were excluded from both. This became the
urban pattern.[84]

It should be noted, nevertheless, that during periods of economic
contraction white workers were not above taking jobs in the San
Francisco cigar industry "at the same rate of pay"[85] as their Chinese
counterparts. In one watershed case in the course of the twenty-year
depression that spanned the 1870s to the 1890s, the Chinese employees of the cigar manufacturing firm of Koeniger, Falk, and Mayer
went on strike to protest what they perceived as a plot to replace
Chinese labor with white labor. San Francisco's Cigar Makers' International Union (CMIU) Local 224 turned the strike to its advantage
by "claiming that its men were more compliant and trustworthy than
the refractory Chinese." About this case, Herbert Hill fittingly added
that "[o]nce again the whites unhesitatingly reversed roles when it
suited them to do so."[86] The final measure taken by white workers to
force Chinese workers out of San Francisco's manufacturing industries targeted the consumption end of Chinese production: the boycott of Chinese-made goods. Chinese workers immediately felt the
effects. "Boycotts of Chinese-made goods by white consumers," remarks Chan, "reduced the number of Chinese factory owners and
workers in San Francisco from 1,023 and 4,264, respectively, in 1880
to only 84 and 1,694, respectively, in 1900. By 1920 there were virtually no Chinese cigar or shoe and boot makers left."[87] "Thus," as Hill
reminds us, "the great tradition of the union label began as a racist
stratagem."[88]

I have included this brief synopsis of Chinese-American social history between the years of roughly 1850 and 1870 to contest Cox's
belief that Asian Americans, like Asian West Indians, entered the
Americas mainly as contract laborers or "coolies," to use the deroga-
tory term. What Cox hoped to achieve by likening nineteenth-
century California events to Caribbean ones in the same period was
to prove that the reactions of both white Californians and, say, black
Trinidadians, to the arrival of Asian workers were not motivated by

racial considerations but by class concerns.[89] As he put it, "[t]his reaction of labor, however, is not peculiarly a racial phenomenon; the conflict is essentially between employer and worker . . . it is a conflict between two exploited groups generated by the desire of one group of workers to keep up the value of its labor power by maintaining its scarcity."[90] Therefore, what may appear on first glance to be manifestations of ethnic nationalism on the part of the numerically dominant groups in California, the Caribbean, and elsewhere, were really nothing other than working people's attacks on capital's latest ploy to reduce their wages and undermine their attempts to organize. This is a serious claim on Cox's part, and it informs his entire understanding of the anti-Asian movement in California.

True to his conviction that the "exploiters of labor" are "responsible for all modern racial antagonism,"[91] Cox began his narrative of Asian Americans in California after 1870, or, at precisely the point when the number of self-employed Chinese began to decline. In beginning the story there, Cox could claim that white Californians were not motivated mainly by racial sentiments in their push to either curtail or end the flow of Chinese and then of virtually all Asian immigrants into the state, but by their desire to break the "alliance" (as they saw it) between capital and Chinese workers. Again, since the pull of the "gold mountain" (the Chinese ideogram for California) did not lend itself to Cox's interpretation of white California's reaction to the Chinese presence, he did not find it useful to begin Chinese American history there.

In line, moreover, with his belief that capitalists are the greatest instigators of racial conflict in the modern era, Cox was sure to underscore the support that southern politicians lent to the anti-Asian movement in California. In addition to the theoretical purposes it served for Cox, he was sure to underscore the political relationship between California labor and southern capital:

> Although the sporadic aggression of the employers gave considerable encouragement and stimulation to the anti-Asiatic movement among white workers, the latter may not have achieved the purpose of Asiatic exclusion so completely had it not been for their favorable alliance with Southern politics. It may seem strange that the politicians of the South, who advocate the interest of a ruling class that has fairly well subdued

white labor through the widespread exploitation of black workers, should deem it advisable to take the side of the white workingmen of California in their struggle against their employers'
desire to exploit cheap Oriental labor. And yet it was probably
the weight of the Southern vote in Congress which made it
possible for California to put over its national policy of anti-
Orientalism.[92]

And what was the common ground that these otherwise class opponents were able to find? Cox supplied one answer:

> [T]he South came to the rescue of California not because of an
> interest in the white workers or dislike for the exploiters of
> Oriental labor but because it wanted to develop a national tra-
> dition to the effect that when the interests of a colored people
> come into conflict with those of white people the former must
> always give way. The problem was defined as a conflict between
> the whites and the Asiatics in California. If this were admitted,
> then white people in the South should be conceded the right to
> control "their" Negroes without interference from the national
> government. This logic was possible in spite of the fact that the
> articulate white people in the South were the masters, while
> those on the Coast were organized workers.[93]

Again, it must be stressed that for southern elites in particular
this alliance with California's white working-class was truly nothing
more than a marriage of convenience. For, as Carey McWilliams
noted, had they not been able to undermine the terms of freedom
for former slaves by the infamous "compromise" of 1877, "the Southern representatives in Congress would almost certainly have voted
against exclusion of Chinese immigration."[94] Why? With the loss of
their most tractable laboring population, southern elites would have
welcomed Chinese or any immigrant population to toil in their fields,
mines, and factories like those who were then engaged in the Caribbean and in South America.

As far as the attitudes of white working-class Californians toward
their Asian counterparts were concerned, Cox again saw these as
similar to Afro-Caribbean sentiments toward East Indian indentured
servants and to those of "native" white American workers toward the

latest European immigrants, save that in this case the victims of discrimination in the east and midwest became its practitioners in California.[95] Echoing McWilliams's thoughts on the subject,[96] Cox described these working-class sentiments as "not unlike the way in which early handicraft workers reacted against the machine."[97] Yet one cannot help but think that even the most militant Luddite recognized the difference between, say, a mechanized loom and an Irish immigrant. In the final analysis, one gathers from Cox's remark that "there is no racial antagonism between Negroes and East Indians in Trinidad,"[98] that anti-Asian attitudes in California, like the "early anti-Irish attitude in the East," are but temporary roadblocks in the path of eventual, if not to say, inevitable, social harmony.

This, however, was only Cox's long-term retrospective projection; in the short-run he considered cooperation between white and Chinese workers "practically impossible."

> The cultural bar between the European and the Asiatic makes it difficult and at certain stages practically impossible for the two groups to reach that common understanding necessary for concerted action against the employer. Moreover, the first generation of Asiatic workers is ordinarily very much under the control of labor contractors and employers, hence it is easier for the employer to frustrate any plans for their organization. Clearly this cultural bar helped to antagonize white workers against the Asiatics. The latter were conceived of as being in alliance with the employer. It would probably have taken two or three generations before say, the East Indian low-caste worker on the Coast became sufficiently Americanized to adjust easily to the policies and aims of organized labor.[99]

Yet, Cox was aware of the dangers in his own argument of Asian unassimilability into American society in the short-term: white workers could conveniently employ it to justify the restriction or termination of Asian immigration into the United States, or, in the worst case, even the deportation of Asian immigrants; while white employers could use it to discourage white workers from attempting to organize Asian workers. As he was forced to admit, "Here again a basic conflict of interest seems to converge in an identical argument, and in this situation it is sometimes difficult to discover the interest behind the rationalization."[100]

Yet again, Cox offered no resolution to the compelling problem he raised. Apart from some tangential remarks about the "gypsification" of Chinese Americans in California by the turn of the century and how the combination of nationalism, religious solidarity, and the military strength of Japan itself enabled Japanese Americans to escape the fate of their Asian American brethren, his discussion of the sociopolitical relationship between Euro-American and Asian American labor breaks off here. Thus it seems fair to conclude that, in Cox's estimation, the anti-Asian statements made by the likes of Denis Kearney, the Irish-born founder of the Workingman's Party of California and by Samuel Gompers, long-time president of the American Federation of Labor (himself a Jewish immigrant), and by countless rank and file supporters of the Chinese Exclusion Act and other such anti-Asian edicts, were fundamentally rallying cries for the "class conflict between labor and capital."[101]

Before we despair of Cox's apparent indulgence of white chauvinism, we should consider alternative ways of reading his position. One such possibility is that Cox adhered to a strict definition of racism according to which working-class people could not be racist.

Racism vs. Intolerance:
Cox on Black and Jewish Experiences in the West

More than one scholar has taken Cox to task for his apparent unwillingness to admit that workers have and act on their ethnic identities independent of the dictates of capital. Robert Miles, for example, concluded that "Cox's analysis . . . does not specifically allow for the expression of race prejudice amongst the working class."[102] And David Roediger, to cite another of Cox's critics, asserts that from Cox's perspective workers "largely receive and occasionally resist racist ideas and practices but have no role in *creating* those practices."[103] Perhaps nowhere is this bias more apparent than in Cox's refusal to entertain that idea that a bipartite situation of race relations operated in the California of the mid-nineteenth century on the grounds that the gold rush "brought a great wave of highly

independent white workers" who effectively delayed the establishment of a "small ruling class," presumably the sine qua non of a bipartite situation.[104] To put Cox's perspective on racism in plainest
terms, those who are hired by capital cannot be agents of racism.[105]

As puzzling as this last statement may seem, it is consistent with
Cox's definition of racism. In *Caste, Class, and Race,* Cox defined race
prejudice as a "social attitude propagated among the public by an
exploiting class for the purpose of stigmatizing some group as inferior so that the exploitation of either the group itself or its resources or both may be justified."[106] Again, this definition suggests
that racism is neither of the working class's own making nor for its
own profit. Of course, this perspective leaves unnamed the conscious
discrimination against workers of color (and periodically against
non-Protestant workers in the American context) by white workers
in the personnel office, the plant, and in the union meeting hall for
the economic gains to be made from either excluding them altogether or from relegating them to subordinate jobs in the division
of labor. As we have already seen, this is precisely what white workers subjected Chinese immigrants to in California and what happened there was tragically similar to Mexican-American experiences
in the southwest generally in the same period and foreshadowed
those of black Americans east of the Mississippi after emancipation.
In short, Cox's suggestion that workers, by definition, cannot be
racist was a puzzling position for a black scholar to take.

Is there any reactionary sentiment, then, which workers can feel
of their own volition? One in particular: intolerance. This is the
label that Cox gave to anti-Asian feelings among white working-class
people in nineteenth-century California and this is also how he cate-
gorized anti-Semitism. However, as the following passage indicates,
he was quick to insist that this last not be confused with racism:

> Anti-Semitism, to begin with is clearly a form of social intoler-
> ance, which attitude may be defined as an unwillingness on
> the part of a dominant group to tolerate the beliefs or prac-
> tices of a subordinate group because it considers these beliefs
> and practices to be either inimical to group solidarity or a
> threat to the continuity of the status quo. Race prejudice, on
> the other hand, is a social attitude propagated among the
> public by an exploiting class for the purpose of stigmatizing

some groups as inferior so that the exploitation of either the group itself or its resources or both may be justified. Persecution and exploitation are the behavior aspects of intolerance and race prejudice respectively. In other words, race prejudice is the socio-attitudinal facilitation of a particular type of labor exploitation, while social intolerance is a reactionary attitude supporting the action of a society in purging itself of contrary cultural groups.[107]

To illustrate further the distinction he drew between anti-Semitism and racism, Cox added that "[p]robably the clearest distinction between intolerance and race prejudice is that the intolerant group welcomes conversion and assimilation, while the race-prejudiced group is antagonized by attempts to assimilate. . . . The Jew, to the intolerant, is an enemy within the society; but the Negro, to the race-prejudiced, is a friend in his place." And even more graphically Cox underscored that a "Jewish pogrom is not exactly similar to a Negro lynching. In a pogrom the fundamental motive is the extermination of the Jew; in a lynching, however, the motive is that of giving the Negro a lesson in good behavior."[108]
These definitions go some way to explain why no fewer than a quarter of a million Europeans of the Jewish faith converted to Christianity in the nineteenth century[109] and why the Ku Klux Klan was formed when it was. Apart from these straightforward examples, however, Cox's definitions of anti-Semitism and of racism can neither address white intolerance of Blacks (in spite of the economic benefits that could be ideally derived from their presence) nor the economic exploitation of Jews as ethnic subordinates. In other words, like all definitions of sociological phenomena based on ideal type scenarios, neither definition can adequately account for all manifestations of anti-Black and anti-Jewish sentiments in the western world. It is difficult, for example, to underestimate the economic dimension of the legal and informal codes against Russian Jews in the nineteenth century when they explicitly aimed at denying the Ashkenazim the means by which to earn a living: their property rights, freedom of movement, choice of occupation, and educational opportunities were all severely curtailed or simply denied.[110] (It is even possible to interpret the loans that the Rothschilds floated to a number of western and central European monarchs and firms in the same

era as little more than "protection rent" to stay the tide of anti-Semitism). Similarly, Cox's definition of racism cannot address the formal and informal codes adopted by many midwestern states in the early nineteenth century that prohibited the further settlement there by Blacks.[111] Neither definition, moreover, calls attention to the political dimension of and parallels between European anti-Jewish and American anti-Black sentiments. For example, in the supposed "emancipation" eras of both populations—catalyzed by the French Revolution for European Jewry and by the Civil War for black Americans—during which time they were supposed to be recognized as indisputable citizens of their respective nations and made to abide by individual rather than group laws, non-Jews and non-Blacks continued to charge them with promoting group interests by cultivating special relationships with their respective governments or political parties.[112] Thus, in the eyes of many non-Blacks and non-Jews, despite the emancipation of Jews and Blacks, western governments and competitors for state power have never desisted from treating them as groups rather than as individuals. Moreover, these critics argue, to the extent that western political leaders continued to conceive of these populations in group terms, they were necessarily acting in violation of the basic precepts of the American Constitution and the Declaration of Rights of Man and Citizens. Of course, that one of the central pillars of the western political tradition was the legal exclusion of Blacks and Jews is conveniently overlooked by the racist or anti-Semite as is the fact that legal "equality" was extended to these populations "in the form and for the purpose of privilege,"[113] be it for loans or for votes.

The point is not to show what Cox "missed" in his comparison of the black and Jewish experiences in the West; something deeper is at issue here. A careful reading of Cox's writings on this theme reveals that the experiences which he believed differentiated the two groups are just as much prescriptive as they are descriptive; that is, his remarks are not merely academic but also consciously political. Cox was not dishonest or deliberately misleading in his presentation of the facts; rather, he factored the political or policy implications of his findings into his sociological formulations. These political considerations are most clear in his treatment of the general social relationship between Blacks and Jews in the United States.

Cox approached the subject in two ways. In the first instance, Cox applied a strict class analysis to the group relationship between American Blacks and Jews:

> In so far as Jews are bourgeois-minded businessmen and manu-
> facturers, they are likely to be, at least implicitly, race-prejudiced.
> They will sooner understand the limiting racial policies of the
> ruling class than the ambition of Negroes for social equality.
> Because the Negroes are almost entirely a proletarian group,
> while the Jews tend to be professional and businessmen, there
> is particular opportunity for the development of a disparity of in-
> terest between them. As Negroes become increasingly assimi-
> lated in the larger society, the likelihood is that they, too, will
> become intolerant.[114]

A couple of comments are in order here. Because of their different collective class positions,[115] Cox believed that Jews have as much
reason to be racist as Blacks anti-Semitic, though their anti-Semitism
is more likely the expression of class resentment than it is of religious intolerance. In addition, to the degree that American Jews become successful capitalists, they would have greater cause to identify
with their gentile class equals than with a minority population of the
working class below them. Moreover, by virtue of both their religion
and class position, Jewish American capitalists would have another reason to ally themselves with their gentile counterparts: to de-intensify
anti-Semitism relative to racism in American society. Here is how
Cox explained this strategy:

> There is a sense in which we may conceive of racial antagonism
> as contributing to the amelioration of anti-Semitism. The po-
> tentialities against which the present-day dominant whites
> struggle in their racial aggression are more dangerous than
> the possible disorganizing presence of the Jews. The threat to
> the entire social system is definitely increased if the black and
> white proletariat are permitted to become unified and class
> conscious—ruling-class Jews and all may be marked for liqui-
> dation. If the Jewish bourgeoisie can keep the fear of this threat
> before the minds of the dominant white Gentiles, it is likely

that they will be able to establish a Jew-Gentile, bourgeois solidarity against the colored people and, of course, against the
white proletariat also. This will tend to allay the intensity of
anti-Semitism. To the extent, however, that the proletariat
gains solidarity and power, to that extent also the Jewish bourgeoisie may come in for its full share of proletarian hatred,
and probably more so from the most exploited group, the colored people.[116]

Still, Cox recognized that the moment that the racist or anti-
Semite employed biological (or biblical) arguments to justify his
or her beliefs, then Blacks and Jews had reason to make common
cause: "When in 1934, for instance, the Nazi party declared that
'the continuation of marriages with bearers of colored or Jewish
blood is incompatible with the aims of the National Socialist party,'
the colored people and the Jews had to come together in opposition to a common danger."[117]

In short, from the vantage point of relative class position, there
was nothing to drive Blacks and Jews to make common cause, but a
lot to make them enemies. Hence the difference between racism
and anti-Semitism, particularly in a bipartite situation of race relations where Jews share the same skin color as the socially dominant
population.

The opening of Cox's second approach to the social bases of
Black-Jewish social interaction begins with disturbing characterizations of both Judaism and Jews. In his last published article entitled,
"Jewish Self-interest in 'Black Pluralism,'" Cox claimed, among other
things, that Judaism is based on "tribal exclusiveness" such that the
Jewish community steadfastly resists "social assimilation" into the
larger society within which it lives. "Social segregation," he added,
"is an inherent element of the structure of [Jewish] culture."[118]
Somewhat predictably Cox argued that "[a]nti-Semitism has been
identified with Jewish behavior in the sense that it is a reaction of
other groups to the Jews' determination to assert and perpetuate
their identity." Thus, anti-Semitism is the non-Jew's "retaliation resulting from a normal Jewish determination to resist merger of their
civilization with that of host peoples."[119] These remarks set the stage
for what Cox asserted is unique about the Jewish experience in the
West: "Jews are unique in that they have been the only people who

have been able to take full advantage of material resources in larger
host societies everywhere without giving way eventually to social assimilation. They have, in other words, maintained divided loyalties—
'dual citizenships.' "[120]

Cox's views on both Jews and Judaism are obviously open to a
number of counterattacks: their disregard of historical change, their
reliance on stereotypes, and, most important, their very serious
implication—that anti-Semitism will cease to exist only when Jews
abandon Judaism, or, in more graphic terms, only when both Judaism and Jews cease to exist.[121] All of these and related points are
of obvious importance in their own right, but for our purposes here
it is important to consider the possible political motives behind
Cox's claims about the Jewish experience in the West; motives, again,
that may have had little to do with that experience in itself but a lot
to do with that of black Americans. The following two passages are
quite revealing when read in this light:

> It seems appropriate to repeat . . . that the Negroes do not have
> a culture in the sense that Jews have one. Jews consider them-
> selves descendants of an ancient Hebrew people, the chosen
> tribes of Judah, a book-devoted people moving in and out of
> great ancient civilizations, and surviving culturally into our own
> times. Negroes, to the contrary, descend from a multiplicity of
> unassimilated West African tribes—most of them preliterate,
> some of them culturally antagonistic, and thus with hardly any
> direct cultural continuity and compatibility—into the United
> States.[122]

> Jews, of course, have been historical 'pluralists.' . . . They have
> both suffered and profited materially from their cultural sepa-
> ration. They have been traditionally a part of the urban West
> where . . . they have been able to specialize in money-getting
> and scholarship. Unlike the tradition of Negroes, then, their
> subculture concentrates on sharpening them for competition
> in those fields.[123]

So much could be said in response to Cox's assertions that one
would hardly know where or how to begin. Still, for our purposes,
the passages provide us with sufficient material out of which to

reconstruct Cox's logic: if black Americans lack a cohesive culture comparable to that of Jewish Americans, then they accordingly lack the ingredient which would enable them to succeed socioeconomically without assimilating into mainstream American society as their Jewish counterparts have traditionally managed to do. Furthermore, through no fault of their own, black Americans, in Cox's opinion, trail their Jewish American counterparts in entrepreneurial and intellectual savvy. Consequently, as he saw it, socially sanctioned pluralism[124] would only serve to "enhance Jewish competitive power"[125] in those domains and to weaken the ability of black Americans to compete not only against Jewish-Americans, but presumably against other white ethnics who are similarly equipped with particular cultural strengths.[126] Here, then, was the basis of his objection to the social scientific use and political encouragement of pluralism in American society and of his assertion that Jewish Americans knowingly stood to gain by the adoption of black pluralism, or, in Cox's rendering of it, black nationalism, on the part of the majority of black Americans.[127] The basis of this assertion, too, is not difficult to discern: to the extent that black nationalists called for the support or creation of predominantly or all-black institutions to address the social needs of black Americans, Jewish American institutions guided by the same philosophy were indirectly protected and justified. (Conversely, the integration of black Americans into mainstream American society ran the risk of constitutionally ending ethnic or denominationally specific religious institutions.) In this light, the title of Cox's article devoted to this issue—"Jewish Self-interest in 'Black Pluralism'"—is less controversial than it first appears. In fact, what is more troubling about the article than the sound of its title is the none-too-subtle claim that even the apparently moral actions of American Jews are ultimately self-serving. If one wanted to charge Cox with being anti-Semitic, I believe that this is the claim that one could submit as evidence.

It should be clear, then, that Cox's primary preoccupation in this article was not Jewish-American responses to either black nationalism or to black integration; his first concern was with how black Americans would fare in a society that promoted white ethnic pluralism (or, as he re-phrased it, the "American Jewish way of life"),[128] over ideally colorblind assimilation. As we have seen, he had reason to believe that they would not fare well. Thus, in light of their cultural disadvantages when compared with white ethnics, Cox counseled Black Americans

> not to look with longing upon these displays of white ethnic culture and nationalism. Already an identifiable culture of superlative design and capacity has emerged in America. Although they are still of relatively lower status, mainly because of persisting racial restraints, Negroes nevertheless are inevitably identified with this culture. In this respect, they are culturally similar to the majority of native white Americans who naturally have no foreign artifacts to display. Indeed, life itself, in the phenomenal mainstream, includes their increasingly indistinguishable folkways. The ethnic celebrations are manifestly attempts to resuscitate, among immigrants, waning nationalism; something Negroes would have to produce largely from scratch.[129]

Among the many comments that this passage may provoke is Cox's apparent failure to distinguish between acculturation and assimilation. Here he provides a fairly comprehensive description of the American acculturation of black Americans, yet he oddly kept silent about the dilemma posed by the persistence of racism and the ideal of assimilation. For if, as he asserted, "capitalist culture is . . . intrinsically racist,"[130] then the most that black Americans can ever claim in American society is that they are acculturated, not assimilated. Moreover, as Harold Cruse correctly remarks on Cox's position, "it was highly questionable and over simplistic to equate black desires for equal inclusion with a social drive toward assimilation."[131] For if assimilation means the acceptance of white nationalism (of whatever persuasion), who could really expect the bulk of Americans of color to embrace assimilation?

Cox has been duly credited for having presented a devastating critique of the caste school of southern race relations, but it is frequently forgotten that he also took on issues such as Asian-white social relations in nineteenth-century California as well as Black/Jewish interaction in twentieth-century America. In all of these cases, Cox wrote his political concerns into his sociological analyses. Thus, among the many reasons for contesting the caste school was to take the responsibility of racism off the shoulders of poor Whites and place it on those to whom it truly belongs, white capitalists. Similarly, though not without abuses, Cox supported the cause of the white working class in nineteenth-century California by presenting their political actions as protection of their class interests and not as discrimination per se against their Chinese counterparts. And finally, in the case of Black-Jewish relations, Cox highlighted the faster social mobility and greater group cohesion of American Jews relative to Blacks in order to dissuade black nationalists, in particular, from continuing to advocate a pluralist political program that is more advantageous to Jews and other white ethnics than it is to Blacks. As we shall see in chapter 6, Cox continued to voice that message in what became his final work — *Race Relations* — but from a different angle.

At this point, however, I would like to introduce in the next two chapters the subject to which Cox devoted virtually all his scholarly energy between roughly the years 1950 and 1965: the capitalist world economy. Cox was convinced that race relations are the product of capitalism, and only of capitalism, and it appears that one of his motivations for undertaking this massive project was to prove this contention.

4

The Foundations of Capitalism

Venice, the Capitalist Prototype

Cox began *The Foundations of Capitalism* with the city-state of Venice, which, like England possessed sugar-producing colonies in the late medieval and early modern era. Yet, for reasons that are unclear, Cox chose not to underscore the obvious parallels between Venice and its Mediterranean sugar colonies and England and its Caribbean ones. Apart from a passing reference to the attempts of this capitalist "prototype" to cultivate cane in the eastern Mediterranean,[1] the most that Cox would say about a related subject was that the "Venetian slave trade was the first capitalistically organized commerce in human beings."[2] In spite of Cox's reticence on the matter, it is worth recounting how Venice came to possess sugar plantations for at least two reasons: one, because it is my contention that Cox was drawn, on some level, to the Venetian case precisely because of the parallel with England; and two, because the story is a revealing example of the manner in which Venice structured its trading world. Let us see how Cox envisioned that world.

Soon after the fall of the Roman Empire, Venice became an ambiguous outpost of the Eastern Roman or Byzantine Empire. The ambiguity of the relationship was due to the occasional inability of Constantinople to defend the lagoon settlement from Lombard invasions in spite of the fact that its leaders or doges were made to pledge Venice's allegiance to the Byzantine emperor. With or without Byzantine protection, by A.D. 1000 the Venetians were able to make of their city one of the principal entrepots of eastern Mediterranean goods in high demand in western Europe: precious metals, spices, and silks. In exchange for these items, the Venetians supplied Byzantium and Fatimid Egypt with locally caught fish, panned salt, timber, and slaves, who "ranked almost with salt and fish as a mainstay of Venetian commerce."[3] At this juncture, however, Venetian merchants were confined to the management of local commerce while "Greeks, Syrians, and other easterners carried most of the trade between Venice and the Levant."[4]

The lot of Venice's merchants would not change for the better until the end of the eleventh century when a normally threatening development proved propitious: a Norman advance which had already claimed Sicily, Bari, Amalfi, and Salerno, compelled the Byzantine Emperor, Alexius I, to call on Venetian aid. Recognizing that Norman designs in the Mediterranean also impinged on its present and future position as a crossroad of continental European, Byzantine, and Arab commerce (despite papal injunctions), Venice heeded Constantinople's call. Once they had successfully rebuffed the Norman advance at Durazzo in 1081, the Venetians were in the moral position to secure from Alexius I a number of trading privileges which entitled them to conduct commerce "in all parts of his empire free of any charge, tax, or duty payable to his treasury."[5] It is in these concessions that Cox located the beginnings of Venice as a capitalist city-state.[6] The Normans would make other attacks on the Byzantine Empire under the pretense of defending Christendom from an expanding Islam, and the Venetians would again be called upon to defend the empire. In these instances, however, their actions were always those of self-interest: the Venetians "were ready to fight the Normans and others to keep the Byzantine Empire intact while equally ready to fight the Greeks themselves, not only for the sake of booty, but also to force the Greeks to renew Venetian privileges."[7]

At this juncture, the Venetians began to employ at least two of the strategies that Cox considered essential tools of a capitalist economy, which he defined as a "system or network of national and territorial units bound together by commercial and exploitative relationships." The first and the one upon which all other capitalist designs depended was the development of the city's primary transportation industry, shipbuilding. "It was in the shipbuilding industry," Cox underscored in his discussion of the Venetian case, "that Venice evinced most clearly the strains of capitalist industrial enterprise. Here emerged large-scale organization for efficient factory production with specialization of skills, under the direction of both private and State enterprise." The most visible proof of the Venetian commitment to shipbuilding was its Arsenal, the shipbuilding and ship-repairing complex that "gradually became the world's largest industrial organization, employing thousands of workers and spreading over sixty acres of 'ground and water.'" The Venetians also protected their shipbuilding industry by enacting a number of restrictions on foreign shipping and trade in those areas they considered under their political-economic hegemony: "They [the Venetians] guarded carefully the secrets of ship construction, limited the sale or rental of galleys to foreigners, regulated the carriage of foreign goods in their ships, excluded outsiders from association with their citizens in overseas ventures, forced 'towns on the mainland subject to the Seigniory [to] dispatch their products only by way of the capital, where a high duty was levied on them,' determined competitive strategy with other communities, and laid down the laws of conduct at sea."[8]

Second, the commercial concessions that the Venetians secured from Alexius I and from subsequent Byzantine emperors enabled them to "export the products of foreign peoples and to supply them with goods from abroad." This type of commercial intervention between social formations Cox termed "provisioning" or "securing the consumptive needs of a [foreign] people,"[9] and by it the Venetians were able to factor into the prices of the commodities they distributed a considerable charge for their services, including "protection rent." Thus Cox concluded that "[o]ne of the characteristics of leadership . . . is that the capitalist nation thus situated controls the most demanded and consequently indispensable articles of world trade."[10]

Yet, the events that bear the greatest responsibility for Venice's entry into the sugar business were those that encouraged medieval European colonial expansion in general: the Crusades. In those wars that European Christians waged against Muslims to reclaim the Holy Land for Christendom, the three leading Italian commercial cities—Genoa, Pisa, and Venice—were hired by the Crusades' organizers to provide transportation to and supplies in the Levant (except in the case of the First Crusade whose enthusiasts took a land route). As the crusaders were frequently unable to pay their suppliers in advance for their services, the bulk of the payments came in the form of booty and conquered lands. In 1123, for example, "the Venetians, who had taken part in the conquest [of Tyre] received some 21 out of 114 conquered villages as well as a few additional pieces of territory in northern Lebanon. Rather then letting out their villages on feudal tenures, the Venetians converted several of them to sugar production, adopting Muslim sugar technology and capitalizing on their own maritime ability to get the sugar to European markets."[11] In addition to their plantations in greater Tyre and Acre in what are today the states of Israel and Lebanon, the Venetians also possessed sugar cane plantations on the islands of Crete and Cyprus. The volume of Cypriot sugar production, for example, was considerable as proven by the crop's "use to pay royal debts, and in the fifteenth century the king [of Cyprus] gave his plantations as securities to private capitalists, to the State of Venice and to the famous Bank of St. George in Genoa."[12] "Crete and Cyprus played the same role vis-à-vis Venice," maintains Immanuel Wallerstein, "that the Indies would later play vis-à-vis Spain, then England."[13] And as in these last-named examples, colonial cane cultivation gave rise to a Venetian sugar industry which supplied Europe with a considerable portion of its sugar needs from the thirteenth to the sixteenth centuries.[14]

As noted, Cox oddly opted to leave the story of the sugar plantation in the margins of his version of Venetian history. Perhaps he felt that to have included it would have raised suspicions of Caribbean-centrism in the minds of his readership or reviewers. Outside of a few pointed comments, Cox's tone is impartial. Though he did not feel so bold to claim in *The Foundations of Capitalism* what Roger Kennedy would in his *Architecture, Men, Women, and Money,* that "plantations worked by black slaves were the source of the wealth of many Venetian patricians,"[15] Cox did not feel inhibited in a public address to contend that "the slave trade and piracy yielded the basic income and motivation for the future development of England as a capitalist nation."[16] The omission of Venice's sugar story notwithstanding, it is doubtful that the historical similarities between England and the Caribbean archipelago and Venice and its Mediterranean island possessions were lost on Cox. For both instances revealed other characteristics of capitalistic international relations.

One of these is fairly obvious: the reduction of many social formations to mere suppliers of raw materials—inanimate and animate—for the commercial and consumptive needs of the capitalist leaders. Colonies like Crete and Trinidad were, by design, just this. Moreover, as a result of the monopoly that capitalist leaders enjoy of the means and mechanisms of the wholesale and, at times, the retail trades of many commodities, even politically independent social formations inevitably become neocolonies of the capitalist leaders. For these reasons, Cox insisted that the "prime object of imperialism is the monopolization of the major productive capacity and foreign trade of weaker countries."[17] He went on to add that "[I]mperialism, therefore, is by no means a nugatory excrescence of capitalism: it has on the contrary, provided its very base, its broad structural underpinning. . . . on the whole imperialism provides the most lucrative and capitalistically significant branch of business enterprise."[18]

Venice's imperialistic relationship with its Mediterranean colonies also illustrates another characteristic of capitalistic international relations: the capitalist leaders' "proclivity to import raw materials and export finished products."[19] Apart from Venice's shipbuilding and sugar refining industries of which we already made mention, "Salt, fish, and some manufactures such as glass and cloth formed a nucleus about which the great commercial structure centered."[20] Thanks to Venice's political-economic position toward its Mediterranean colonies and neo-colonies, commodities originating in that city were typically valued well above those imported from its satellites.

Though an important commodity, sugar was only one of many in the Venetian commercial exchange between the eastern and western Mediterranean. From their resident German merchants, the Venetians procured "gold, silver, copper, iron, lead, tin, furs, and manufactured goods of leather, wool, linen, and cotton."[21] "From Romania to Venice," noted Lane, "came raw silk and, above all, silk fabrics and other products of Constantinople's skilled craftsmen, alum, kermes (the red dye from Morea), wax, honey, cotton, wheat from various ports according to the harvest, furs and slaves from the Black Sea, and sweet wines from the Greek islands."[22] The Venetians also "exported wine, oil, fruits, and nuts from the Greek islands to Egypt and brought back wheat, beans, sugar, etc."[23] To Mamluk-ruled Egypt, the Venetians supplied Slavic, Greek, Tartar, Russian, Mongolian, Ukranian, and Caucasian (that is, from the Caucasus mountain region of Eurasia) slaves who were in high demand given that "[o]nly non-Muslims, particularly pagans, could be enslaved for military and governmental service . . . [T]he awlad al-nas (literally, the children of the people) born of Mamluk fathers and native women were theoretically excluded from the Mamluk governing elite."[24] Also eagerly sought after in Egypt were German silver and copper, both of which were undoubtedly processed into military hardware, though the arms trade with Muslims was prohibited by Rome. Reciprocally, in the Holy Roman Empire, France, and in the Low Countries, sugar, wheat, alum, gold, and spices coming by way of Egypt and the Levant were greatly valued for both practical and profit-seeking purposes. These last three commodities were, moreover, the dearer ones at the Champagne fairs; their values rendered the Venetians all the more important as economic players at these French clearinghouses.

The "local" Adriatic economy was less lucrative than the Mediterranean one, but it was never neglected by Venice. "[F]rom Zara [now Zadar]," explained Lane, "came food stuffs, from Ragusa [now Dubrovnik] hides, wax, and silver and other metals mined in its Balkan hinterland."[25] Apulia, the region located at the heel of the Italian peninsula, was a "main source of wheat and also of olive oil, cheese, salt, meat, and wool for the Venetians. In return Venice sent iron, copper, cloth, and oriental wares and also considerable quantities of gold and silver, often needed to clinch purchases of wheat."[26] And closer to home:

Venice sent onions and garlic as well as salt to Aquileia; Aquileia exported to Venice pigs as well as wheat. Istria sent Venice wood, charcoal, and stone. Trieste, which by the thirteenth century was competing with Capodistria in importance, sent skins, hides and meat. The Marches sent their wines. In return, the metropolis met the needs of the countryside and of small towns for specialties in woodwork, leather, pottery or glass, and metalwork. Once Venice had become a large city, it was the natural market for farms over a wide area and their main source of fine manufactured goods. This inter-regional trade was a mainstay of the Venetian economy throughout the centuries.[27]

Cox did not place the same value on local or domestic trade as he did on foreign trade. Still, what is important to note about this trading world, in which Cox saw the "foundations of capitalism," was the Venetian Republic's ability to structure the incipient capitalist "world" economy by supplying surrounding polities with the most important of their service and commodity requirements. To these social formations, Cox gave the names, *subsidiaries, progressives, dependents,* and *passives.* In this hierarchical schema, the Hanseatic League and perhaps Genoa, rated as subsidiaries of Venice, which was "least subject to the economic restraints and plans of other nations, while it [was] most influential in altering the affairs of others in its own interests."[28] Into the category of the progressives, Cox placed the urban republics of Florence and Amalfi, for "each [had] . . . ambitions and capabilities for development somewhat similar to those" of Venice. The various kingdoms, principalities, duchies, and even caliphates with which the Venetians conducted trade, he considered the dependents and passives of the system. Dependents exhibited "little self-initiative in foreign commerce and [were] subject to the immediate, self-interested, economic calculations of the great powers." Passives were "regarded by the leading powers as having no international rights . . . and their resources were organized directly with a view to the enhancement of the economic welfare of any active capitalist nations that was able to establish and maintain control."[29]

Cox did not believe, however, that Venice's success was due to superior economic strategy alone; the republic's political structure had also to reflect its economic requirements. In assessing the merits of

Venice's political organization, which he thought "constituted the kernel of her capitalist organizations,"[30] Cox underscored three aspects of it: one, that Venetian government leaders or doges were chosen by election and subject to numerous aristocratic checks on their political prerogatives; two, that Venetian government was ruled "by law and not by persons," such that law makers themselves had to abide by their own laws; and three, that in "subdu[ing] and restrain[ing]" both monarchical and democratic rule, the Venetian "ruling class openly took over the membership of the national legislature; achieving thereby such a degree of consistency between capitalist economic power and the law as has never been matched in the annals of capitalism."[31] Each point warrants a brief discussion.

Perhaps the most striking feature of the republic's political system was its apparent "balance between monarchy, aristocracy, and democracy"[32] (though this did not include rule by the "people" without money and status). The position of the doge before the fourteenth century gave the Venetian government the façade of a monarchy, but the limitations put upon him in the fourteenth pointed Venice in the direction of a republic. In his official capacity the doge was charged with "commanding the armed forces, conducting foreign affairs, dispensing justice, and supervising administrative officers."[33] In contrast to the selection of European monarchs from among the great noble houses, one of whose members was designated to rule by birthright, the doge was chosen by a "general gathering of the people" called the *Concio* or *Arengo,* that is, the general assembly.[34] The intervention of the general assembly was the result of popularly perceived abuses on the part of a number of earlier doges who attempted "not only to perpetuate themselves in the dogeship but also to make the office hereditary."[35] Other restrictions on the doge's prerogatives similarly came in the wake of an incumbent's abuses.[36] As a last measure against the monarchical tendencies within the dogeship, the Venetian aristocracy both broadened and lengthened the oaths to which the newly named doge swore at his inauguration:

> It was impossible to prevent a successful doge from enhancing the status of his family through the glory which reflected on them from his notable achievements, but the Venetians attempted to restrain his use of the position for either personal

or family gain by adding restrictions to the oath of office of each new incumbent. These oaths (promissioni) record a continual limiting of the doge's powers and freedom of action. At the death of each doge, a committee was appointed to consider additions to the oath before it was taken by the new doge to be elected. Later, another committee was appointed to examine the record in office of the dead doge and to prosecute him so that his heirs might be forced to pay compensation if he had wrongly received any gifts and to pay fines for any derelictions of the duties specified in the doge's oath.[37]

Curiously, the Venetians neither opted to commute the life tenure of the dogeship to a shorter period nor to rotate it as they did in the case of the ducal councilor who held his position "for only six months or a year and [was] debarred from being re-elected to the same post."[38] The actual average length of doge incumbency may have made time limitations unnecessary. "Between 1172 and 1354," Frederic C. Lane specified, "doges were in office eleven to twelve years on average."[39] Still, in so limiting the political room within which the doge could maneuver, the Venetian aristocracy turned the doge into a "mere magistrate" as the republic's government moved from an "elective monarchy"[40] to a full-fledged aristocracy.

Cox was less interested in the Ducal Council, however, than he was in the Great Council, which he equated with the English Parliament. Comprised of anywhere from 300 to 2,000 members throughout the republic's history, the Great Council was charged with "elect[ing] all magistrates and the members of all other councils and settled disputes between them. It passed laws, decreed punishments, and granted pardons."[41] By 1323, moreover, its members pronounced the Great Council "fully hereditary."[42] For Cox, what was most impressive about this legislative body was its uniform class composition that ensured that the laws made by it in no way impeded the republic's economic ends.

The political role that the Great Council played in the Venetian republic provided Cox with the primary political requirement of a capitalist society: that business interests, if not business people themselves, must dominate the sites of policy making in that society.[43] Like the mercantilists, Cox argued that republics (be they aristocratic or bourgeois) are better guarantors of these ends than are monarchies on the grounds that shared governance typically erects more impediments to collaboration with foreign economic interests than does rule by a single person. This point was of utmost importance to Cox since he was particularly interested in the mechanisms by which one polity becomes, or avoids becoming, a neo-colony of another. In addition, the practice of shared governance not only quashed any monarchical pretensions, but it also gave rise to promising speculations on the role of the governed in legitimizing government rather than vice versa.

Though it was the leading pole of capitalism in medieval Europe, according to Cox, and the city-state to which he devoted the most pages in *The Foundations of Capitalism,* Venice was not the only one. What the Venetians were able to do in the Aegean and then in the Mediterranean Seas, the Hanseatic League was able to do in the Baltic. Nevertheless, "powerful as they were in the north," Cox was sure to comment, "they were still pupils among the Venetians."[44]

Hanseatic Hegemony

The Hanseatic League or Community, as Philippe Dollinger prefers,[45] can be thought of as a coalition of German-speaking merchants that dominated Baltic Sea trade throughout the late-medieval–early modern era and at its height could boast of representatives from more than 150 cities. The Hansards drew on two inspirations: the seafaring warrior-trader tradition of the Vikings; and what we may call the northern crusade, equal in intensity and ferocity as that waged against the Moors. The northern crusade entailed both the forced conversion to Christianity of the "pagan" Slavic populations east of the Elbe River and the settlement of these lands by Germanic populations from northwestern Europe. Thus the Hanseatic conquest was both by land and by sea.

Apart from those instances of outright military conquest, the Hansards won their position in the Baltic arena through a combination of tactics: the transshipment of western Baltic goods to the eastern Baltic and vice versa; the provision of loans to insolvent monarchs; and the ability to boycott effectively any trade partner that expressed economic nationalism or class contentiousness. The effectiveness of each of these measures relied on the strength of the Hansards' shipping industries.

We can be sure, once again, that Cox took note of the parallels between Trinidad's economic relationship with an imperial England and a younger England's economic relationship with the Hansards. It must have been an illuminating discovery for Cox to have read about England's humble apprenticeship in colonialism in, say, Henri Pirenne's *Economic and Social History of Medieval Europe.* It would be more accurate to call the political-economic relationship between the English crown and the Hansards neocolonial since the Hansards never occupied and governed English territory in the manner that England would in Trinidad in later centuries. The Hansards did not reduce the English population to mere units of labor, nor did they constitute a nation-state. They were rather an "organization for maximizing the economic capacity and diplomatic power of its membership."[46] Still, the Hansard–English crown relationship did fulfill three indispensable criteria of classical neo-colonialism: one, it was founded on a contract between a "local" or "indigenous" elite and foreign merchants; two, the host territory "agreed" to supply agricultural and mineral raw materials to those foreign merchants who coordinated the processing or manufacture of those materials; and three, those same foreign merchants owned and operated the means of transportation which distributed the primary and secondary goods, in this case, throughout the Baltic Sea.

The Hansards began in England with the extension of loans to the crown. In return for keeping various monarchs solvent, the Hansards were awarded an impressive number of commercial privileges at the expense of local English merchants:

> The tale of the privileges is staggering to consider. They had their fortified Guildhall with its wharves and store houses on the riverside; they were free of most, if not all, English taxes, both municipal and national, and paid less in customs than native Englishmen; they had not only their own court and alderman for the government of their own affairs, but they had special judges to settle their disputes with natives; they were above English juries and English law; they were exempt especially from that ancient custom of (hosting) which prevailed

not only in England but throughout at least Northern Europe; they held their houses in London and other parts in freehold; they had control of one of the gates of the City of London, and were free to go in and out without paying municipal duties; they dealt not only in gross but in retail, in defiance of English custom. They were thus favored not only over other foreigners but over Englishmen.[47]

Though considerable in themselves, these privileges were only of secondary importance to the Hansards; they were in England for wool. Superior in quality to most other grades, English wool fed the fine woolens industries of Flanders and northern Italy. Before the eleventh century, English pastures supplied a national woolens industry that had achieved international renown. However, with the growth of Flanders' productions after that date, English wool farmers, thinking more in monetary than nationalistic terms, did not hesitate to supply Flanders' woolens manufacturers by way of foreign merchants, some of whom became Hansards. This incipient neocolonial relationship between the Hanseatic League and the English crown had reached maturity in the fourteenth century when Edward III awarded a select group of English wool merchants (who became the Fellowship or Company of the Staple) not only the exclusive right to export English wool, but also an exclusive site where foreign buyers could purchase English wool. "By 1361," noted M. M. Postan, "the English Company of the Staple was in possession of a virtual monopoly of wool exports to northern Europe; by 1399 it was safely and permanently launched in Calais."[48] By this agreement, company merchants were effectively protected from competing with independent merchants and wool farmers. Clearly, then, the Hansards had strong English supporters.

In spite of the fact that Hansard merchants were generally prohibited from engaging in local retail trade in either Bruges (the site of their most important *kontor* or trading post) or in other Flemish cities, they could and did hire local workers to process English wool into broadcloth. Those hired by the Hansards were not local guild members, and this absence of corporate protection made them resemble as Henri Pirenne observed, a "modern proletariat."[49] Still, what separated the experience of the Flemish working class from that of their counterparts in nineteenth-century Europe was the location of the workplace: the former continued to work at home and not in factories. They could do so because the Hansards were not interested in the management or supervision of the work practices of their employees, but primarily in the final product. As Cox commented on the subject, "the Hansa encouraged foreign industry and manufacture if only it had the privilege of handling the international commerce in them."[50] This was the medieval putting-out system turned international not unlike much of today's industrialization in the "Third World."[51]

Before the fourteenth-century revival of the English woolens industry,[52] the excellence of Flemish woolens undoubtedly caught the eyes of English elites who purchased them over home productions. Woolens were, however, only one of the Hansard's offerings to English consumers: amber, furs, honey, wax, timber, iron, tar, and wheat were among the eastern Baltic goods exchanged for salt, salted herrings, butter, beer, copper, raw wool, and tin from the western Baltic arena (the last two commodities constituted the bulk of England's exports). The Hansards, moreover, shipped these items and Flemish woolens in the same bottoms that carried English wool to Flanders in classic neocolonial fashion. Thus, in the absence of a shipping industry to rival Hanseatic and Italian carriers, every increase in England's raw wool production was, in effect, a greater net gain for the Hanseatic and Italian carrying trades than it was for English producers.

The important economic point to be drawn from this scenario is that as long as the Hansard arrangement with the English crown endured, England remained both a supplier of raw wool, and later, even of woolens, to the Baltic economy, and not a distributor of its own products. The English economy was only able to come "out from underdevelopment" to borrow James Mittelman's clever title, after the crown chartered in the fifteenth century the Company of Merchant Adventurers to rival the Hanseatic League; closed the Hansard's London kontor at the end of the sixteenth; outlawed the "export of English wool in 1614";[53] and assigned England's extra-European colonies the task of supplying agricultural and mineral raw materials to be processed by English manufacturers and distributed by English merchants. In other words, it was at the moment that English merchants, like the Hansards before them, secured "among foreigners all the commercial advantages [the English crown] denied them,"[54] that the process of England's economic development began. This perspective explains Cox's contention that "the Germans thus served as the immediate, though unwilling, instructors of the English in the capitalist practices and organizations."[55]

Before I attempt to name the "structural designs" or "principal attributes"[56] of capitalism that Cox drew from his reconstruction of these histories, something should be said about the geographic and ideological contexts from which these early capitalist city-states emerged.

Cox and Pirenne

If, as Cox maintained, "the miraculousness of capitalist culture is due to the fact that it seems to create wealth from nothing,"[57] then it is fitting that the loci of its origins should have been in places lacking natural resources. Venice and Lubeck, the principal Hanseatic city, were initially founded as marginal maritime settlements that grew to become important cities to the degree that they entered into the carrying trade of shipping eastern commodities to the West and western commodities to the East. Lacking landed material endowments and otherwise "isolate[d] . . . from feudalism,"[58] Venice and the Hanseatic cities had recourse only to what the sea had to offer, thus making maritime commerce the mainstay of their respective economies and also the source of wealth of their respective ruling classes. With wealth derived from merchant's capital, as Marx termed it, neither city-state could literally afford to attach the then-prevalent social stigma to engagement in commerce as was the case in the feudal societies that surrounded them. Moreover, maritime commerce provided more economic opportunities to a wider range of social climbers (at the outset, at least) than feudal society offered possibilities of land acquisition. "[T]he greatest gift of the Commercial Revolution," Robert Lopez maintained with some hyperbole, "was the continuous creation of new opportunities for everyone to climb from one class to another."[59] Just as the vow of celibacy on the part of the priesthood "precluded the possibility of its achieving the solidarity of a caste,"[60] in feudal Europe, so too the vow of commerce made "room for social mobility."[61]

In the 1940s Cox had decided on the what and where of capitalism but not the when. At that time he settled for a simple definition of it—"buying and selling rationally for profit"—to which he appended a number of characterizations of its "way of life": "[t]rade, profit, the indispensability of money, inventiveness, mechanical power, money-making as an end in itself, factory manufacture, efficiency, individualism, competition, bourgeois freedom, utilitarianism, ambition, plutarchy, capital accumulation, exploitation, nationalism, humanitarianism, idealism, and so on."[62] To this he added that capitalism "developed in the urban communities of Europe" in the postfeudal era but he did not specify where. Nevertheless, in his address at the golden jubilee meeting of the Missouri Association for Social Welfare in St. Louis, Missouri, a couple of years after the publication of *Caste, Class, and Race,* Cox did specify "certain medieval Italian cities"[63] as the sites of capitalism's origins. Roughly a decade later, he narrowed down the sites to Venice and specified the "early thirteenth century as the period when capitalism became definitely established in the world."[64] What, then, precipitated Cox's decisiveness on the question of capitalism's origins in the decade separating the publications of *Caste, Class, and Race* and *The Foundations of Capitalism?*

My guess is that the explanation lies in Cox's re-reading of Henri Pirenne. Cox was familiar with Pirenne's work and drew heavily on his *Economic and Social History of Medieval Europe* to describe feudal society in *Caste, Class, and Race.* Apparently Cox did not initially agree with either Pirenne's characterization or periodization of capitalism. However, a second reading of the following passage may have forced him to reconsider Pirenne's position:

Strange though it may seem, medieval commerce developed from the beginning under the influence not of local but of export trade. It was this alone which gave birth to that class of professional merchants which was the chief instrument of the economic revival of the eleventh and twelfth centuries. In both parts of Europe where it started, Northern Italy and the Low Countries, the story is the same. The impetus was given by long-distance trade. This is clear directly when we examine the nature of the goods carried, for all were of foreign origin, and indeed early medieval commerce bears a certain resemblance to colonial trade.[65]

Cox would advance the date by a century, otherwise, the passage encapsulates the process by which he came to "refer to the Venetian experience as capitalism."[66] What follows are the constituents of the world capitalist system according to Cox:

(1) The capitalist world economy is composed of *leaders, subsidiaries, progressives, dependents,* and *passives* and is structured such that the first two named supply the rest with the most important of their service and commodity requirements.
(2) "Provisioning" is an essential role of a capitalist power.
(3) Transportation industries must be the leading sectors of all a capitalist power's industries.
(4) Colonial or neocolonial trade relations with commercially weaker social formations are the base of a capitalist power's economic strength.
(5) In a capitalist society, business interests, if not business people themselves, must dominate the sites of political power within that society.

This is hardly an exhaustive list and another reading of Cox's work could well add another five principles of the capitalist system to this one. Nevertheless, I believe that Cox would have found it an adequate summary that makes it clear why the Venetian example served as an enviable model. It was precisely the moment at which other nations began to consciously imitate aspects of the Venetian example that Cox dated the foundations of capitalism:

> One reason for our accepting the early thirteenth century as the period when capitalism became definitely established in the world is that by this date the culture had become irreversible. The pump had been primed, hence the capitalist development proceeded on its own momentum. The culture, in other words, had become not only irrepressible but also covetable. The unwavering endurance of so pure a pattern of capitalist society as Venice gave to many subcenters in Europe a stable model for imitation . . . By this time capitalist culture

had demonstrated one of its most remarkable traits: its inordinate tendency to diffuse, its imperative pull upon imitators. Furthermore, already in the thirteenth century, diffusion had advanced so far that cultural continuity was assured. At this period, soon after the Fourth Crusade, Venice had become so powerful and she had projected herself among the great nations with such force and drama that from then on the eyes of the world were turned toward her. Her type of social organization took the spotlight and kept it, in various more elaborate designs, to our own day.[67]

The "eyes of the world" was a rhetorical exaggeration, but his point was made.

Cox and Marx

Cox's conception of capitalism takes as its point of departure the locations to which Marx alluded but on which he did not elaborate in *Capital.*[68] Yet, in beginning *The Foundations of Capitalism* in Venice, Cox was consciously challenging a number of Marx's positions: the primacy of the nation-state over the city-state; commercial agriculture over commercial shipping; and industrial capital over merchant's capital.[69] On this last point, Cox did not consider merchant's capital the "antediluvian" form of capital, but its principal form.[70] It was largely this position that baffled Charles Tilly. In his review of *Capitalism as a System,* in which he called Cox's theory of capitalism "mediocre," guilty of "pseudo-history"[71] (a risky criticism for a historical sociologist to make), and altogether inadequate, Tilly is most troubled by the absence of a significant treatment of industrialism in Cox's work, the phenomenon which is typically considered the hallmark of capitalism. In my reading of Cox he had no choice but to downplay the significance of nineteenth-century English industrialism for at least two reasons: one, because he recognized that earlier capitalist leaders were also industrial powers; and two, because he found that capitalist firms ultimately preoccupy themselves less with the labor terms under which a commodity is produced than how it is moved from the point of production to the consumer. The Hanseatic attitude is most illustrative of this point. It was certainly

the herald of a new era when the merchant, first, supervised commodity production rather than simply "put out" raw materials to an
artisan, and second, applied machinery to the labor power of an
assembly of people under one roof, but slaves and prisoners have
labored under the same regimes. Historically, most firms have turned
blind eyes to the conditions under which the commodities bearing their labels have been manufactured (though not, by extension, to the "quality" of the products), but they have consistently
concerned themselves with the control of the movement and wholesale trades of those commodities.

The confusion on this subject is due in no small part to the coin-
cidence of merchant's and industrial capitals in the same nation-
state in the English case, Marx's site of full-fledged capitalism and
the claimant of the first industrial revolution. In that case, goods that
bore an English label were made in England, were carried in British
bottoms, and were sold wholesale, and sometimes even retail, by
English firms at home and abroad. In short, the commodity chains
of a number of goods were all British. Few economic historians,
however, have appreciated all the components of the economic formula that nineteenth-century English capitalists successfully put
into practice: many still insist that industrialism alone is the mainstay of capitalism. A plausible hypothetical scenario makes the limitations of this perspective readily apparent: if English manufactured
goods had been transported and marketed by another European
power or even by an African, Amerindian, or by an Asian power for
that matter, we would now retrospectively applaud this last power's
prescience and England's exploitation. In fact, this last scenario is
a fairly accurate if skeletal description of much of "Third World"
industrialization.

Along these lines, what I believe that Cox "discovered" in his research on Venice and the Hanseatic League was the birth of the
western firm. And it is imperative to note that he found that the
business partnerships of various kinds (joint ventures and commis-
sion arrangements) were not outgrowths of domestic commerce but
of overseas trade. For Cox, the multitude of Venetian fleets named
after ports of call—Tanan, Syrian, Roumanian, Egyptian, Flemish—
and the Hanseatic League's kontors, or branch offices, throughout
the Baltic arena, were the precursors of the English Company of
Merchant Adventurers, the Dutch East and West India Companies,

the Levant Company, the Russia Company, the East India Company, the Royal Africa Company, and the West India Company. These names were testaments to the fact that the western firm looked outward before it looked inward.

From Venice to Amsterdam

The best description of how Cox explained the passing of the capitalist torch from Venice to Amsterdam was not supplied by his own pen but by Fernand Braudel's:

> The northern countries took over the place that earlier had so long and so brilliantly been occupied by the old capitalist centers of the Mediterranean. They invented nothing, either in technology, or in business management. Amsterdam copied Venice, as London would subsequently copy Amsterdam, and as New York would one day copy London. What was involved on each occasion was a shift of the center of gravity of the world economy, for economic reasons that had nothing whatever to do with the basic or secret nature of capitalism. The definitive shift at the end of the sixteenth century from the Mediterranean to the North Sea represented the victory of a new region over an old one.[72]

Cox similarly placed greater emphasis on the Portuguese entrance into the Indian Ocean and on the Spanish crossing of the Atlantic than he did on the Ottoman challenge marked by that fast-growing empire's seizure of Constantinople 250 years after Venice's own example. Cox's omission of the Ottoman Empire may ironically reflect an unconscious acceptance of certain aspects of Eurocentrism despite his attempts to surmount it, or, conversely, he might have partially agreed with the conclusion that "[n]either the fall of Constantinople nor Portuguese explorations . . . had much to do with Venetian decline."[73] Whatever Cox's position, the explanation that he undoubtedly found in need of substantial revision was Marx's categorical claim that Venice's decline was due to the "economic development" of the states, empires, and city-states between which it conducted its carrying trade. What Marx meant by economic development in this instance was the transformation of a society's economy such that industrial capital directs merchant's or commercial capital, and not vice versa. According to Marx, commercial or carrying trade capital becomes a mere branch of the capitalist mode of production in its mature stage, the index of which is the growth of industry.[74] Yet, the challenge that both Dutch and English merchants posed to their Venetian counterparts in the Mediterranean world of the sixteenth and seventeenth centuries was based just as much on their investments in their carrying trades as it was in industrial expansion, particularly in textiles.

On the commercial front, for example, Dutch and English merchants sought, like their Portuguese counterparts a century and a half earlier, "to go behind their [Mediterranean] middlemen and enter directly the import markets of the Near and Far East."[75] This aim became particularly compelling when the Eighty Years War and Venice's struggles with the Ottomans disrupted the arrival in Antwerp of Mediterranean and eastern commodities, namely spices, silks, and cottons. Direct access or more direct access to these commodities also served two purposes: it reduced the cost of these commodities in northern European urban centers; and it enabled Dutch and English merchants to increase the percentage of the mark-up that they could pocket from the sale of eastern commodities in each of their respective domestic markets as well as in those they supplied overseas. Perhaps the most significant testament to Dutch and English success in their combined commercial mission in the Mediterranean was the fact that "[b]y the turn of the sixteenth century Holland was building the larger part of Venetian ships."[76]

On the industrial front, Dutch and English manufacturers "flooded the area with clever imitations of the excellent southern textiles and even marked them with the universally reputed Venetian seals in order to sell them under that 'label' on the usual Venetian markets. As a result, Mediterranean industry lost both its clientele and its reputation."[77] However, before any pity is felt for the fate of Venice's industries we must recognize that the Dutch and the English were merely following Italian practice. For example, in the case of fustians (originating in the Egyptian city of Fustat) or wool-cotton blends, the Italians managed to make such effective copies of the Egyptian originals that "these Italian fustians were sold back to the inhabitants of the region from which their name derived."[78]

The Italians also did the same in their manufacture of cheaper imitations of Near Eastern glass, paper, inlay, and silk products.[79]

The social factor that hamstrung Venice's ability to respond to their northern challengers was the Venetian guilds' successful defense of the value of their labor (as reflected in the prices of their commodities) and the high quality of their manufactures. "While in England the level of real wages at the beginning of the seventeenth century was noticeably lower than one hundred years earlier," noted Carlo Cipolla, "in Italy real wages did not show any substantial deterioration in the course of the sixteenth century."[80] As can be observed in this modern seventeenth-century example, in the capitalistic order of things, a victory for the working class is considered bad for business. In refusing to either relinquish control of the work-place or to reduce the standards of their crafts (even in face of the threat of being undersold by cheap imitations), Venetian guilds ironically hindered that city-state from taking advantage of "the new mass markets that were emerging in the sixteenth century—the middle farmers of northern Europe, the artisans, the lesser bureaucrats—all of whom had some money because of economic expansion and the general inflation, and who wished to purchase inexpensive and stylish (albeit less durable) cloths."[81]

Taken together, the decline of the Venetian economy was due just as much to its "over-development" as it was to the development of the Dutch and English economies. From Cox's perspective, the gains of the Dutch and English merchant classes at the expense of the Venetian economy were testaments to what they had learned from Venetian practices. Furthermore, in a seemingly unpatriotic and counterintuitive fashion, Venetian capitalists "exhibited another typical characteristic of declining capitalist society" and "export[ed] capital to the new leader for more efficient uses. . . . The former industrious merchants now largely became rentiers, investing in foreign securities and land, and living in luxury."[82]

It was to the Dutch republic that Venice and other Italian city-states sent their surplus capital. In spite of English endeavors in the Mediterranean textile market, the formation of the Merchant Adventurers in the mid-fifteenth century, and the closing of the Hanseatic Guildhall in the early seventeenth century, English merchants, statesmen, and publicists recognized that their nation's economy was still second to the Dutch republic's in the seventeenth century. Consequently, much English energy in that century was expended in determining the strategems by which the Dutch republic managed to amass its wealth. Cox devoted a sizable portion of *The Foundations of Capitalism* to mercantilism, or, if a more pragmatic definition is required, the economic philosophy that developed primarily in England out of the attempt to imitate the Dutch example and to avoid the failures of both the French and the Spanish.

The Dutch Century

Cox wrote about the Eighty Years War and the subsequent formation of the Dutch republic with three themes in mind: one, that it was an anti-imperialist revolt that pitted the Low Countries against imperial Spain; two, that even within the united ranks of the soon-to-be Dutch republic there existed a political-economic split between mercantile and landed interests; and three, that Protestantism, or more specifically, Calvinism, became the rallying cry of Dutch nationalism in obvious opposition to the Catholicism of the Spanish Empire, but it was not the official, religious denomination of capitalism. Each of these dimensions of the Dutch revolt warrants its own discussion.

Most modern revolutions or anticolonial movements begin as contestations of some combination of three impositions: inordinate taxation, commercial restrictions, and inadequate local political representation. Though the Dutch revolt "served as a model in all great capitalist revolutions: the English, American, and French,"[83] in Cox's estimation, it was curiously not guided by the usual motives for rebellion. Taxation was not excessive though the billeting of Spanish troops and the lately levied "Tenth Penny" was a source of annoyance;[84] far from constricting the growth of the Dutch economy, Spanish imperialism before and during the war was ironically a boon to it; and rostra from which Netherlanders could voice their political concerns were not lacking. Rather, what chafed these imperial subjects were the antiheretical decrees that targeted Protestantism. Apart from the economic damage that these decrees affected in the way of capital flight, was the local objection to religious prerogatives shaping state policies. This local objection by itself squarely places the Dutch revolt in the modern era. Netherlanders felt that to concede their religious authority to Spain would have been the first step in the eventual compromise of other elements of their autonomy. In short, Netherlanders sought the separation of church and state, a goal that ultimately meant their separation from Spain.

In an age in which any and every sociopolitical entity could not "exist accept by authority of some feudal lord,"[85] the prerogatives of local merchants constantly ran the risk of being compromised by landed interests. Therefore, one of the issues that had to be resolved by Dutch elites in the course of the Eighty Years War was in whose political-economic interest the future society would be established. Generally speaking, the commercial interests of the economically dominant provinces of Holland and Zeeland were represented in the States-General or representative council composed of "the mayors of the towns besides the responsible lords of the seventeen provinces," while the interests of the agricultural provinces of Guelderland and Friesland were voiced through the office of the Stadtholder (literally "lieutenant or representative of the king in the provinces"[86]), hereditarily held by the House of Orange. Given that Holland "carried in theory 58 per cent of the republic's financial burden and in practice far more,"[87] commercial interests frequently won out in what was at bottom the contest between Amsterdam and the House of Orange. However, when urban workers were added to this mix, matters became more complicated. The Low Countries' urban proletariat was wont to lodge its protests against the burgher-oligarchy by rallying around the banner of the Stadtholder—more than one prominent Dutch nationalist had been consumed by popular rebellion for his opposition to positions taken by the House of Orange. Still, in the course of the Eighty Years War, the States-General "brought" the Stadtholder "to recognize that he must not be master of the States."[88] On this subject, Cox continued: "Historians seldom fail to remark upon the contradictory division of authority struck by this compromise. From a list of nominees, the Stadtholder appointed the chief officers of the cities—the aldermen, burgomasters, and sheriffs of the town councils—but these in turn, appointed the electors of the Stadtholder." In short, "[t]he Dutch cities were the first to integrate their feudal ruler into their capitalist social structure; though, not yet completely so"[89]—an intimation of what the English would come to achieve.

In explaining the political division of the Low Countries into the ten southern provinces (now Belgium) that remained loyal to the Spanish Crown and the seven northern provinces that successfully secured their independence from it, Cox appears to suggest that the Calvinism of what would become the Dutch republic not only sustained its uncompromising resolve against Spain's armies, but was moreover a calculated ideological response to the Catholicism of the Habsburg Empire: "Everywhere in Europe the capitalist cities had sought to limit the secular powers of the Church, then to restrict the appointment of religious leaders to natives, and ultimately to nationalize the Church by adopting some form of Protestantism."[90] The facts suggest, however, that the Calvinism of the Dutch republic was the result of the Eighty Years War and not its cause.

Nevertheless, while it is true that Roman Catholicism was the doctrine "to which the great proportion of the common people conformed,"[91] contrary to the supposed association between Calvinism and capitalism, "Calvinism had originally found more adherents in the southern Netherlands than in the northern provinces."[92] In other words, if Protestantism itself was largely responsible for Low Country resistance to Spanish imperialism and its embrace of capitalism, then demographically speaking, the southern Netherlands should have become the home of the Dutch republic. Simply put, the concentration of Calvinists in the Dutch republic was due to their forced migration in wartime. It was the Spanish occupation of the southern Netherlands that drove

> people of Protestant sympathies [to] emigrate northwards and eastwards, and Calvinism became extinct in the provinces governed from Brussels. These embittered Calvinist refugees from the south greatly strengthened the influence of their militant co-religionists in the north, who were only prepared to accept the reunification of the Seventeen Provinces on the basis of uncontested Calvinist supremacy in the Church and State. Thus the Low Countries were split, not along a geographical, a linguistic, or an ethnic boundary, but along a purely artificial one determined by the military vicissitudes of an eighty years war and by the parallel outgrowth of mutual religious intolerance.[93]

In short, the Calvinism of the Dutch republic was not an intended outcome of the struggle against Spain.

Fortunately, the religious moderates were able to stay the fervor of uncompromising Calvinists who sought to disenfranchise all but devout Calvinists in the new republic. Sentiments such as these and the potential policies inspired by them would have had disastrous effects on future economic development. Instead, the burgher-oligarchs established in the republic one of the most religiously tolerant societies of modern Europe (in marked contrast to the inquisitorial atmosphere that their former monarch created at home), offering a safe haven to many of Europe's persecuted. "Among the streams of refugees—French Protestants, Antwerpers, Jews from Spain and Portugal—were many merchants often in possession of substantial capital . . . No less than one-third of the city's [Amsterdam's] population was of foreign birth or extraction in 1650."[94] Little wonder, then, that it was widely believed in the Dutch republic that religious tolerance encourages prosperity and that prosperity lends itself to religious tolerance.

Of course, we cannot end this discussion without a word about Max Weber's thesis on the supposed relationship between Protestantism and capitalism. In my assessment, the accidental manner in which Calvinism assumed political dominance in the northern Netherlands is sufficient evidence to dispel the putative relationship between the two. Though Cox approached the subject from a different angle, he, too, rejected Weber's thesis, stating dryly that "Calvinism in Holland, at least, was no producer of capitalism."[95]

Appearances are often deceiving, as the proverb warns us, but at times what one sees is an accurate indication of what one gets. When Amsterdam, the economic heart of the Dutch republic, began to be referred to as the "Venice of the North," it was more than a reference to Amsterdam's striking physical resemblance to Venice, it was also a statement about Amsterdam's economic development. For if water was so much the "matter and substance"[96] of Venice such that it directed that city's economic strategies, the same was true of Amsterdam. Thus, in Amsterdam's case, too, its shipping industry was the mainstay of Dutch leadership of the world capitalist economy in the seventeenth century.

"[I]t may be said," Pierre Goubert suggested, "that the Dutch fleet of anything from eight to nine thousand vessels represented— with the exception of China—at least half of the world's shipping."[97] In comparison to the volume of shipping in the rest of Europe, Cox noted that "[i]n the middle of the seventeenth century the Republic had a larger number of ocean-going vessels than the combined shipping of all the other countries."[98] Such was the order of Dutch shipbuilding that it was not uncommon for the Dutch to sell their ships to rival powers, including to Spain during the Eighty Years War. Due perhaps to the fact that he largely viewed Amsterdam as following in the footsteps of Venice, Cox did not elaborate on some of the special contributions the Dutch republic made in the domains of shipping and shipbuilding, of which we should name three. First, its shipbuilding industry "was highly mechanized and used many labor-saving devices—wind-powered mills, sawmills, powered feeders for saws, block and tackles, great cranes to move heavy timbers— all of which increased productivity."[99] Second, the Dutch had designed a new cargo ship, the fluit (or *flyboat* as the English then called it), which though slower was cheaper than faster ships since it "mounted few or no guns"[100] and "needed a smaller crew."[101] Finally, Dutch sailors (of whom a significant portion were foreign-born immigrants) were typically "low-paid and frugally fed,"[102] factors which further reduced the costs of the commercial voyages. It should be added that members of the republic's maritime proletariat received a partial monetary compensation from the small amount of merchandise they were permitted to sell on their own account on each voyage.

Cox's decision not to discuss these contributions notwithstanding, he did draw attention to the related or "linked" industries to which the shipbuilding industry gave rise. Commenting on the sail-making, rope-making, metallurgy, salting, provisioning, and lumber industries in the republic, he noted: "As we have already noticed, great industries of leading capitalist nations tend to engender a multiplicity of dependent and minor servicing industries. They ranged all the way from those supplying the consumptive needs of concentrations of workers to the manufacturing of "parts" for the principal product. . . . Shipbuilding indeed was one of the large-scale industries employing specialized labor-groups and large capital investments."[103]

This instance would not be the last time that Cox would under-score the role of linkages in the historical development of capitalism.

Similar to the political-economic conjectures foreigners made about Venice during the course of its leadership of European capi-talism from the thirteenth to the sixteenth centuries, the remarks made by seventeenth-century observers of the Dutch Republic also sought to solve an apparent paradox: how such a resource-poor land could amass in such abundance the very things that it lacked naturally. They noted that though the bulk of the goods found on Amsterdam's docks, in its storehouses, and its shops originated else-where, it was still to Amsterdam that these goods came. To some, like William Petty, the secret of Dutch success was to be found in the most obvious place: in its shipyards. In "reviewing the advantages of secure title to land, the use of banks, and the reduction in ship-building costs through the division of labor, [Petty] finally decided that Dutch prosperity rested on shipping."[104] Writing in the next century, Daniel Defoe deepened Petty's conclusion, stating that the "Dutch must be understood as they really are, the Middle Persons in Trade, the Factors and Brokers of Europe. . . . They buy to sell again, take in to send out, and the greatest part of their vast commerce consists in being supply'd from all parts of the world that they may supply all the world again."[105] And to do so, the Dutch traveled to the ends of the earth, making the capitalist system of which they were the center, a truly global one: "This busy, enterprising fleet, kept at the peak of condition by continual rebuilding, was con-stantly at sea carrying Nordic herrings, salt from Brittany and Por-tugal, wine from the Loire and Aquitane, grain, flax, timber and tar from Muscovy and the Scandinavian countries as well as the trea-sures of the Indies: ebony, sugar, molasses and tobacco."[106] To these we must also add Indonesian and Indian spices and cottons as well as Chinese and Japanese porcelains and silks. In short, Dutch ship-ping enabled the Republic to become the carrier of the world's imports and exports, a role which also served to make Amsterdam the great entrepot of the world's products.

Many scholars of the Dutch republic would agree with Cox's claim that the "key to [its] success inhered not in the quantity or quality of output from its manufactures, though improvement in these went hand in hand with the general growth, but rather in its monopoly of *distant* foreign trade."[107] They would differ with him, however, on the order of importance of the United Provinces' maritime arenas. Whereas Cox underscores the republic's trade relations with Indonesia and India, other scholars highlight the Baltic trade that the Dutch themselves referred to as the "mother trade." Of course, from the standpoint of economic survival, it was logical that the Dutch should privilege the Baltic trade: it provided the timber, pitch, tar, hemp, and flax necessary for the republic's ship-building industry. If, for example, "one warship required 2000 oak trees that needed a century of maturation so the wood would not split too easily and 2000 oak trees required at the time 50 acres of woodland,"[108] out of sheer necessity the Dutch republic would hold the sources of its commercial requirements in the highest regard. Yet, of comparable importance to the republic's role as Europe's provisioner, was the Baltic grain trade. On this matter, too, Cox was surprisingly less than forthcoming, providing no indication that according to one recent estimate the "Dutch share of the [Baltic] grain trade fluctuated around a long-run average of about 75 per cent."[109] We cannot claim that Cox's omission of the Baltic grain trade in the making of Dutch prosperity was a function of insufficient secondary material given that we do know that at least one important source on the subject—Violet Barbour's *Capitalism in Amsterdam*—to which he made reference in *The Foundations of Capitalism,* unambiguously stressed its importance. The Baltic grain trade is significant for our purposes here due to its relationship with the bullion drawn from the Americas. The Eighty Years War provides a graphic illustration of its features. Even in the throes of military conflict, each side recognized that it required (even to conduct war) the exports and reexports of the other such that despite temporary embargoes, trading with the enemy flourished:

> After the great change in the Netherlands in 1585 and following the catastrophe of the Spanish Armada in 1588, Philip II pursued a policy—except for a brief embargo in 1595—of permitting trade between the mother country and the rebellious subjects in the northern Netherlands (the Dutch Republic). This was due on Spain's part to her need for the goods which the Dutch carried from the Baltic and Norway to Spanish ports (grain, wood produce and naval store) and also merchandise for the American trade; on the part of the Dutch

it was prompted by their need above all for silver from Seville and Cadiz (gold was collected by the Dutch themselves from the Guinea region of Africa), as well as Portuguese salt and Spanish wool and wine.[110]

In failing to mention how the Dutch (or even the greater Netherlands before the outbreak of the Eighty Years War) paid for their Baltic needs, Cox missed an opportunity to incorporate the Americas into otherwise seemingly intra-European affairs. Grain for bullion was the indispensable exchange that the Dutch conducted with their Spanish opponents, and it was the means by which the former gained entry into all of the latter's commercial networks. "Holland's fortune," remarked Braudel, "was evidently built on both Spain and the Baltic. To neglect either of these would be to fail to understand a process which wheat on the one hand and American bullion on the other played indissociable roles."[111] Furthermore, the European circuit of Amerindian bullion afforded the Dutch republic three other economic opportunities: the purchase of raw materials for its shipbuilding industry or "the production of the means of production;"[112] the monetary means by which to enter into both the intra-Asian and Asia-Europe carrying trades, which typically required cash payments; and the ability to loan money at half the going rate of interest in the rest of Europe.[113] In fact, contemporary observers (particularly English ones) were convinced that the republic's low interest rate throughout the seventeenth century was the key to Dutch economic success.[114]

Based on the language he used to describe it and to a lesser extent on the number of pages devoted to its discussion, Cox was clearly of the opinion that the Dutch republic's trade with Asia was "the most dramatic and even spectacular branch of Dutch commercial expansion in the seventeenth century."[115] Though some disagree with this position, privileging instead Dutch commercial activities in the Mediterranean and the Baltic Seas, Cox would have found Immanuel Wallerstein's characterization of the Vereenigde Oost-Indische Compagnie (VOC, or the Dutch East India Company), more than satisfactory: "It was a model of capitalist trading company, part speculative enterprise, part long-term investment, part colonizer."[116] Cox credited the VOC with having "set the pattern of modern colonization in the lands of colored peoples, which has persisted to our own day."[117] This last assertion was an exaggeration on his part, since both the Portuguese and the Spanish undoubtedly led the European field in colonialism for at least a century before any of their rivals had any colonies of note in the extra-European world.

Like the Dutch republic itself, the VOC was born in the Eighty Years War. Roughly twenty years after the union of the two Iberian crowns in 1580, the VOC charter was issued by the republic's grand pensionary, Johan van Oldenbarnevelt. Apart from the desire to pose a visible challenge to what was fast becoming a Portuguese monopoly of spices and other Asian commodities highly sought after in Europe,[118] the establishment of the VOC was designed to unify individual Dutch merchants whose independent efforts in the Asian trade "so expanded the supply of pepper as to send the price plummeting, threatening the competing Dutch investors with ruin."[119] However, in the process of coordinating the commercial efforts of Asia-looking merchants within a single corporation, the VOC did not ensure the equal participation of either all its members or investors despite the name *participanten* given to all investors. The decision-making structure of the company reflected the "old money" or patrician bias in Dutch politics which deemed that this class should furnish leadership just as it had traditionally supplied the urban regents. Governed by a board of "seventeen directors elected from various [six] local groups or chambers,"[120] the Heeren XVII, as they were called, "were drawn from subscribers with a minimum holding of FL. 6,000 for most of the regional chambers [Amsterdam, Zeeland, Rotterdam, and Delft] and of Fl. 3,000 in the smaller ones of Hoorn and Enkhuizen."[121] In practice, this privilege enabled fewer than 80 investors (from among whom were drawn the Heeren XVII) to direct the monetary commitments of a "total of 1,800 individuals."[122] Clearly, neither the corporation nor its structure is a product of the twentieth century.

Charles Boxer's claim that the VOC "was . . . virtually a state within a state" is hardly an exaggeration when the privileges that it was accorded in its charter are taken into account.[123] The Heeren XVII were "empowered to conclude treaties of peace and alliance, to wage defensive war, and to build 'fortresses and strongholds' in that region. They could also enlist civilian, naval, and military personnel who would take an oath of loyalty to the Company and to the States General."[124] Decisions made in Amsterdam, however, were not always followed to the letter in Asia. This discrepancy between orders and implementation had less to do with a laissez-faire attitude on the part of the Heeren XVII toward their subordinates in the field, as Cox suggested,[125] than it did to a compelling logistical constraint: it took eighteen to twenty-four months for either a directive or a request originating in either Amsterdam or Batavia to make a round-trip voyage.[126] Thus, it was due to the insurmountable time delay in the communication relay that the "Governor General had wide latitude for discretion and action," as Cox correctly asserted.[127]

Cox's tripartite claim that the "ultimate purpose of the Dutch was to gain sovereignty over more and more of Indonesian territory, to subordinate the native rulers to their regional governors, and to reorganize production monopolistically through the authority of these native rulers," is also in need of both qualification and expansion. [128] In order to do this, however, we must take a larger perspective on Dutch designs in Asia.

While most of the Heeren XVII and participanten were of the opinion that the republic needed to assume an aggressive stance toward the Portuguese and their Asian allies, a significant number were desirous of peaceful trade in the Indian Ocean arena, at least with Asian societies if not with the Portuguese. The idealistic and perhaps naïve vision on the doves' part envisioned Dutch shipping so impressing Asian potentates that they would naturally be led to choose Dutch services over those of Portugal. Yet, at bottom, both the men in the field and those in Patria (including the majority of the peaceful traders) "believed that neither the Portuguese nor the powerful Asian rulers in whose kingdoms they traded would allow them to do so [i.e., trade peacefully] without the sanction of arms. This argument was of course only a part of the current ideology."[129]

Consequently, for the first two-thirds of the seventeenth century, the Dutch had open hunting season on Portuguese possessions in Asia. Within three years of its founding in 1602, the VOC captured from the Portuguese one of the principal spice islands of the Moluccas, Amboina. In 1641, they captured Malacca, and "in 1656 the Portuguese garrison in Colombo surrendered after a long siege."[130] Portuguese Ceylon fell to the Dutch in 1658; Portuguese Cochin was overwhelmed by Dutch forces in 1663; and the 1667 offensive against the Iberian power in Macassar secured it for the

VOC. That the majority of Dutch military successes against Portugal's Asian possessions occurred in the latter half of the seventeenth century is largely explained by the Dutch conquest of Batavia (Jakarta) on the Indonesian mainland. Taken in 1619 from the indigenous Indonesian state of Mataram, Batavia became the Dutch equivalent of Portuguese Goa: entrepot, repair station, and socio-cultural enclave. Yet, contrary to what Cox implies, Batavia was one of the few Dutch territorial acquisitions in Asia, which is why the Indonesian example should not be taken as a model of the VOC's political-economic activity there. "It must be emphasized," Boxer underscores, "that although the Dutch East India Company became a territorial power in Java, Ceylon and the Moluccas, it always remained an alien body on the fringe of Asian society, even in the regions which it administered directly."[131] Had the Dutch been the first Europeans in Asia and had they also enjoyed a larger population, perhaps the VOC would have pursued a territorial empire in Asia with greater resolve. Yet the actual limits on Dutch imperialism in Asia worked to the VOC's advantage: it minimized the already significant protection costs demanded of Dutch shipping in Asia among which were "customs duties, presents, and bribes where occasion demanded such costs, . . . [t]he expense of constructing fortresses overseas and heavily arming the ships."[132] Though these costs were in large measure offset by "monopoly profits earned in Europe by selling Asian goods, from payments received for issuing safe-conduct passes to Asian shipping,"[133] and from conducting the lion's share of the intra-Asian carrying trade, a Dutch colonial empire in Asia would have significantly cut into the VOC's returns. Therefore, in order to avoid these outlays, the company abandoned many of the colonial pretensions it formerly held and opted instead for "administered"[134] or neocolonial trade. In short, the manner in which Cox characterized Dutch motives in Indonesia and elsewhere in Asia, were more representative of those of the nineteenth-century republic than those of its seventeenth-century precursors.

Nevertheless, Cox's assertion that "[t]he United Provinces was as much and perhaps even more involved in war than any of its capitalist forerunners,"[135] was hardly an exaggeration. We have already noted that in the anticolonial struggle out of which the Dutch republic was born, the Dutch "took every opportunity to prey upon the commerce of the enemy, to trade illegally but profitably with the

latter's territory, to carve out an empire from the Portuguese possessions in the East, and to isolate the Spanish Netherlands." War was
thus a mainstay of Dutch capitalism in the seventeenth century, notwithstanding occasional Dutch lip service to the theoretical pairing
of peace and prosperity. "The warlike necessities of capitalist societies," commented Cox on Dutch bellicosity, "are here clearly illustrated: wars of liberation, wars of commercial rivalry, wars among
backward peoples, and wars for survival."[136] For the Dutch republic,
in short, peace would have ensured poverty, not prosperity.

Cox apparently subscribed to the view that the force that made
the Dutch republic was ultimately responsible for its undoing. Given
that military success like capitalist leadership itself is always time-
bound, the republic's humbling was explained, in his opinion, by
the emergence of better armed and better manned rival powers
out to replace it. It was, of course, the fast-expanding British Empire
that posed such a challenge, and in the first of four Anglo-Dutch
Wars, Cox felt that "the fate of the Dutch was already decided."[137]
He was specifically referring to the first of England's strictures
against the Dutch carrying trade in the North and Baltic Seas as well
as in the Atlantic and Indian Oceans, steps which Cox took to be
proof of the fact that the "territorial base of the Dutch nation was
too thin to withstand the larger [national] units."[138] With a population of roughly a million and a half,[139] the Dutch nation was a mere
fraction of that of the British Isles.

Cox was likely tempted to explain the movement of capitalist
leadership from the Netherlands to England much as he did that
from Venice to the Dutch republic. In the first instance, he attributed the transfer not merely to the rise and role of war that now
posed the nation-state against the city-state, but also to the favorable
audiences that native merchants increasingly held with their national
rulers to counteract Hanseatic commercial interventions. Though
these factors were undoubtedly at play in the Dutch republic's decline, Cox's sensitivity to historical accuracy compelled him to recognize that the effects of the Anglo-Dutch Wars on the republic did
not compare to those that pitted the Hansards against Denmark,
Sweden, Russia, England, and the Low Countries in the fifteenth and
sixteenth centuries, nor did they compare with the socioeconomic
repercussions of the Thirty Years War on the league in spite of its
neutrality in that contest. Yet, here too, the decline of the Hanseatic

League like that of Venice, was really a relative one. The Dutch republic's decline was little different:

> The falling back of the United Provinces was gradual; indeed, in some respects, she moved forward only more slowly than her great rivals. Her colonial possessions were so extensive and rich that, even with the loss of leadership, the country rested upon a great cushion of prosperity; grass did not grow in the streets as in Antwerp. . . . Thus, like Venice and Florence previously, Holland entered her rentier stage. As we should expect, capital was exported mainly to England, and at double the interest rates available in Holland on probably better security.[140]

Thus, until England emerged as the new leader of the capitalist world economy in the aftermath of the French Revolution, the relative decline of Dutch hegemony was obscured by that nation's ability to live off of the returns of its past economic dynamism and to invest in those nations that now displayed those same capabilities.

Whatever were his precise reasons for having ventured to the late-medieval world to uncover the roots of capitalism, in the course of that journey Cox discovered a hierarchy of economic actors and roles that has been reproduced with a remarkable degree of consistency over the course of eight centuries. To summarize what Cox considered the main event of capitalism's first scene, commercial aristocrats with marked republican inclinations, took center stage and began a monologue previously unheard. According to Cox, these protagonists first appeared in Venice and in the cities that constituted the Hanseatic League. Maritime islands in a vast feudal sea, the Venetians and the Hansards were able to develop what some would now term neocolonial relationships with more powerful feudal kingdoms by securing commercial concessions from financially strapped or militarily challenged monarchs and emperors. Ironically, their ability to profit from monarchical rule elsewhere was the primary reason why both the Venetians and the Hansards refused to be ruled by a monarch: without a body of legislators who shared political power, there was no safeguard against the possible dissipation of the nation's wealth by the prerogative of a monarch. Both powers subscribed to the view that oligopolistic rule promotes economic nationalism in ways that monarchical rule cannot. The Dutch experience with the Spanish monarchy proved the same point.

These lessons were not lost on the English, leaders of the capitalist world economy between roughly the mid-eighteenth century and the end of the First World War. In fact, many of that country's most influential minds spent much of the seventeenth century trying to determine the bases of Dutch wealth. It was for this reason that Cox devoted nearly a hundred pages of *The Foundations of Capitalism* to that topic, which, as he understood it, evolved into the doctrine of mercantilism. In the English Revolution of the same century, Cox similarly saw the triumph of commercial interests over feudal prestige, of republicanism over monarchy. Therefore, before turning our attention to the era of England's leadership of the capitalist world economy, we must address these two related themes, since they fundamentally frame Cox's interpretation of English events.

Capitalism from the English Revolution to the Twentieth Century

Mercantilism

For Cox, mercantilism was first and foremost an anti-neocolonial strategy. Among its many economic goals, mercantilist doctrine posited that foreign merchants should no longer enjoy commercial privileges at the expense of local merchants in a given nation. In the English case, mercantilism meant that the Hansards would no longer carry the lion's share of the country's raw wool and unfinished woolens throughout the Baltic since English merchants would now assume that role. In other words, the nation-state would adopt the economic strategies of its city-state precursors by which "foreign merchants were encouraged only in so far as their commerce contributed

directly to the profit of native merchants."¹ Moreover, mercantilism
entailed the prohibition of foreign merchants from "dealings with
[local] consumers or primary producers."²

A change of this sort, however, could not be confined to the domain of economics. In light of the commercial privileges enjoyed
by foreign merchants and granted by the crowns of host nations, the
rise of mercantilist doctrine was also an indication that English merchants in particular were fast becoming political agents in their own
right. These processes (that is, the economic and political dimensions of mercantilism) were complementary: to the degree that the
commercial strength of a national bourgeoisie grew, the more its
crown turned to it (instead of to foreign merchants) for loans and
tax revenues; while in order for its commercial interests to expand,
the national bourgeoisie required the protection and allegiance
of the crown.

Since economic cooperation is typically the result of a mutual recognition of political power, it is not hard to imagine how agreements
between crown and national bourgeoisie could create the expectation on the latter's part of acting as political consultant on pressing
issues (particularly on the subjects of commercial policy and of taxation), an expectation which could ultimately threaten the prerogative of the throne. Unheeded appeals from merchant politicians,
moreover, could quickly become uncompromising demands, justified on the grounds that their economic activities provided the king-
dom with a significant portion of its wealth. The next step—taken
in the Dutch, English, American, and French Revolutions—was for
the bourgeoisie to "supersed[e] the authority of entrenched feudal
power" and to make the "purpose of the State itself in the capitalist
interests of its citizens."³

The foregoing comments largely explain why the mercantilist writers equated political regime type with the economic policies pursued by a given polity. "[T]he early capitalists," observed Cox, "put so
much stress upon its significance [political organization] that they
seemed to think that, given favorable institutions, the economic ends
would follow as a matter of course."⁴ Republics, in their eyes, tended
to pursue lucrative commercial ends, while monarchies sought territorial acquisition through war. In a footnote to *The Foundations
of Capitalism*, Cox cited Davenant's relevant observation that where
there is good government,

[t]hat country will always increase in wealth and power. Have we not before our eyes the example of Spain, labouring under the publick and private wants, occasion'd by nothing but a long series of misgovernment? What has preserv'd the Venetians for thirteen centuries against such potent leagues as have been frequently form'd against 'em, but that the goodness of their Constitution has enabl'd them to do great things with a very little? Would people under a tiranny, or indeed under a better form of government ill manag'd have defended themselves with such courage as Venice and Holland have done?[5]

Davenant's judgments make it clear that mercantilist doctrine, as disparate as it was, drew, nevertheless, on concrete examples. "The principal method of the mercantilist, then," Cox commented on this point, "was that of direct observation and imitation of the capitalist practices in successful models."[6] To seventeenth-century English observers, the Dutch republic appeared to have found the right formula of political and economic elements to make the compound of economic success. On the political front, for example, despite the retention of nominal feudal authority in the person of the Stadtholder or Prince of the House of Orange, in the Dutch republic "[t]he upper bourgeoisie openly monopolized the government of the cities and largely the opportunities for making profit in foreign commerce."[7] On the economic front, the republic similarly demonstrated to contemporary observers the benefits that could be derived from the carrying trade between Asia, Africa, America, and Europe as well as from the sale of domestically manufactured goods abroad. The obvious advantage in the latter activity was that manufactured commodities (before industrial mass production, that is) commanded higher prices than did raw materials, given the additional labor and transport costs embodied in the former. Yet, in order to capture foreign markets (in the areas of both manufacture and commercial shipping) for their own domestic producers, the cost of Dutch labor had to kept below its competitors' industrial pay scales. The capitalist imperative of low domestic labor costs was all the more necessary when raw material inputs came from overseas (the case for most Dutch industries) the transport of which necessarily increased their cost. Therefore, it was probably argued and applied in the Dutch republic before the same process crossed the Channel that "[t]he worker . . . was indispensable but he should be paid only so much as would be sufficient to keep him alive and able to labor—a subsistence wage."[8] Cox explains the absence of any "serious strikes or riots, let alone revolutionary movements, initiated by the Dutch proletariat," as the result of two factors: one, that Dutch workers "tended to participate, though passively, in the foreign exploitation directed by their ruling class"; and two, that "[p]ressure was constantly put upon the welfare funds of the gilds and other societies in aiding the numerous poor and necessitous workers."[9] Thus, when petty investments in Dutch overseas firms failed to pay sufficient returns, Dutch workers had to rely on their mutual aid societies to take up the slack.

The foregoing illustrates why Cox rejected the academic division of mercantilism "into stages such as the 'bullionist,' the 'balance-of-trade' and other 'stages,'"[10] for he understood that "[e]conomics, religion, government, law, family life, education: the whole social context had meaning to these architects of society." In short, Cox understood mercantilism to be what Gustav Schmoller made of it:

> [I]n its innermost kernal [mercantilism] is nothing but state making—not state making in a narrow sense, but state making and national-economy making at the same time; state making in the modern sense, which creates out of the political community an economic community, and so gives it a heightened meaning. The essence of the system lies not in some doctrine of money, or the balance of trade; but in something far greater:—namely, in the total transformation of society and its organization, as well as of the state and its institutions, in replacing of a local [town] and territorial economic policy by that of the national state.[11]

In the eyes of English observers, to the degree that the Dutch republic had succeeded in both state and national-economy making, Spain had failed on both fronts. "Just as they [the English mercantilists] looked to the Dutch as a prime example of commercial wisdom," noted Cox, "they frequently took an alternate glance at Spain as the dolt and weakling in the commercial system."[12] The great puzzle for the mercantilists was to determine just how the bullion of the Americas impoverished rather than enriched the Spanish Empire. But for the memory of Venice, Genoa, and Florence, the mercantilists could easily have resorted to a religious argument to explain the differences in economic performance between Spain and the Netherlands: Protestantism promotes prosperity as Catholicism constrains commerce. Yet, the mercantilists were not fooled by denominational appearances and were fully aware that even the reformed church could stifle economic development if checks were not imposed on it. Instead, the mercantilists subscribed to a political-economic theory that equated monarchy with the feudal passions of territorial acquisition, and republicanism (or some semblance of shared governance) with the capitalistic interest in commerce, to borrow Albert Hirschman's terminology.[13] Thus, the Spanish monarchy's shortcoming was to have allowed "feudal aggrandizement at home and the booty of extractive capital overseas . . . [to] disincline it to promote the growth of manufactures or foster the spread of mercantile enterprise within its European empire."[14]

The French provided a third mercantilist model that stood midway between the Dutch success story and the Spanish tragedy. As it was for the English mercantilists, the obvious target of French mercantilist policies was also the Dutch. At the behest of Louis XIV, Jean Baptiste Colbert, then Intendant of Finance, prohibited the Dutch from carrying French goods between France and its colonies as well as between France and the rest of Europe. The *exclusif*, as it was known, made it formal policy that French commodities must be carried in French bottoms by French merchants, hence the plethora of companies founded during Colbert's tenure. In France as in the rest of western Europe, mercantilist policy was also designed to promote metropolitan manufacturers, the quality of which should match the grandeur of the French state: "France must astonish the world by producing mirrors as fine as those of Venice, cloth as fine as that of Haarlem, serge as fine as that of Florence, tapestries as fine as those of Brabant, ironwork as good as that of Germany or Sweden, as many ships as heavily laden as those of the United Provinces, or all these things finer and better still. In this way glory and prosperity should come together, each supporting the other."[15]

Unfortunately, seventeenth-century French mercantilism failed to realize many of its goals. Dutch ships, for instance, "still carried the bulk of French and international trade. French cloth and textiles could not compete with the Dutch, even when they were manufactured 'in the Dutch style.' Arms, munitions, cannon, ships and military supplies continued to come from Holland, or through Dutch middlemen and it was still Dutch ships that carried the trade in wine and brandy from the west of France."[16]

French mercantilism was successful in some arenas, nevertheless. In the French Caribbean, for example, where Dutch shipping was dominant in the seventeenth century, Colbert's program recorded some gains. "The success of Colbert," remarked Eric Williams, "can be gauged from the fact that French ships trading with the Caribbean, which numbered four in 1662, amounted to 205 in 1683." Moreover, "[b]y 1683 there were twenty-nine refineries in France, consuming 17,700,000 pounds of sugar."[17]

Yet, even more significant than the Dutch challenge for French mercantilism, was the king himself. Like the kings of Spain a century earlier, Louis XIV clung to the monarchic view that territorial acquisition was the basis of economic growth, an ideology which justified military ends regardless of their costs to industry and commerce. Cox phrased the same idea in more explicitly political terms: "More than individual freedom, however, Colbertism tended to strengthen the hand of the king. Not having a capitalist parliament, the king was able to use his augmented income toward non-capitalist ends. Colbertism was thus in service of the monarch and not a direct instrument of capitalist enterprise."[18] Clearly, the mercantilists were of the same opinion.

The English Revolution

Our second preliminary remark on Cox's handling of the British case centers on his interpretation of the English Revolution (1640–88). Combining both the Whig and Marxist interpretations of seventeenth-century events, Cox read the English Revolution as the marker of the political arrival of the engineers of England's commercial transformation. "In the process of this change in England," he remarked, "the motive force naturally centered in the Commons of the Council. It was here that the merchants and gentry had representation; hence the story of the rise of capitalist government in

England is the story of how the initiative was won by the House of Commons."[19]

Cox divided the main contestants of the English Revolution along these social lines: "on the one hand, the great merchants, their lawyers, and the Puritan ecclesiastics; and on the other, the king, the majority of the peerage and the ministry of the Anglican Church." Of course, to a scholar who maintained that the "vital life processes" of England "had come to be determined by the devices of great merchants in foreign trade," it is not difficult to surmise whom Cox took to be the prime movers of the revolution. From his perspective, the English Revolution was the culmination of the political challenges posed by the crown–native merchant alliance: to the degree that the economic strength of native merchants grew so too did their impatience with "debat[ing] only questions submitted to [them] by the ruler with the sole concern of assisting him in the realization of his policies." In short, English merchants and their representatives in parliament wanted to "select [their] own questions and formulate governmental policies."[20]

Taken to its logical conclusion, however, Cox's pitch for the revolutionary role of England's wealthiest merchants lent itself in equal measure to an argument for their political conservatism: if their commercial monopolies were maintained by royal protection then there was little to justify the abandonment of a lucrative economic alliance for the uncertain promise of usurping political power.[21] Consequently, if any sector of the English bourgeoisie played an instrumental role in the revolution "it was the merchants in *domestic* trade, not the major overseas merchants, who supported Parliament in the 1640s."[22]

However, Cox was not unmindful of the apparent historical difficulties posed by his interpretation of the English Revolution, which is why he was quick to add certain qualifiers to his account, such as: "Yet still, England was no capitalist city. The new government, fashioned and supported by a determined minority of great merchants particularly in London had to assimilate not only the intractable nobility and a largely agricultural population but also the rising masses of workers. There was by no means an overwhelming flight of the people to the new capitalist freedom; indeed, ominous spells of popular resistance began forthwith to appear."[23]

In spite of these obstacles, Cox's conviction that the English Revolution was a bourgeois one was bolstered by two developments that emerged during its course: the Navigation Acts and the seating of William of Orange on the English throne. The importance of these first lay in their "limit[ing] [of] the importation of goods originating in Europe either to English ships or to those of the country of origin; and insist[ing] that ownership of vessels engaged in the coastal trade be restricted to English subjects. Thus no capitalist nation could profit from the carrying trade of England; while English shipping was shielded from Dutch and Hansa competition." On the significance of the second consequence of the English Revolution, Cox remarked: "By a stroke of good fortune England in her Glorious Revolution was able to import the most highly conditioned capitalist prince in all the world, the Stadtholder of the Dutch republic whose illustrious ancestor had sponsored the authorship of the Act of Abjuration, and who . . . received his education under John de Witt." This last comment refers to the fact that William III knew that the Crown should, above all, "serve the interests of capitalist enterprise."[24]

Yet, in spite of his exaggeration of merchant capital's revolutionary role in the English Revolution, Cox was not mistaken in insisting on its economic role in the industrial revolution. It was his position that "[a] continually expanding foreign market and monopoly of the home market were essential to the progress of industrialization in England."[25]

The English Round

Cox shared Eric Hobsbawm's opinion that the industrial revolution's "technical innovations were exceedingly modest, and in no way beyond the scope of intelligent artisans experimenting in their workshops, or of the constructive capacities of carpenters, millwrights and locksmiths: the flying shuttle, the spinning jenny, the mule."[26] For his part, Cox asserted that "[I]n so far as the essentials of capitalist communities are concerned, it should be said again for purposes of perspective that this contribution [the industrial revolution], though important, was rather developmental than original."[27] Moreover, what was of greater importance to Cox than the inventions or mechanical "improvements" that marked the industrial revolution, were the "social situation and set of attitudes characteristic of capitalist social organization" out of which they emerged. In his opinion, the failure to address the social context within which the industrial inventions were produced hinders the student of the industrial revolution from addressing the equally pressing question of "[w]hy, for example, they seem to have arisen spontaneously at the time of the industrial revolution and not previously."[28]

Yet, for a scholar who never tired of repeating that industry is a function of commerce and not vice versa, Cox was not always as emphatic as he could have been in proving his case. He did maintain, as Hobsbawm succinctly put it, that "[t]he British, like all other cotton industries, had originally grown up as a by-product of overseas trade," and that "[c]otton was the first industry to be revolutionized."[29] However, he underscored the relationship between foreign commerce and industrialization neither to the degree that Hobsbawm did in a general survey of the epoch nor to even a fraction of that which fellow countryman Eric Williams detailed in *Capitalism and Slavery*, with which Cox was familiar. At most, he acknowledged that "[a]ll sorts of subsidiary industries from bleaching, dyeing, and printing to railroad construction, shipbuilding, machine making, and mining responded to the progress of this major industry."[30] These understatements are particularly curious in light of the fact that the overseas areas that were vital to the first phase of British industrialization (that is, the mechanization of the cotton industry) were both the indigenous and adoptive homes of people of African descent: Africa and the Americas. However, as I suggested earlier, it may well have been the fear of appearing "nationalistic" before a Euro-American academic audience that forced Cox to shy away from expressing the same degree of enthusiasm for the Williams's thesis as did, say, W. E. B. DuBois in *The World and Africa*.

Still, omitted or not, Williams's thesis only corroborates Cox's position: industry cannot be separated from foreign commerce. In the chapters devoted to the English case in *The Foundations of Capitalism*, Cox repeats this point on numerous occasions. Time and again he underscored the fact that a successful capitalist country must profit not only from the manufacture of commodities but from the distribution of them as well. In fact, it is typically the case that when a capitalist polity has passed its economic peak, it first relinquishes control over production, not over distribution; the choice itself suggests that production is frequently the least lucrative enterprise for capitalist accumulation. This insight into the workings of capitalism provided

Cox with a unique perspective on England's economic history within which he detected two strategies that eventually coalesced in the eighteenth and nineteenth centuries. The first pivoted on the twin efforts of the woolens manufacturers and the Merchant Adventurers, who, as we stated earlier, captured the domestic textile market by the mid-fourteenth century and "transferred the commercial exploitation of England to Englishmen."[31] Yet, while Cox felt that "[t]his was an indispensable stage in national-capitalist development," he went on to add that "[I]t was by no means, however, the ultimate objective of capitalist enterprise."[32] Thus what the second strategy sought to do was to insinuate English merchants into ever widening carrying trade circuits:

> In England, therefore, such trading organizations as the Russia Company, the Spanish, the African, the Eastland, the Hudson's Bay, and the East India Company, constituted the new dynamic force of capitalism. They imported in order that they might export either the same products or commodities manufactured from them. They made England the outstanding market for *raw materials* intended for workshops whose customers lived abroad. Moreover, they engaged in profitable commerce which had absolutely no relationship to supplying any direct wants of England.[33]

And it bears repeating that for Cox (echoing Rosa Luxemburg in certain measure), this insinuation of English merchants was a function of the "acquisition of foreign privileges and concessions." He went on to add that

> [t]he securing of commercial and industrial opportunities by dealing directly with foreign chiefs and princes now sought to put the human and natural resources of vastly inexperienced peoples at the disposal of merchant companies. . . . Concessions ranged all the way from those filched from simple folk peoples, such as certain tribal groups around the coasts of Africa and in Asia, to those negotiated with powerful feudal lords such as the Czar of Russia and the Manchu Emperor. . . . These privileges were acquired partly by force, but their significance

lay in the fact that they provided an opportunity for unprecedented capitalist exploitation.[34]

From Cox's perspective, then, whether domestic industry "takes
off" before foreign commerce, as was the case in England's woolens
industry, or follows it, as was the case in that country's cotton industry, successful capitalist practice requires the conjunction of the two.
And in many respects the close relationship between trade and industry only stands to reason:

> In assessing the nature and extent of this new "organizational
> revolution" of capitalist world-economy, it is important to bear
> in mind that the distinction between "trade" and "production"
> is not as clear-cut as it is often assumed to be. The reshuffling of
> goods in space and time, which is what trade is all about, can
> involve as much human effort and can add as much use-value
> ("utility") to the goods so reshuffled as does extracting them
> from nature and changing their form and substance, which is
> what we understand by production in a narrow sense. . . . The
> capitalist organizations that specialized in long-distance trade
> were always involved in some kind of production activity. Besides
> storage and transport, they often engaged in some processing
> of the goods they bought and sold, and in the construction of at
> least some of the means and facilities required by the storage,
> transport, and processing of commodities. . . . In addition, capi-
> talist organizations that specialized in long-distance trade en-
> gaged in, or closely supervised, the manufacture of goods.[35]

These sensible remarks by Giovanni Arrighi aptly explain Cox's
refusal to separate merchant's from industrial capitals.

Another of Cox's omissions in the British case is entirely understandable given his position that it is the structure of foreign trade
that dictates the course of capitalist development: the eighteenth-
century agricultural revolution is wholly absent in his three volumes
on capitalism.[36] The most that Cox said about British agriculture
was that the enclosures of the fourteenth and fifteenth centuries
introduced "larger units utilizing capitalist techniques."[37] Even the
second movement of land consolidation beginning in the eighteenth

century does not enter into Cox's discussion of the industrial revolution though its magnitude was greater than the sixteenth century's enclosures: "Some 300,000 acres were enclosed between 1710 and 1760 and 7 million between 1760 and 1843."[38] How, then, do we explain Cox's silence on the matter that some scholars contend *had to* precede the industrial revolution?

One reason is found in Cox's position that past capitalist leaders have always been able to secure adequate food supplies for their home population as well as for the inhabitants of other nations, without those sources necessarily coming from domestic agricultural production. "[A]ll previous leader nations," Cox underscored in his brief discussion of English agriculture, "from Venice to Holland . . . were under the strict necessity of importing food."[39] He went on to add that Venice "had no land for the production of corn; and yet, through her trade, she became most abundantly supplied with it."[40]

Cox, then, would have found Ralph Davis's argument wholly untenable that "if British agriculture had not found the means to double its production between 1780 and 1830, Englishmen would have starved, with incalculable consequences to industry."[41] Similarly unconvincing would be the contention that it was thanks only to the agricultural revolution that then present and future industrial workers were released from the hold of agricultural pursuits. For even if English agricultural production remained at its prerevolution levels with the same tenure system intact, thereby ostensibly limiting the number of agricultural workers who could have been "freed" from farming, British industrial labor requirements could still have been met by the immigration of continental European workers, just as it fulfilled the woolens industry's needs in the fourteenth century.[42]

Yet, one aspect of Cox's discussion of the English case seems particularly odd. For a scholar who was undoubtedly influenced by Marx, his discussion of the quality of life of the English working class is remarkably brief. Although the decision not to elaborate on the industrial worker's travails could be justified on the grounds that "[t]he revolting facts of his exploitation are well known," as Cox himself added, one is still led to question the extent of his outrage when a couple of pages later he remarked that the British working class attained a "higher standard of living than ever" under the industrial capitalist regime. It is possible that Cox was simply guilty of having conflated two distinct epochs of industrial working-class conditions: the 1790–1850 degradation with the post-1850 "improvement." However, the full quote from which the above excerpt is taken suggests something else: "It was this general fact of the superior efficiency of the machine, the increased utilization of native resources (such as coal and iron), and the exploitation of the labor and wealth of foreign peoples which greatly augmented the national income and allowed the British worker a higher standard of living."[43] Of all people, Cox should have known that "under early industrialism . . . there was no effective mechanism for making the distribution of the national income more equal and several for making it less so."[44] Moreover, the fact that the British nation was collectively implicated in the underdevelopment of its imperial possessions should not have led Cox to minimize, in any way, the exploitation of the metropolitan working class by British capital, which had proven itself quite adept in profiting on two fronts.

Still, this passage reveals perhaps better than any other, Cox's break with orthodox Marxism. Given his belief that the main source of capital accumulation on a world scale was that drawn from the economic interaction between leader capitalist nations and the "backward" social formations of the world (or that Marx's *primitive accumulation* "is none other than fundamentally capitalist accumulation"),[45] Cox consciously chose not to employ the conceptual tools that Marx developed to both describe and analyze the socioeconomic meeting of capital and the wage worker in the English, or more generally, the advanced industrial setting. Thus, Cox used terms such as "commoditization," "alienation," "social misery," "degradation," "oppression," and "privation," but rarely if ever such terms as "surplus value," "constant capital," or "the declining rate of profit." Cox should not be reproached for having decided not to make use of Marxian categories on the grounds that they were derived from the "industrial" or "factory" mode of capitalist production, but in failing to supply his own alternative language, he deprived himself of a conceptual vocabulary with which to critique industrial capitalist exploitation in more than moralistic terms. In other words, if "Marxian economics is [not] broad enough to embody" imperialism, then he should have provided his own brand.[46]

As far as Cox's assessment of English capital's pursuit of profit-motivated war is concerned, some of his oversights are again puzzling. Certainly his reticence on the subject is partially justified by the reduction of intra-European conflicts during the Pax Britannica. But the peacefulness which characterized European history between the final defeat of Napoleon and the outbreak of the First World War applied only to the political relations between European states, not to those between European and African and Asian polities. Though apparently aware of the limits of the Pax Britannica, as his comments on British imperialism in India confirm, Cox did not see fit to mention British designs in China and, above all, in Africa. Whatever Cox's reasons for deciding not to pursue these cases (the omission of the scramble for Africa in particular seems, once again, to have been due to an overriding antinationalistic preoccupation on his part), they were nevertheless missed opportunities for further elaborating on the mechanisms of capitalist leadership during England's tenure.

The American Century

At the outset of *Capitalism and American Leadership,* his second volume on the history of capitalism, Cox made it clear that two themes guided his approach to the subject: one, the United States' political-economic relationship with the "backward" (as he labeled them) social formations of the world, many of which were still under colonial rule; and two, the centrality of domestic race relations as a primary determinant of American capital's political and ideological positions. In a slightly different context in the same volume, Cox remarked that "[t]hese two, then, colonialism and racialism, by their very nature involve the heartbeat of capitalism."[47] While certainly an unorthodox understanding of the "American century," these themes were consistent with Cox's expressed reasons for embarking on the study of capitalism: to demonstrate that racism is a product of capitalism and of that system alone. We have already addressed Cox's treatment of American race relations; here we will direct our attention to the United States' interest in what would later be artificially termed the Third World.

Cox's treatment of nineteenth-century American history was noticeably brief. Of it he said little more than that once what would become the American West was won from indigenous peoples, rival European claimants, and Mexico, and capitalist institutions successfully established there by the end of the century, "[t]he American vision had now to be urgently refocused overseas" to capture other sources of raw materials and other consumers. This return to colonial North America's original investment direction would have come sooner had American attention throughout the nineteenth century not been committed to simultaneously expanding, defining, and even, preserving, the union, privileging in the process, the domestic market over the foreign one. We might note as did Cox that "in 1790 the area of the continental United States was approximately 892,000 square miles, already twice as large as the area of the [thirteen] colonies; in 1850 it was 2,997,000 and in 1900 3,026,000. Territories and possessions added about 597,000 square miles." Cox provided as proof of American capital's relative abandonment of foreign trade in the nineteenth century the fact that "American shipping . . . was allowed to vegetate during the great westward expansion."[48]

It was only in the aftermath of the First World War that the United States assumed the leadership position of the world capitalist economy, and this more by default than by economic prowess in the near past; for it is probable that without the war, the next capitalist world leader would have undoubtedly been Germany. This is not to deny that the United States was a major industrial power before the Great War, but it was nonetheless the damage done to the past leader (England) by the contender (Germany) that provided this country with the opening to take its place in the sun as of the 1920s. American capital quickly learned, however, that provisioning the world is an endeavor vastly different from that of supplying the domestic market; one that, at the very least, calls for unprecedented scales of production and organizational adjustments. To facilitate the transition, the U.S. Congress passed the Export Trade Act in 1918 "and, to this fundamental instrument, the Edge Act, which provided for the creation of banks, investment trusts incorporated by the Federal Government to finance exports, was added in 1919. American business men now had the way cleared to bring into play powerful weapons of monopolistic competition against their foreign rivals. . . . By the middle of the twenties more than 500 firms had formed some 50 associations to cooperate in foreign markets." And if American industrialists were to meet the challenge of supplying

the world with its wants, the "Third World" would be "converted into
more or less specialists in production of raw materials for American
factories and thus made dependent upon the latter for manufactured consumption goods."[49]

Securing the institutional and material requirements for commerce on a world scale was, however, only part of the American capitalist equation: another part was the need for solvent consumers.
The American domestic market provided some of the demand for
its industries' prodigious output of retail goods, but larger markets
had to be found for the sake of long-term profitability.[50] The most
logical market, the European one, could offer very little in the way
of meaningful consumer demand given that Europe was fresh from
the experience of a devastating global war. Therefore, if American
capital planned to prosper, it could only do so through the artificial
mechanisms of loans and other credit extensions to customary and
potential consumers. These recovery funds were not initially supplied by either the federal government or by American commercial
banks as one might expect. As a result of a successful propaganda
campaign that equated the purchase of foreign securities with patri-
otic duty, roughly a million Americans offered loans to a world in
need of capital.[51] The volume of their response was impressive: "for
the interval between 1920 and 1931 the American capital market
disposed of over 11.6 billion dollars of foreign securities or 9.9 billion exclusive of refunding." And "[o]f the foreign bonds issued
in the United States between 1920 and 1931, it has been estimated
that Europe claimed about 40 per cent; North America, especially
Canada, 29 per cent; Latin America 22 percent; and the Far East 9 per
cent." In short, an extraordinarily small sector of the American public "financed the sale of [American] goods abroad."[52]

However, in lending money to capitalist rivals, a capitalist leader
must face an unavoidable contradiction: its debtors' ability to service their outstanding debts depends on the increase of their exports
and the reduction of their imports, a combination which ultimately
and necessarily undermines the goal of the creditor in the first place.
"The problem," summarized Cox, "may be restated simply as follows: outlets for the manufactures of the advanced industrialized
nations are an immanent necessity, but payment for these exports
is obviously also required; since payments must be made with imports,
the larger the exports the greater must be the freedom to import;

and the eventual outcome of this process must be 'free trade.'" American industries, however, were far too young for the bulk of their owners to become vocal advocates of free trade. Generally speaking, capitalist leaders only advocate free trade in two instances: in mid-career when their services and industries have surpassed those of their rivals; and again in the final (rentier) stage of their hegemony when the objective is to realize the highest return on their investments regardless of site of production. In the 1920s, American capital did not yet believe (if it ever has) that the world's consumers (including its own) would freely choose its products over European makes. "A country in such an early stage of capitalist development as the United States," Cox asserted, "is not yet ready for rentier status."[53]

It was precisely this split economic personality of American capital that ultimately predisposed the capitalist world economy both to the Great Depression and to the Second World War. On the one hand, American capitalists were compelled to provide capital to the former leader (England) as well as to their other European rivals (France and Germany) rather than devote the bulk of it to the monopolization of "the markets of the raw-materials producing countries," as was the case for all previous capitalist leaders in their early years of economic dominance. Not only did Cox consider this investment reversal of American capital "uncapitalistic" in the sense that "[n]ormally . . . capital moves from mature capitalist nations to the new leader nation," but he went on to add that "[t]he economies rebuilt in Europe through American aid are, in fact, artificial growths; they are not the natural products of the characteristic processes of the capitalist system." Thus, the United States was "assuming primacy in the [world capitalist] system at a point where important markets for manufactured goods could only be secured through large investments in the very foreign projects calling for use of those goods."[54] On the other hand, the fact that American industrialists lobbied their political representatives to enact protectionist measures while their investors lent money to their economic rivals, was ample proof that American capital was not yet mature enough to assume the role of capitalist benefactor:

As the country assumed leadership, however, a remarkable reversal of policy ensued. Three successive laws—the Emergency

Tariff of 1921, the Fordney-McCumber Act of 1922, and the Smoot-Hawley Act of 1930—ran the tariff barrier up again to a new high level. Thus while commercial leaders campaigned intensively for augmented exports and foreign investments, the doors to imports were being shut tighter. This policy of protection, of course, tended to be imitated all over the world. . . . Still other tendencies, not characteristic of traditional capitalist leadership, intensified the dilemma. These were marked by such legislation as the Buy American Act of 1933 . . . [which] roughly limited the Federal Government to purchases of its vast supplies in the United States unless domestic prices were 'unreasonable,' a condition which proved to be heavily biased against foreign suppliers.[55]

Thus, if American capital was unwilling to share the domestic market with its debtors, then the sustainability of the capitalist world economy remained dependent on three factors: the continued willingness of American investors to lend; the ability of politically independent yet economically dependent countries (particularly those in Latin America) to purchase European and American goods; and the intensification of European exploitation of its colonial possessions.

Unfortunately, yet inevitably, American "[l]ending began to contract in 1928, when the stock exchange boom diverted American funds from foreign investment to domestic speculation."[56] Cox underscored that "[w]ith this reduction in foreign investments a critical point in the American economy was also approached: the point at which repayments on past loans became greater than additional exports of capital."[57] Some figures provide perspective on the severity of the American credit reduction:

[T]he United States export surplus diminish[ed] from plus 1,037 in 1928, to plus 842 in 1929, plus 782 in 1930 and plus 333 in 1931 (in millions of dollars). . . . In 1929 the U.S.A. made available to the rest of the world through imports and investments the sum of 7,400 million dollars (world imports amounted to 35,601 million dollars); this sum contracted in 1932 by 5,000 million dollars to as little as 32 per cent of what was made available in 1929. It is hardly necessary to look much further for the causes of world wide depression.[58]

One immediate effect of the American credit withdrawal was the decline of global consumption that, in turn, drove down commodity prices. "From 1929 to 1930 the average price of wheat fell 19 per cent, cotton 27 per cent, wool 46 per cent, silk 30 per cent, rubber 42 per cent, sugar 20 per cent, coffee 43 per cent, copper 26 per cent, [and] tin 29 per cent." Given that "[m]ost debtor countries were primary producers,"[59] when their export prices fell so did their ability to service their debts. "By 1934," recorded Cox, "some $22 billion in foreign obligations besides $12.5 billion in interest had defaulted."[60] The defaults "[a]lso provoked a crop of bank failures, with their trebly deflationary effects in destroying money, in encouraging hoarding of currency, and in discouraging further investment."[61] Primary producers were consequently forced to reduce their orders for American and European manufactured goods, forcing, in turn, those affected industries to curb output. "Thus the slowing down of lending," Cox summarized, "affected not only the capacity of foreigners to repay with safety, but also the power of our domestic economy to dispose of products. The system, therefore, became primed for retrenchments."[62] As a result, by 1932 the number of unemployed worldwide bettered thirty million; half of that population lived in the United States.[63]

The national capitalist economies, furthermore, turned in on themselves; international trade was now considered suspect and each social formation strove toward autarky. "Restrictions were applied especially to imports of food and imports of manufactures," noted W. Arthur Lewis.[64] About the economic mechanisms employed to cope with the Depression, Cox noted: "Demoralization consequently overtook capitalism, and nations individually sought expedients to exist or to become self-sufficient. They looked to such devices as international barter, tariffs, bilateral trade agreements, development of native industries in the direction of self-sufficiency, exchange controls, import quotas, regulation of currencies, and so on, sometimes to save their economies from complete collapse; and these very devices made it even more difficult for the United States to exercise classical leadership."[65] The ultimate marker of a profoundly transformed economic order was the English government's decision to quit the gold standard in September 1931.

War and Capitalist Progress

Cox's remark that "war is the 'sovereign remedy' for capitalist depression,"[66] suggests that even if Germany had not made a bid to establish itself as a colonial power equal to England in the first half of the twentieth century, a war of similar magnitude to the Second World War would eventually have taken place anyway. That is, if capitalism is prone to depression, it is also dependent on its antidepressant. To their credit, American business leaders and their political proxies devised a way to capitalize on this sad capitalist truth in the aftermath of World War II: wage a constant total war. In Cox's opinion,

> Militarization and preparation for the eventuality of open conflict are extreme measures but they may provide many important subsidiary values in the crisis: they entail enormous expenditures and siphon off manpower, thus contributing to the stabilization of the domestic economy; they are flexible enough to provide for the economic and military support of subsidiary nations; they may create optimistic expectations of recapturing the non-capitalist areas of the world; they ordinarily present a forbidding posture toward restive colonial and dependent areas of the world; and they serve as a restraint upon any precipitate attempt to advance socialism by the U.S.S.R. or China.[67]

In short, Cox interpreted the Cold War as an effective marketing campaign for the institutionalization of the military-industrial complex, a mélange of the New Deal and a simulated wartime economy. For its part, the American public had its own self-interested reasons for buying their government's exaggerated advertisements that Stalin intended to impose his political-economic regime on larger and larger portions of the globe:

> It would be misleading to leave the impression that only the oligarchy has favored the steady increase in military spending

during these years. If one assumes the permanence of monopoly capitalism, with its proved incapacity to make rational use for peaceful and humane ends of its enormous productive potential, one must decide whether one prefers the mass unemployment and hopelessness characteristic of the Great Depression or the relative job security and material well-being provided by the huge military budgets of the 1940's and 1950's. Since most Americans, workers included, still do assume without question the permanence of the system, it is only natural that they should prefer the situation which is personally and privately more advantageous. And in order to rationalize this preference, they have accepted the official ideology of anti-Communism which appears to justify an unlimited expansion of the military establishment as essential to national survival.[68]

"This massive absorption of surplus in military preparations," added Baran and Sweezy, "has been the key fact of postwar American economic history."[69] Cox certainly agreed.

Ultimately, however, the Cold War's battlegrounds were neither in the United States nor in the Soviet Union, but in the world surrounding them. Whereas the extent of Cold War posturing that actually involved American and Soviet citizens in conflict was limited to acts of espionage and occasional high-profile defections, of which the number of people effected numbered in the hundreds, the Cold War consumed tens of thousands in military engagements outside of the Great Powers' respective borders. For both sides, the sites of conflict were quite logical for at least two reasons: one, neither power was willing to risk the potential nuclear destruction that could have resulted from a direct confrontation by one on the other's national territory; and two, neither socialism nor capitalism can exist solely in one country despite Stalin's and bourgeois political economists' claims to the contrary. This last point warrants some elaboration.

If, as Cox maintained, "the existence of capitalism is unthinkable in complete isolation from their peculiar, sometimes indirect, economic affiliations with these [backward] countries,"[70] then any political movement that calls into question those economic relationships, threatens, in this case, American hegemony. Accordingly, U.S. foreign policy "tends to be determined by concern for the welfare of free enterprise especially in Europe and by fear of progress toward governmental economic planning in the backward countries."[71] So-cial planning, incidentally, was for Cox the essence of socialism. Simi-larly, if the "spread of socialism, taken by itself, does not imply any reduction of the trading area open to the capitalist countries,"[72] then neither should it suggest any less trade between socialist states. In fact, as Baran and Sweezy argued, it is probable that former colo-nies or neocolonies that have embraced socialism would enjoy more trade opportunities than they did as colonial appendages since eco-nomic planning typically promotes greater economic diversifica-tion.[73] Therefore, any restrictions put on the trade options of social-ist states (particularly ones that impinge on the procurement of food, fuel, or necessary raw materials) can be as detrimental to the prac-tice of socialism as the same limitations placed on capitalist states can be to the practice of capitalism.

Apart from the different motives for engaging in foreign trade, what, for Cox, separated American and Soviet foreign policies were their different social foundations. Whereas the foundations of the capitalist world economy are imperialism and racism, those of so-cialist society are self-determination and social equality. In Cox's mind, a global economic system based on "the commercial and in-dustrial imbalances among the backward and sophisticated units of the system"[74] cannot help but develop implicit, if not, explicit, racial (or "ethnic") reasons to account for some states' prosperity and the poverty of most other social formations; structural explanations would necessarily require the admission of an unequal playing field in the leader nations' favor. It was for this reason that a central ob-jective of the 1955 Asian-African Conference held in Bandung, In-donesia, was to lodge an international protest against colonial and neocolonial racism and the concomitant "concept of the right of capitalist powers to hold peoples in subjection until they are 'civi-lized.'"[75] Though it can be argued that the United States has not been an imperial power to the same extent that most all western European nations have been (excepting, of course, the occupation of its national territory, Hawaii, Puerto Rico, and Micronesia), Cox was still of the opinion that by virtue of its position as global capi-talist leader, it must be imperialist. On this point he wrote:

Nothing could be more misleading, it seems not amiss to re-mark, than to suppose that since the United States was originally formed by colonies which had to liberate themselves by war, she would *ipso facto* become the champion of all colonial peoples. Given a world in which major areas of exploitation were being preempted by other imperialist nations, we should expect this country, developing according to capitalist tradition, to be critical about colonialism and insistent on its legitimate share by demanding an 'open door' everywhere. This policy, manifestly, was not intended to exclude backward countries from exploitative transactions. Indeed, it sometimes resulted in even more severe exploitation, as in China, than that associated with some forms of colonialism. When anticolonialism tends to lead, as it currently does, not to open door, but to a rejection of all forms of foreign capitalist exploitation, we should expect, to the contrary, the leader nation to consider traditional colonialism the lesser evil.[76]

Accordingly, in the post–World War II era, American interests, both public and private, have done everything in their power to stifle the attempts of Third World progressives to attain economic freedom of choice whether or not the country in question had already achieved political independence. The tactics have been predictably effective: installation or support of client dictators; large investments in colonial or neocolonial enterprises; Congressional indulgence of colonial and neocolonial interests, both American and foreign; establishment of regional and international organizations to counter nonaligned or socialist precedents; aid to convince recipient nations that the "processes of the free market constitute the most acceptable instrument of economic development" (regardless of the fact that the very need for economic aid itself belies the theory); and military intervention for those leaders or movements that are harder to convince. Naturally, these last-named political-economic options have "left the immanent differences between the western countries and the backward peoples largely intact."[77]

Socialism in Theory

In light of his thoughts on capitalism's global historical record, Cox could not see equating the political-economic activities of the Soviet

Union as either state capitalistic domestically or imperialistic externally. Furthermore, implicated as capitalism is in the exacerbation or creation of "illiteracy, superstition, disease, low standards of living, and 'stone-age culture,'"[78] it seemed only logical to Cox that any social movement that sought to combat these challenges would necessarily question capitalism; and this was precisely the formal position taken by the Soviet Union. In the African-American intellectual community, others shared Cox's political assessments: W. E. B. Du-Bois and Paul Robeson, for example, were also of the opinion that social planning was the only conceivable response to the abuses of capitalism. They also maintained that to the degree that the central underpinning of capitalism—colonialism—was in retreat in the post–World War II period, socialism had but to fill in the breach.

For other commentators, however, including the many partisans of the Left, state planning by itself hardly suffices for a society to earn the socialist label. For these critics, it was not only possible that the Soviet Union never was a socialist society in spite of the state's direction of its politics and economy, but that it was unconscionably repressive both within and without its borders. And their positions were ostensibly justified by the evidence: an industrial regime no less Fordist than the American original; compulsory collectivized farming, the rewards of which were probably less than those realized by agricultural laborers on United Fruit plantations in Central America; Siberian labor camps, when not a bullet, for Stalin's critics; the "assertion of Russian control over the Baltic states, the pushing westward of the Polish-Russian border, the elimination of East Prussia, and the acquisition of territories from Finland, Hungary, and Rumania"[79] in the immediate aftermath of World War II; and Soviet military interventions in East Germany, Hungary, and Czechoslovakia in 1953, 1956, and 1968, respectively.

Yet neither these facts nor the public admission of Stalin's failings at the 1956 Communist Party Congress in Moscow seemed to shake Cox's or DuBois' or Robeson's faith in Soviet socialism. Apparently, there were a number of factors that shaped their reasoning. First, in their collective opinion the "Soviets had solved the minorities question,"[80] precisely the supposed goal that continued to elude capitalist society. Second, the Soviet Union supported Asian and African desires to liberate themselves from the political-economic straitjackets of colonialism and neocolonialism. Third, that capitalist imperialism, not Soviet socialism, fomented the two world wars of the twentieth century and countless others in previous ones. Fourth, the preservation of Soviet socialism required the establishment of buffer states in Eastern Europe to hinder a capitalist assault on it like the German one during World War II. And finally, employing a biological metaphor by which to explain Soviet imperfections, Cox wrote:

> The troubles of the planned economies are those of infancy and childhood. They involve problems of 'passing the worst'; setbacks due to ignorance and foolhardiness; and stoppages resulting from blows administered in contests with oldsters. The new system displays some ugly scars left by burns from deliberately playing with fire. But underneath it all seems to surge the irrepressible recuperative vigor of youth. The study of the development and of the social pathologies of modern socialism thus seem to call for a different set of hypotheses.[81]

In short, whatever the abuses of socialism, they are the result neither of the profit motive nor of racism.

Racism and the American Order

Cox and others on the American Left, both black and white, felt that racism hindered American workers from building a socially transformative labor movement. The legacy of both settler colonialism and slavery, racism enabled American capital and its political representatives to circumscribe the economic and political rights of all workers by encouraging the popular belief that prolabor policies promoted the pretensions of Blacks to "social equality," including the one-time southern shibboleth against the black male–white female intimate relations that the equal application of the law would supposedly engender. Rather than compromise the monolith of white supremacy in any fashion even if it ultimately disadvantaged them economically, white workers have typically settled for the lower wages (as a percentage of total profit, higher in relation to those earned by workers of color) and compromised bargaining rights that are the consequences of a racially divided working class. This result can be thought of as racism's opportunity or operational cost. Still, when viewed with the understanding that racial discrimination satisfies certain ineffable psychological needs as well as relative economic ones, it pays off. At midcentury,

> Despite the gains scored here and there, the industrial scene in 1955 showed little in the way of improvement of black workers' conditions. . . . Although the gap between the annual wages of black families and white families had narrowed somewhat, the annual earnings of black families in 1955 were still only 56 per cent of white family income. . . . In 1955, only 7 per cent of all black workers were in skilled crafts as compared with 17 per cent of all white workers. On the railroads, nine out of every ten black workers were in service, unskilled, and common-labor jobs; in the auto industry, at least 40 per cent of the foundry workers were blacks and less than 3 per cent were in the tool and die division; in the steel industry, almost all black workers were in the eight lowest-paid of some thirty-two classifications. Only a handful of black workers were employed in textiles, and in tobacco they were still mainly in the low-paid stemming and drying plants. Six out of every ten black women workers were in domestic and service jobs, and only 20 per cent of black women held industrial, sales, and office jobs, as compared to 59 per cent of white women workers.[82]

Though Cox maintained that "[t]he dominant economic class has always been at the motivating center of the spread of racial antagonism," he did not deny that "organized labor can be less democratic than the citizenry at large."[83] Craft unions (as opposed to those in mass industries such as auto, mining, steel, and meat packing) were particularly notorious. "As late as 1950," Cox noted, "there were some eight AFL unions having clauses in their constitutions specifically excluding Negroes; while all the big railway unions: Locomotive Engineers, Railroad Trainmen, Railroad Yardmasters of America, Railway Conductors and Train Dispatchers (which are not AFL affiliates) proscribed them in their fundamental documents. Many other unions exclude Negroes either by tacit agreement or by stipulations in 'rituals.'"[84]

Yet, the even greater impediment to progressive politics in the United States was the South's attitude toward and treatment of its black inhabitants. In order to deny black southerners their civil rights as American citizens "the Bill of Rights and other crucial amendments to the Constitution guaranteeing civil liberties had to be circumvented by ingenious social devices and by a succession of *ad hoc* local statutes."[85] When "Negroes beg[a]n to show signs of unionization, of movements for normal political status, and of desires to bring themselves up to cultural parity . . . the articulate [southern] ruling class revived Ku-Klux-Klan type, vigilante organizations, of which the alert White Citizens' Council became most pervasive, to restrain and intimidate by extra-legal means such as mob violence, bombings, economic boycott, and political ostracism."[86] From the personal experience of having lived in both Texas and Alabama, Cox was well aware that the reverberations of southern politics were felt far beyond the Mason-Dixon line and the Mississippi River.

Sometimes, especially when there is a weak President and a Democratic Congress, the South may effectively rule the nation. It has power to do so because (a) the relatively small political participation of Southern people strengthens the hand of the demagogue. Since the [eighteen] eighties the most momentous political issue in the area has been the recurring demand for strict white supremacy. It has been repeatedly pointed out that representatives are elected in the South by a decidedly smaller number of votes than in any other section of the country. In 1952, for instance, about 74,000 votes elected a Congressional Representative there as compared to 164,000 in the Northeast and 156,000 in North Central states. (b) The one-party system limits debate and opposition, providing thereby an excellent opportunity for the unprincipled politician to exploit biased arguments and to arouse mass emotions in favor of himself as a person. (c) The tenure of Southern politicians in Congress tends, consequently, to be relatively continuous; and this, according to Congressional tradition, gives the group a critical advantage in building up seniority and influence. In 1956, of the 15 Standing Committees of the Senate, 11 were controlled by chairmen from the South; and of the 19 such committees in the House 14 had chairmen from this area. (d) Although the voting power of the South is minor relative to that of the rest of the country—in 1950, of 435 seats in the House, 17 Southern and border states held 145 and, of course, this group had only 34 of the 96 seats in the Senate—it can and has stopped by filibuster in the Senate almost any civil rights legislation. For some 80 years before 1957 not a single piece of civil rights legislation managed to get by the Senate.[87]

And as many labor leaders were begrudgingly forced to admit in the 1950s, a vote for a southern democrat was not only an anti–civil rights vote, but an antilabor one as well. Southern politicians could brand Labor communist with the same effect its use had on black southerners fighting for civil rights.

Apart from the fact that black Americans increasingly found intolerable the racially motivated social humiliations to which they were subjected not only in the South but in all other regions, unabashed American racism was also bad for American business overseas in the aftermath of World War II. In the wake of the fascist menace and in the initial phase of Asian and African decolonization, people of color throughout the world were justifiably sensitive to any hint of racist doctrine in either Western domestic politics or foreign policy. When the association between colonial capitalism and racial exploitation was added into the postwar, global ideological mix, recently and soon-to-be politically independent Asian and African peoples were all the more suspicious of Western political-economic intentions in their regions. It takes no leap in logic to comprehend why the images of billy-club wielding police officers threatening black picketers, of German shepherds set on peaceful demonstrators, of high pressure water cascading on civil rights protestors, of counterprotest signs bearing slogans such as "Niggers go home!" and of charred black corpses suspended by ropes might be perceived as detrimental to American economic interests in Africa, Asia, and Latin America.

In the final analysis, however, even Cox felt that the efforts of black Americans to force American society to abide by its constitutional principles would not guarantee a similar transformation of the country's economic system. For this last to occur, "[t]he initiative must come from still more disadvantaged groups abroad,"[88] he believed. We will address the viability of this formulation in the next chapter.

Although English and American businessmen and politicians undoubtedly drew on the political-economic experiences of their immediate predecessors during their respective tenures as leaders of the capitalist world economy, both groups had to contend with unanticipated social developments during their eras of leadership. In the English case, the most important was obviously the industrial revolution. However, as we noted earlier, Cox insisted on situating even this continuing ensemble of momentous advances in the processes of production in the context of England's international commerce. For Cox, in order for the intensification of production to be of any economic consequence for a particular country, it must be accompanied by the expansion of distribution. It is for this reason that Cox was not especially impressed by the technological innovation of the industrial revolution in itself.

During its tenure as leader of the capitalist world economy, the United States was forced to respond to three major challenges: a post–First World War international economy, a decolonizing non-European world, and its own racism. As far as the first challenge was concerned, Cox argued that American elites contributed to the Great Depression by protecting domestic industries at the same time that they sought to rebuild a war-torn Europe economically through loans and grants. This and other capitalist contradictions came to a head in the 1930s.

The Second World War and its immediate aftermath provided temporary resolutions of these contradictions. However, in the process, that conflagration discredited two mainstays of the capitalist world economy: colonialism and racism. American responses to these challenges were only partially successful. To the first, American elites fomented, in Cox's estimation, the Cold War by which the United States could proclaim itself anti-imperialist while cultivating neocolonial relationships with "backward" nations. To the second challenge, however, American elites did not see fit to respond for nearly a decade despite having fought and denounced the racism of Nazism. That American tardiness in confronting its own racism made non-European nations suspicious of American intentions in their countries is hardly surprising. As a result, socialism remained an attractive option to non-European nationalists as well as to the most respected black Americans.

In the next chapter, we will take a closer look at the prospects of socialism in "backward" countries based on Cox's understanding of particularly economic development. We will also return to a theme raised in chapter 3—Cox's critique of black nationalism—in order to show that it, too, was ultimately grounded in his vision of the transition to socialism in capitalist leader nations.

6

Black Nationalism and Socialism

I ended chapter 3 with the hypothesis that Cox's criticisms of pluralism (as both social scientific model and as political program) were not a guise behind which he camouflaged his anti-Semitism, but rather were motivated by the political position that the societal adoption of pluralism as the basis of social policy can only work to the disadvantage of black Americans. I also intimated that within his antipluralism arguments are some stereotypical ideas about "culture" and which groups supposedly exhibit certain cultural traits. On this matter, Cox felt that the cultures of Jewish and black Americans were polar opposites: where one benefits from a common religion to promote group cohesiveness, the other lacks a common belief system to support group solidarity. To put Cox's position in yet other terms, whereas Jewish Americans identify themselves on the basis of a common religious tradition whose roots date more than two millennia, black Americans[1] cohere by color (when it is made an "issue") whose label is just over five hundred years old. That Cox exaggerated both the socioreligious unity of American and global Jewry and the diversity of sociopolitical opinion of black Americans should be clear. It should also be clear that, in his eyes, his political conclusion—that white Americans stood to gain more economically and politically than black Americans could ever hope to from the national embrace of pluralism—required such hyperbole.

Another of Cox's political exaggerations aimed to discredit all variants of black nationalism not, however, for the express purpose of encouraging the assimilation of black Americans into mainstream American society, but with an eye to how that process will facilitate the advance of socialism even in this country. As will become clearer, Cox both steadfastly remained an advocate of socialism throughout his life, and, like Marx, he maintained that socialism would emerge from the bowels of capitalist society. Where he parted company with Marx was in his belief that the transition from capitalism to socialism did not require the catalyst of clashes between workers and owners of capital, but rather the entry of ever-larger numbers of working people into the ranks of the middle class. This was socialism by class imitation, not by class struggle. Utopian, perhaps, but no more so than other prescriptions for social improvement.

The Troublesome Legacy of Slavery

Cox's second argument against black nationalism begins with the assertion that its advocates equate black culture with ghetto culture. This is how he described the association: "An important current definition of Negro self-respect is total respect for the Negro lower-class subculture. The size of this class is relatively so large that its ethos, rather than that of the Negro middle class, has been frequently assumed to be the dominant orientation of all Negroes. . . . In the ghetto, lower-class culture becomes so pervasive and stable that achievement of middle-class status may be regarded, by at least a section of the leadership, as a mark of apostasy."[2]

Contrary to appearances, however, Cox exhorted black Americans to pursue the "American dream" not as an end in itself, but as a means to a more radical end. For the moment, though, it is im-

perative to bear in mind that Cox considered ghetto culture the
retention of the worst patterns of behavior developed during the
slave era and its immediate aftermath. On this matter, Cox was particularly emphatic.

> It was the culture associated with American bondage that
> Negroes brought into freedom. And this let it be noted, was not
> merely the culture of a lower class but of an extremely perverted
> lower-lower class. The Negro *masses* became freedmen condi-
> tioned to a tradition of the most degraded form of family irre-
> sponsibility, with a distorted conception of the nature of prop-
> erty, with relatively little personal motivation for work, with the
> slave's orientation toward division of the day regarding rest,
> work, and relaxation; with feeble and restricted powers of reach-
> ing out toward the motivating forces of the larger culture. The
> Negro was almost entirely illiterate. He had a telltale drawl,
> servile rhetoric, and comparatively little use for quiet and clean-
> liness; he was trained for the crudest form of agricultural manual
> labor, and subject to the ambivalent control of his former mas-
> ter. All this was bound up in a cultural pattern that held him out-
> side the normal structure of the American social status system.
> And yet, his was inherently an American culture with an Ameri-
> can future.[3]

Put this way, slave culture—the roots of ghetto culture—is to be
avoided at all costs by those afforded the opportunity to do so. From
Cox's perspective, moreover, middle-class American culture, being
"commercial, thrifty, scientific, technological, Christian, dynamic,
orderly, [and] sanitary," (that is, point-for-point the antithesis of
slave culture), should be the aspiration of all Blacks just as "on the
whole, lower-class whites respect it as normal, proper, and worth
striving for."[4]

However, Cox's recommendations to his fellow black Americans
did not aim at mere imitation of middle-class ways. On the contrary,
he argued that the advance of capitalism in this country, as elsewhere, ultimately spurred its "direct outgrowth," socialism, for even
the "socialist countries" recognize that they have to "develop in [their]
people attitudes for hard work, honesty, efficiency, sobriety, and
upward cultural motivation such as that which made possible the

development and maintenance of the phenomenal American productive system." Therefore, in light of the fact that socialism "seeks
essentially to modify and render capitalist culture more effective in
the service of its people,"[5] the more that black Americans participate in and master that culture, the closer they bring American society to the adoption of the social system that aims to provide for all
its members, regardless of physical or cultural distinctions within
the population.

Here, then, is a sketch of the theory that moved Cox to insist that
black Americans identify with the larger American society in spite of
the humiliations, resistance, and setbacks along the path toward
assimilation. Let us now dissect the components of his theory.

It is obvious that Cox's point of departure is the notion of "lower-
class," a term he used repeatedly in the passages cited above. Just
who or what is meant by it, however, Cox never specified in *Race Relations*. A likely candidate (given his repeated quips about Malcolm
Little's criminal activities[6]) is the black *lumpenproletariat* or that portion of the "reserve army" of the working class that furnishes goods
and services (frequently by illegal means) to its fellow class members
and to others above it when its ranks are laid off from or refuse to
find new wage work.[7] In this sector we would include anyone from
petty thieves to prostitutes, from numbers runners to drug dealers.
From the tone of his remarks, it is clear that Cox felt little sympathy
for their plight (which, in itself, suggests that he did not see them as
victims of capitalism, but as conscious scavengers of already picked-
over labor power) and, unlike Frantz Fanon, incapable of any heroism, political or cultural. In his eyes, the black lumpenproletariat is
neither the custodian of black culture nor the definer of the political
direction of black Americans. It is, simply put, an embarrassment.

It is possible, then, to interpret Cox's refusal to define "lower-
class" as deliberate: it avoided the awkward situation of discussing its
intimate ties to both working-class and bourgeois life. In addition,
more than intellectually distancing the black lumpenproletariat
from its social "betters" by skirting the discussion of the former's
roots in the structure of industrial capitalism, Cox sought to distance its "cultural" practices from those of the black working and
middle classes. If we refer to one of the passages cited earlier, we see
that Cox supplied a laundry list of the cultural characteristics that
the black lumpenproletariat continues to share with its pre- and

postemancipation forebears: an emasculated family structure, ignorance of economic matters, lack of a work ethic, illiteracy, boister-
ousness, and uncleanliness. Of the six characteristics, the one with
which Cox headed the list was the most important in his mind. This
variable has been and still is commonly used by commentators of all
political persuasions to explain the incidence of the other variables
just named in urban black communities.[8]

Cox concluded that male-absent family life was the inheritance of
former slaves. If, under the slave regime, human chattel were, by
law, the property of their "owners," there was little, if anything, that
slaves could do without the "interference" of their masters. Under
these circumstances, Cox thought it grossly misleading to call the
romantic unions between male and female slaves, marriages, for
most unlike marriages between free men and women, slave unions
denied the male partner the ability to assume his "rightful" role as
family patriarch:

> During the time of bondage . . . the institution of marriage
> tended to limit the chattel interests of the master, hence he
> relied upon his legal power to disregard it. He controlled pro-
> creation; and children inevitably became his property. In the
> process, the basic social rights and duties infringed upon were
> particularly those of the Negro man. Coition for him lost its
> customary significance. Indeed, sexual promiscuity was often
> encouraged; he thus gained a degree of sexual freedom but
> lost self-respect, a sense of possession, and the responsibility of
> manhood.[9]

Apart from the decidedly patriarchal bias of his position (that the
denial of the male slave's manhood was somehow more significant
than the denial of the female slave's womanhood), it is possible to
argue that Cox's reconstruction of slave life ultimately denies the
humanity of the enslaved perhaps more than most slaveholders' actions did themselves. Cox's legal training may have been a hindrance
on his perspective of the "peculiar institution": he took the statutes
(or lack thereof) governing the relationship between masters and
slaves as the course of everyday practice.[10] What more recent scholarship (that is, roughly since Cox's death) "on the world the slaves made"
has revealed is that a significant number of slaveholders understood

that they advanced their own economic interests by making certain social concessions (within limits, of course) to the enslaved, one of which was to recognize slave unions.[11] But countering Cox's position on this matter misses what I believe to be his penultimate objective: to make the case that one component of ghetto culture, the woman-headed household, has its roots in slavery and that now, like then, it is a "perversion" of the familial norm. His ultimate objective in providing a cultural explanation for the relatively high incidence of black families without adult males in urban communities was to justify his assertion that the children of such families were socially maladjusted and therefore unqualified to be political actors. In other words, by indirectly attacking their "mamas," Cox hoped to deflate the bravado of black nationalists and their sympathizers. The problem with that strategy was that he was knocking on the wrong doors. "Most Black Power spokespersons," remarks Manning Marable, "came from upwardly mobile working-class or middle-class backgrounds, were trained at universities, and had been groomed for ultimate assimilation into the existing system. . . . Only one small fraction of the major proponents of Black Power had the gritty background of Malcolm X."[12] Thus, Cox himself could have fathered a black nationalist.

Still, it is likely that these facts would not have compelled Cox to change his positions on either the roots of the lower-class black family or on the segment of the black population to whom, he felt, black nationalism appeals most. These were political matters and as we have already seen, Cox could be relentless where politics was concerned. However, attacking black nationalism in this way was a costly strategy and one from which political opponents more ruthless than black nationalists could profit. For both in naming the woman-headed household as the independent variable of the host of disadvantages that inhibit the social mobility of black urban and rural families and in tracing its incidence in the twentieth century to the era of black enslavement and its immediate aftermath, Cox had effectively absolved government, employers, and unions of virtually any responsibility for the socioeconomic conditions of the black poor since emancipation. Even more debilitating politically than the presentation of an academic endorsement of this view is that it guaranteed that federal, private, and labor institutions could interpret (except in the most blatant of cases) as mere excuses (to avoid dealing with the real source of their social problems) any charge made by black accusers that the representatives of these institutions are racist and discriminate against people of color. For once a "cultural" variable is identified to explain, in this case, the social stagnancy of the black poor, then structural factors (over which they exercise least control) could be conveniently avoided by the policymakers of the institutions named above. In effect, Cox's political strategy to counter the appeal of black nationalism could be used to blame the poor for being poor.

In all fairness to Cox, however, it must be said that he did not entirely fail to mention a number of the structural forces that have taken and continue to take their toll on the lives of the black poor. In *Race Relations* in particular, he underscored the impact of job discrimination (on the part of both employers and unions), housing discrimination (on the part of both the federal government and local real estate associations), and the "flight of industry from metropolitan centers to suburbs." Taking these factors into consideration, Cox posited that "[t]he core of the Negro subculture in American metropolises constitutes an unassimilated way of life: the conjunction of black, southern plantation conditioning and the individualistic, highly motivated, racist spirit of modern urban society. Ecologically, the ghetto is the outcome of nation-wide physical mobility and racial ostracism."[13]

Cox could not have written a more marked departure from the passages we cited earlier! Here, in no uncertain terms, he asserted that "ghetto culture" is a combination (implicitly in equal measure) of social approaches and practices retained from slavery and those developed as a result of capitalist racism in the long postemancipation era. If, however, this was Cox's sincere position on ghetto culture, how, then, do we explain his unyielding emphasis on the vestiges of slavery in the passages cited earlier?

As I have said elsewhere in this study, Cox wrote his politics into his academic work. In this instance, I believe that he targeted two very different audiences in *Race Relations*: social scientists and "lay" readers in the first half of the book and black nationalists in the second.[14] Thus, given his feelings on what black nationalists espoused, they were treated to an intellectual fare that attributed "their" communities' social problems to its denizens' retention of patterns of behavior formed in slavery, whereas the first audience was told that "[g]hetto culture

is not critically lower-class despite its poverty, substandard housing, family disrepute, static outlook, storefront churches, slum conditions, and so on—it is lower-class culture subject to implicitly
planned degradation and repression. By and large, the cultural failure and low reputation of Negroes may be thought of as the de-
siderata of the white ruling elite, especially in the traditional home-
land of the Negro, the plantation South." It was similarly told that
the "strength of the Negro family ordinarily derives not essentially
from operations within the family itself but from less direct social
gains which are still limited and opposed by elements in the larger
society—especially those determined by southern leaders. Prospec-
tive benefits must include such values as freedom of economic opportunity, educational equality and encouragement, societal respect
for open housing, political equality, and freedom from racism." And
of no less consequence, Cox underscored that the incidence of both
woman-headed households and out-of-wedlock births declines with
the increase of employment, family income, and educational attain-
ment for both black and white Americans.[15]

Of course, read with his life-long allegiance to the promise of assimilation in mind, Cox's decision not to highlight structural forces
as much as cultural ones in his explanation of the persistence of black
poverty since emancipation, was understandable: if he had stressed
the former, it could have been used by black nationalists to support
their claim that the root cause of black America's social ills are white
racism. Little wonder, then, that Cox would write about the decision
in 1954 *Brown v. Board of Education of Topeka, Kansas,* to desegregate
the nation's schools in this spirit:

> The decision implicated the federal government directly. The
> Court, moreover, obligated itself to supervise the desegrega-
> tion of public schools in the United States and especially in the
> South; and it implicitly bound the administration to use force
> in the process. Thus, race relations suddenly became head-
> line news; the public was awakened, and protest leaders be-
> came champions of national morality. The decision involved so
> wide an area of racial discrimination that the NAACP seemed
> to have its hand full merely in helping to support the man-
> date of the Supreme Court. For the first time resolution of
> the "Negro problem" had become an obligation of the United

States. And blame for the social conditions of Negroes became increasingly centered upon "American institutions."[16]

In an equally important description of the meaning of the 1954 ruling, Cox added later in *Race Relations* that "[w]ith the federal courts assuming leadership in the struggle for civil rights, the trend toward Negro assimilation was not only expedited but also, for the first time, societally confirmed. The group now possessed their citizenship status not on sufferance but by inherent right. Activist Negroes and white sympathizers thus sought confrontation after confrontation and repeatedly forced conservative whites to retreat."[17]

Accordingly, Cox praised the nonviolent tactics—boycotts, marches, sit-ins, pickets—and liberal agenda of the civil rights movement to secure access, above all, to voting booths, schools (funded, in large part, by the very tax dollars of those excluded), employment opportunities, and public accommodations for particularly black, but generally for all, Americans. It must be noted, however, that these were Cox's sentiments in the late 1960s and early 1970s. Just three years before the landmark court decision, Cox was highly critical of the ideology driving the organization that spearheaded the movement to have the case reviewed by the Supreme Court: the NAACP. In his 1951 article, "The Programs of Negro Civil Rights Organizations,"[18] he characterized the "protest" tactics of the NAACP and like-oriented organizations in this manner: "Although in achieving its ends it must inevitably entail a significant modification of the status quo, protest ideology never brings the social system itself into question. It envisages only an indiscriminate inclusion of Negroes in the general society as it is. Indeed from the point of view of the sufficiency and final excellence of the American social order the Negro protest leader is perhaps as reactionary as even the Southern oligarch."[19]

Cox could not have made a more serious declaration of the long-term limitations of the NAACP's liberal agenda. We can imagine that leftists even more radical than Cox and other NAACP sympathizers found his remarks on the organization's work unduly harsh. Despite his criticism then, Cox neither made reference to nor repeated these sentiments in *Race Relations*.

Had Cox been asked to reconcile his apparently contradictory assessments (separated by no less than fifteen years) of the objectives of the NAACP, it is conceivable that he would have responded by saying something to the effect that different times warrant different analyses, but that his commitment to socialism is unchanging. Thus, whereas in the early 1950s he continued to hold to a vision of socialism realizable only after the working-class revolution(a belief he had held since the mid-1930s), in the mid-1960s he switched to a vision of socialism achieved through a middle-class revolution. Still, the manner in which he chose to espouse this alternative theory of the transition to socialism—by attacking the cultural milieu from which black nationalism emerges—undermined, to a large extent, his great expectations of the civil rights movement. For if the factors most responsible for the proportionally large number of poor black Americans are cultural in nature, then there is little that either the civil rights movement or the entity to which the movement appealed for social redress, the federal government, could do to keep that population from vitiating programs designed to improve its ranks. This has been precisely the argument that political conservatives have made to justify the reduction of welfare disbursements (typically expressed in the superficially coded language of "anti-big-government" and "tax relief"), particularly to single mothers of color.[20] Again, I think that Cox exercised poor political judgment in critiquing black nationalism on cultural grounds, since his political opponents could use it to justify the abandonment of the black poor at all levels of government.

Moreover, what was most ironic about Cox's running battle with black nationalists was that his own sociological findings supported the basis of their sociopolitical philosophy. Who, among black nationalists, would disagree with Cox's claim that the American economic order is racist; that residential segregation is the normal course of American neighborhood life; that "official" and informal violence and physical intimidation against black people and other people of color is so routine that only the most heinous are taken notice of; that while white liberals are typically condescending toward people of color, white conservatives can only tolerate the sight of them in subordinate positions and in small numbers; and that discrimination on the basis of race in all areas of American social life is the rule, not the exception? These (and a host of related) observations can be gleaned from Cox's own writings. Why, then, his relentless verbal pillory of one apparently justifiable, black response to American social injustice that even he, in an admittedly generous mood, described as "seek[ing] to develop among Negroes dignified and meritorious conceptions of themselves?"[21]

The Many Limitations of Black Nationalism

In addition to his antipluralist position that we discussed in chapter 3, I believe that there were five other reasons why Cox disparaged black nationalism: one, his rejection of the internal colony thesis to which some black nationalists subscribed; two, his concern that black nationalism could be used to justify the continued neglect of particularly black urban areas; three, his application of a model of social change derived from (Caribbean) ruling-class situations of race relations to a society where a bipartite situation of race relations is operative; four, his belief that the population of black Americans as a percentage of the country's total is too small for black Americans to be significant political actors in American society; and five, his contention that there is what we may call a "middle-class road" to socialism. We will address the first four of these points in this section; the fifth requires a lengthier analysis in its own section.

It is unfortunate but not surprising that in his critique of the internal colony thesis Cox did not provide an adequate definition of the concept. It is not uncommon for scholars to make strawmen of the positions of their opponents. Although I do not believe that this was typical of Cox's approach to the ideas of his political adversaries, it does characterize his approach to black nationalism. At most, then, he defined the internal colony thesis as the "contention" that "Negroes . . . constitute a colonial people exploited by a foreign American nation as an imperialist power."[22] Cox clearly thought the details of the thesis irrelevant and therefore unworthy of elaboration. Among the many detailed descriptions of the internal colony thesis that he opted not to cite, however, was William K. Tabb's, which we would do well to quote at length here:

The economic relations of the ghetto to white America closely parallel those between third-world nations and the industrially advanced countries. The ghetto also has a relatively low per-capita income and a high birth rate. Its residents are for the most part unskilled. Businesses lack capital and managerial know-how. Local markets are limited. The incidence of credit default is high. Little savings takes place and what is saved is usually not invested locally. Goods and services tend to be 'imported' for the most part, only the simplest and the most labor-intensive being produced locally. The ghetto is dependent on one basic export—its unskilled labor power. Aggregate demand for this export does not increase to match the growth of the ghetto labor force, and unemployment is prevalent. As consumer goods are advertised twenty-four hours a day on radio and television, ghetto residents are constantly reminded of the availability of goods and services which they cannot afford to buy. Welfare payments and other governmental transfers are needed to help pay for the ghetto's requirements. Local businesses are owned, in large numbers, by non-residents, many of whom are white. Important jobs in the local public economy (teachers, policemen, and postmen) are held by white outsiders. The black ghetto, then, is in many ways in a position similar to that of the typical underdeveloped nation.[23]

Here, again, there is little in this passage that cannot be found in Cox's own work. And here, too, we can surmise that he chose not to underscore his own indirect contributions to the internal colony thesis because he feared the policy "remedies" that black nationalists could propose based on it. Thus, more important than Cox's conclusion that the "chances . . . of a black nation arising within the larger American society seem illogical and unrealistic,"[24] and his conviction that the "destiny of Negroes is cultural and biological integration and fusion with the larger American society,"[25] was his concern that the "[a]rguments based on colonial assumptions often lead to preposterous conclusions and merely serve to justify socially erratic behavior among American Negroes." His vision, then, of specific American cities governed by black elected officials (where Blacks are in the majority) was predictably dire: "Left to Negroes alone, the city would probably crumble and vanish; indeed, left to white labor alone, the city would also quickly perish. There is, however, a peculiar functional continuum between labor and white entrepreneurship in the city, a phenomenon still largely missing in the Negro relationship. The distorted, temporary reaction to this limitation has been ghettoization, or development of a black community on the periphery of main-stream culture. The ghetto is anything but self-sufficient."[26]

In addition, Cox thought that the timing of the black nationalist thrust could not have been worse. Heartened, as we noted earlier, by what he took to be indications of the federal government's steadfast commitment both to the guarantee and protection of the civil rights of the nation's black citizens and by what he saw to be the future educational needs of American industry, Cox felt that the socio-economic prospects of black Americans to "enter the mainstream of urban life . . . [and] to become in practice and in attitude, part of the imperialistic tradition of American capitalism," had never been better than what they were in the mid-1960s:

> What then? Are Negroes to be forever excluded from the core of American patriotism? Three considerations seem to modify the negative implications of this question: (1) Negroes are not currently being deprived of market positions previously held by them—these positions are indeed recognizably improving; (2) the center of creativity in the system seems to be moving gradually from rampant competitiveness for economic domi-nance abroad toward reliance on technological progress and efficiency in domestic production; and (3) all signs seem to indicate that social inclusion will be increasingly a matter of education and absence of racial discrimination in the distribu-tion of jobs. These trends are not entirely new; they may be considered projections on an upward turning curve.[27]

It must be said that no matter what his rationale for making such remarks, it still strikes one as bizarre to read Cox call on black Ameri-cans to join in the "imperialistic tradition of American capitalism" given what that implies in the way of both domestic and global race relations. Equally puzzling was his failure to consider that the tech-nological revolution which he thought held so much promise for black Americans could "eliminat[e] . . . the menial, unskilled, and semi-skilled jobs which have been [traditionally] left to Negroes."[28] Or, perhaps Cox was not thinking about the fate of the black work-ing class when he made those remarks.

Another reason for Cox's negative assessment of black national-ism was that he feared that self-segregation or separation could be

further exploited by political and economic conservatives to continue to allow the nation's inner cities to become de facto urban reservations or "native reserves" of the type imposed on Amerindians
and, until recently, indigenous Africans in the apartheid-era Republic of South Africa.[29] It is generally the case that these supposedly "self-governing" territories are economically nonviable such
that the bulk of the people living there are forced to eke out a mea-
ger existence with minimal state aid, while a "lucky" few are able to
secure low-paying jobs in the service or manufacturing industries in
need of unskilled labor. With these models in mind, Cox was of the
opinion that a pivotal tenet of black nationalism—the acceptance
of racial separation— "conforms to the historic wishes of the southern oligarchy who have constantly insisted that Negroes in the United
States ought to live in their own societal enclaves."[30] Moreover, Cox
felt that the black nationalist "idea of . . . constituting the territory
of a nation from the multiplicity of black urban enclaves . . . con-
tributes . . . to the perpetuation of ghettos," by its "abandon[ment]"
of the "idea of the ghetto as a temporary social situation similar to
that experienced by other unacculturated immigrant groups."[31] And
to the likely black nationalist counterclaim that black people's stay
in the ghetto has neither been temporary nor is it similar to that of
white ethnic immigrants, Cox would have responded that, as bad as
current conditions in the ghettos are, they would indeed be worse
if ghettos were governed by black nationalists. What we have here are
competing visions of American society and consequently conflicting
assessments of *realpolitik*. Where black nationalists felt that Cox subscribed to the view that "there is nothing of value in the black community and that little value could be created among black people,"[32]
Cox thought the goals of black nationalists impracticable.

A third reason for Cox's low opinion of black nationalism stems
from his belief that it is an inappropriate political philosophy as
much for the American bipartite situation of race relations as it is
for the Caribbean ruling-class situation of race relations. In other
words, I am suggesting that when Cox critiqued the expression of
black nationalism in the United States he may have frequently had
the demographic context of the Caribbean foremost in mind. This
point requires some elaboration.

As we may recall from an earlier chapter, when other socioeconomic variables are constant, the variable that separates ruling-class

from bipartite situations of race relations in the Americas is the historical and current size of the European settler population in its polities: in the first case it is negligible, and in the second it is substantial. Given, then, the small number of people of European descent
in ruling-class situations of race relations, it is easy to envision (as I
believe Cox did) the gradual entry of those populations traditionally deemed ineligible for consideration into positions of social prestige. In other words, the inability of the white elite to reproduce itself in sufficient numbers to occupy all the coveted economic and
political positions of power inevitably required the recruitment of
social subordinates with relatively little political fanfare.[33] In short,
assimilation is not merely possible in a ruling-class situation of race
relations, but over time it is socially necessary.

Moreover, this admission of token numbers of social subordinates into select prestigious posts necessarily undermines the racist
position that people of any visible African (or Amerindian) descent
are categorically inferior. By virtue of the limited assimilation of
some people of color, nearly everyone who lives in a ruling-class
situation of race relations recognizes, either consciously or unconsciously, that within the racial categories of "black" or "brown" are
found representatives of a relatively wide range of class identifica-
tions. Thus, the variability of pigmentation in a number of class categories in ruling-class situations defies the relatively neat correspondence between "race" (narrowly defined) and class that typifies race
relations in, for example, the bipartite situation. In the ruling-class
situation context, then, appeals to racial nationalism can only receive limited support; racial lines are often too blurry. It was with
this reasoning in mind that Cox once remarked that only in the
United States could Marcus Garvey's black nationalist movement
have been a mass movement, for the "racial situation in his native
country, Jamaica, could not have been approached in this way."[34]

Conversely, in bipartite situations of race relations where, as Cox
maintained, there exist substantial white populations and where
comparatively absolute definitions of racial membership obtain and
are enforced, those white populations are able to occupy virtually all
the positions of social prestige to the near exclusion of nonwhites.
Under these conditions, even the token assimilation of racial subordinates into "mainstream" society is typically perceived by Whites as
entailing the displacement of some of their numbers. Therefore, if

racism is just as hard (if not harder) to mitigate as classism in any capitalist social formation, then in a bipartite situation of race relations in particular, the token assimilation of individuals from the most subordinate "race" is clearly the exception and not the rule. It seems, then, that when taken to their logical conclusion, Cox's sociological findings on race relations (as opposed to his political pronouncements) suggest that the "complete" assimilation of black and other American racial minorities into American society must await the era when the white American population becomes a mere fraction of the national total or, in other words, similar in number to that found in ruling-class situations of race relations. Cox may have had this in mind all along.

Although large enough to make race relations in the United States bipartite according to Cox's typology, the black American population is too small a percentage of the country's total in order for it to serve as an independent political force. This was Cox's fourth objection to black nationalism: not only is it an erroneous social philosophy but, more important, it seeks to make into a political force a minority whose numbers are insufficient for the role. His critique of black nationalism on this score was unyielding. "An imperishable ecological fact of [American] race relations," he declared in his final opus, "is that the Negro population will remain approximately one-tenth of the total." Consequently, "[I]n the United States, it seems clear, Negroes may participate to advantage in the larger movement for social change but they cannot realistically hope to lead it."[35] This political reality based on long-standing demographic patterns is nothing new in this country, as Cox was sure to underscore in his survey of black leaders and their ideologies, "Leadership Among Negroes in the United States." For another "imperishable" fact, to borrow Cox's strong adjective, is that virtually all political movements in this country whose primary goal has been the improvement of the lives of black people have counted white activists in their ranks. From the abolitionists to the missionaries "who followed the Federal armies into the South and began the systematic education of the Negroes," during Reconstruction to the birth of the NAACP to the Civil Rights Movement, "white men [and women] have been outstanding leaders in the Negroes' struggle for political freedom."[36] From this indisputable fact, Cox drew two conclusions: one, that "in the United States racial conflict has never been between white people and black people as such; rather it has been between a particular class of white people and Negroes virtually as a whole;" and two, that the "common cause of Negroes in the United States is not fundamentally limited to Negroes. It is in fact an aspect of the wider phenomenon of political-class antagonism inseparably associated with capitalist culture. A principle involved in the process of democratic development is at the basis of the Negro's cause; and for this reason leadership among Negroes is likely to be as effectively white as black."[37] To the degree, then, that black nationalists were unwilling or unable to come to terms with these two propositions because they insisted on viewing the world through the prism of race membership rather than through political-class stance, Cox had no sympathy for their cause.

Cox's critique of black nationalism was ultimately grounded in his belief that socialism is attainable in the capitalist leader nations through the collective upward mobility of historically excluded groups. Though Cox provided few clues about the practical workings of this process, the implicit idea is that as a capitalist leader nation is forced to accommodate larger numbers of middle-class entrants, that society will necessarily adopt more socialist measures (presumably to ensure the fair employment of those who have been historically discriminated against) such as greater state direction of the economy and a wider distribution of capitalist income. Moreover, as we stated at the outset of this chapter, it was Cox's contention that capitalist values such as discipline and thrift would increasingly be used to further socialist objectives in this transitional period.

The Middle-Class Road to Socialism

It must be said at the outset of this discussion of Cox's "middle-class road" to socialism in the capitalist leader nations that the likelihood of its fruition is highly remote given two of his other contentions: one, that the most lucrative economic relationships in the capitalist world economy are those between leader and backward nations; and two, that in light of the "impossibility for backward countries to develop along the historic lines of the leading capitalist nations," more of them will increasingly opt to "withdraw from the [capitalist] system."[38] Taken together, these propositions suggest that over time both the volume of earnings in capitalist leader nations and the related size of their middle classes will contract. Under these circumstances, a likely response of a representative middle class would be to heighten the barriers of entry to the institutions to which it owes its life: universities and professional schools. It could achieve this objective by employing one of two methods or both: the raising of academic standards for entrance into these institutions or raising tuition costs. In short, in trying economic times we would expect to see the middle classes of leader capitalist nations abandon any pretense of liberalism and embrace the most selfish characteristics of their lives: competitiveness and snobbishness. It seems almost unnecessary to state that periods of economic contraction are hardly promising circumstances for those populations which have historically been excluded from the middle class to make bids to gain entry into its ranks.

Assuming, nonetheless, for the sake of Cox's argument, that both profits and the size of the middle classes are expanding in capitalist leader nations, we must still consider the attitudes of the middle class toward newcomers, for Cox appears to assume that the reception, if not warm, will neither be prohibitively hostile. One way of gaining insight into middle-class reactions to new entrants is to explore its own modern entrance into American society.

In light of their structural position between a miniscule elite and the mass of industrial and service workers, it is not surprising that representatives of the American middle class are typically both arrogant and insecure. The first because, like the "power elite," to borrow C. Wright Mills' designation of that exclusive population, they are prone to believe that their station in life is largely due to their own, individual efforts; the second because, unlike the power elite, they lack the income that would make work voluntary and a few bad investments inconsequential. We must be sure, however, not to exaggerate the extent of middle-class economic insecurity, for their members possess a collective blanket that their counterparts in surrounding classes need not or do not possess: university and professional school degrees. The rise of the requirement of higher educational certificates for entry into the ranks of the middle class dates from the birth of the large, multidepartmental corporation in the wake of the Civil War. Between 1870 and 1920, in industry as well as in the professions, university degrees or, simply put, professionalization, "was presented as a reform, a bold new measure aimed at replacing guesswork and tradition with science and rationality." However, professionalization was more than merely the generation, collection, or application of "scientific" knowledge in a variety of fields, it was also the "carving out [of] . . . occupational monopol[ies] restricted to the elite minority who could afford college educations and graduate degrees."[39]

Thus, unlike the power elite who owns capital and workers who create it, middle class "capital" is "knowledge and skill, or at least the credentials imputing skill and knowledge." In Barbara Ehrenreich's words, the collective self-conception of the middle class can be summed up like this: "We know more, and are therefore entitled to positions of privilege and authority."[40] A self-conception based as this one is on the supposed monopoly of intelligence lends itself to the vigilant guarding of its gates. Nor is it unreasonable to assume, as I suggested earlier, that arrogance and insecurity are virtually inherent character traits of the middle-class personality. With that said, we can now return to our original question: how do members of the American middle class receive new entrants from populations whom they have traditionally excluded?

Recent studies on the social experiences of middle-class Blacks have found that they have encountered consistent resistance from their white counterparts with regard to their right to hold white-collar positions. In both surveys and interviews, significant numbers of middle-class Blacks have maintained that "race worked to their disadvantage when it came to ratings, pay, assignments, recognition, performance, appraisals, and promotion." Contrary to what we might expect "[t]hey consistently report more encounters with racial prejudice and voice stronger reservations about the country's success at delivering on the American dream" than poor Blacks.[41] Apart from the role of competitiveness in the middle-class world, the resentment of black middle-class newcomers appears to be due, in the main, to two interrelated beliefs: that Blacks are fundamentally intellectually inferior to Whites (for genetic or cultural reasons) yet have "force[d] themselves into places and positions where they were not wanted or for which they lacked the competence."[42] The first of these beliefs we can call the thesis that middle-class Blacks are an undeserving middle class; and the second, a simple *status quo ante* argument.

One of the factors that distinguishes the structural position of the black middle class before and after the emergence of the civil rights movement pivots on politics. The black middle class of the first half of the twentieth century and earlier was a kind of "second string" middle class. Unlike its white counterpart, in its ranks were included many blue collar and service workers. This was so because, in many respects, the class system of black Americans was based on what white Americans felt themselves too good to do. Thus, at this juncture, the status of middle-class black Americans derived from a combination of racism, custom, and paternalism, not from the enjoyment of political-economic rights. These could only be won by mass political action and it was the aim of some of the federal programs that the civil rights movement catalyzed to make the class structure of black America approximate that of white America. However, because this still-incomplete objective grew out of political struggles (as it had to), it is considered by many Whites, regardless of class identification, extortionist. For their bedrock belief is that one's class standing should be the result of one's individual effort, not of special political measures. By this overriding logic, sympathy for those who historically have been denied access to middle-class positions for no other reason than special political considerations could only be but sparing and short-lived on the part of its current holders and rival aspirants. It is hardly surprising, then, that the objectives of affirmative action (to name but one federal initiative designed to correct today past policies of exclusion) are habitually under attack.

What can be termed the conservation of custom is, I believe, the second most important factor shaping white middle-class attitudes toward black newcomers. What is and has been customary in this regard is that self-identifying white people have been and continue to be the overwhelming majority of the middle class. As a result of this long-standing monopolization, it has become natural for many Whites to believe that their racial kith and kin are the rightful occupiers of middle-class positions. Speaking in more general terms, Robin M. Williams Jr. described this phenomenon like this:

> Whenever a number of persons within a society have enjoyed
> for a considerable period of time certain opportunities for get-

ting wealth, for exercising power and authority, and for successfully claiming prestige and social deference, there is a strong tendency for these people to feel that these benefits are theirs "by right." The advantages come to be thought of as normal, proper, customary, as sanctioned by time, precedent and social consensus. Proposals to change the existing situation arouse reactions of "moral indignation." Elaborate doctrines are developed to show the inevitability and rightness of the existing scheme of things.[43]

Where, then, does this leave the prospects of the middle-class road to socialism? Clearly at an impasse. For if there is successful resistance to the admission of new entrants on the part of current middle-class status holders then not only will the class structure of the capitalist leader nation remain unchanged, but so too the promise of the transition to socialism. That Cox did not entertain this possibility in writing is perhaps due to the fact that after *Brown v. Board of Education* he sincerely expected the federal government to remain committed to the provision of equality of opportunity for all, in most spheres of public life, until equality of outcome between Blacks and Whites is achieved (measured, presumably, by the racial composition of the middle class as a percentage of respective population totals). Sadly, much of American politics in the post–civil rights movement era can be understood as white American resistance to the advancement of Blacks and other people of color into the ranks of the middle class. All the same, for Cox to have advised fellow black Americans to aspire to middle-class status without taking into account the potential reaction of that class's current membership to that goal was a glaring omission, to say the least.

Before turning to Cox's alternative road to socialism, however, it might be of interest to compare his views on black nationalism with those of fellow countryman, C. L. R. James.

Cox vs. James

For a number of reasons—among which are their common place of birth, year of birth, and political leanings—it is worthwhile to

compare Cox's position on the black power movement to that of
C. L. R. James. Unlike Cox, who in James's words in the late 1960s
thought it "some racist eruption from the depths of black oppression and black backwardness," James conceived it as "represent[ing]
the high peak of thought on the Negro question which has been
going on for over half a century."[44] Why the difference of opinion?
Perhaps the foremost reason is that James took a Leninist approach
to struggles outside the labor movement, which, in the case of black
America, enabled him to discern that "American Negroes in fighting for their democratic rights were making an indispensable addition to the struggle for socialism in the U.S."[45] This was a summation
of a formulation that James had first made as early as 1939,[46] and
further refined in a 1948 document entitled, "The Revolutionary
Answer to the Negro Problem in the USA." In that position paper
he persuasively demonstrated that throughout American history,
the independent political activities of black people for social justice
have either "stimulated" or abetted the movement of larger progressive forces in that society, only to be betrayed by them. For these
reasons, James put forward the following propositions as those that
should guide, in this case, the Socialist Workers Party's approach to
the "Negro question," as it was then called:

> We say, number one, that the Negro struggle, the indepen-
> dent Negro struggle, has a vitality and a validity of its own; that
> it has deep historic roots in the past of America and in pres-
> ent struggles; it has an organic political perspective, along
> which it is travelling, to one degree or another, and everything
> shows that at the present time it is travelling with great speed
> and vigor.
>
> We say, number two, that this independent Negro move-
> ment is able to intervene with terrific force upon the general
> social and political life of the nation, despite the fact that it is
> waged under the banner of democratic rights and is not led
> necessarily either by the organized labor movement or the
> Marxist party.
>
> We say, number three, and this is most important, that it is
> able to exercise a powerful influence upon the revolutionary
> proletariat, that it has got a great contribution to make to the

development of the proletariat in the United States, and that
it is in itself a constituent part of the struggle for socialism.[47]

In short, James's position on independent black political movements
was the same in the 1940s as it was in the 1960s.

For all his intellectual genius and political insight, Cox refused
to conceive of independent black struggles for social justice as acting as catalysts of broader social transformation in the societies in
which they occur. We have already reviewed the many reasons why
he came to this conclusion. Nevertheless, Cox did name the specific types of social movements that he thought most promising of
social transformation both within particular societies and on a global scale.

Social Movements of Promise

In order to address this matter, we must recall Cox's understanding
of the structure of the capitalist world economy. As he conceived it,
"the wealth of a leading capitalist nation is not entirely, or sometimes even mainly, accumulated from the exploitation of domestic
workers," but is "based significantly on economic relations with backward countries."[48] Cox advanced two related propositions from this
assertion: one, that "[I]n leading capitalist nations . . . workers tend
to become participants in foreign exploitation;" and two, that the
"backward peoples are the real exploited and exploitable proletariat
of the system."[49] More important, however, than even these structural observations were the political ideologies to which Cox maintained the working classes of the two types of nations adhered. In
the first case, he posited:

> The working class in a leading nation . . . has sufficient reason
> to walk arm in arm with its oligarchy against the world. On im-
> perialistic questions, we should ordinarily expect this class to
> be nationalistic, because a threat to the imperial position of
> the nation tends to become a threat to its own welfare. The class
> struggle thus goes on at home . . . for a larger share of the na-
> tional income. But it is a struggle that tends to stop at the water's

edge where antagonisms with rival imperialists and exploited backward peoples begin. The working people of a leading capitalist nation are likely to rise up in wrath against those of their fellows who disclaim the imperialist actions of the government, regarding them as traitors.[50]

In short, on the whole, the working classes of leading capitalist nations are reformist, not revolutionary, and as such, will remain, along with their employers, imperialistic in outlook and in business practices. Conversely, the working classes of what Cox calls the "backward" nations of the capitalist world economy tend to be revolutionary—i.e., socialist—because unlike their wealthier counterparts, "they have no valuable exploitative claims abroad to relinquish." Consequently, the "social situation in the major backward countries is such that revolution is not only indicated, but also feasible and largely profitable. Hence revolutionary solidarity seems far more easily attainable among them. Their successes will bring not only a change in the economic orientation and organization of the advanced capitalist nations, but also a new perspective on the benefits of planned economies to workers everywhere."[51]

In the ultimate sentence of the above passage, we see that Cox took a Leninist position when it came to working-class movements in the former colonial world and underscored their ability to encourage similar movements elsewhere, including those in the leading capitalist nations themselves. The relationship was not unidirectional. Though limited in scale and frequently reformist, movements for social change in the leading capitalist nations can be beneficial to their equivalents in the backward nations:

Although the social situation in leading nations tends to limit developments conducive to radical societal change, it would be a mistake to underestimate the importance of radical movements in these countries. The continuing general dissatisfaction with the morality and operation of capitalism, the attempt to find ways out by Utopian or by realistic socialists, the unrest of anarchists, and the parliamentary struggle of the common people for increments of democracy have reduced capitalist freedom of action at home and abroad. This movement provided not only an ideology, but also inspiration and encour-

agement for defiance of the imperialists by the subjected countries. Its existence, moreover, frequently helped to buy critical
time for revolutionaries in those countries to consolidate socialist gains.[52]

Summarizing his position, Cox remarked that the "two movements . . . in the backward economies and in leader nations, thus
supplement each other."[53]

Still, I do not believe that Cox provided convincing reasons why
he could not see fit to include black nationalist movements in the
United States with other status quo-challenging initiatives in leading
capitalist nations, although they too could have encouraged revolutionary movements in the "backward" nations. In any event, in light
of the fact that Cox maintained that it was in these developing countries where socialism is most likely to emerge, it is to that subject
that we should now turn.

Socialism in Practice

As I have stated throughout this study, Cox had surprisingly little
to say about the actual practice of socialism in any one of the then
numerous countries whose leaders labeled themselves socialist. Surprising, because it would only seem logical that his ideal would warrant serious, intellectual investigation. However, fear of what he
might have found in the endeavor may explain Cox's evasion of a
close study of socialism in practice. Then, too, it is more comforting
to criticize certain systems, institutions, and ideologies with alterna-
tives in mind (if not, in fact) than without them. In any event, in addition to being uncharacteristically terse on the subject, the little that
Cox said about socialist society was equally wanting. For example,
in discussing the social requirements for establishing a socialist society, he stated that there are no more than six: "A viable socialist
society demands a relatively large, sophisticated governmental bureaucracy, a tractable military establishment, at least a nest egg of
native scientists and technicians, a certain critical size of population
and quantity of resources, and a people capable of being inspired
and motivated to endure privation and to labor unremittingly for a
millennium which they may never live to enjoy."[54]

Although we have no reason to assume that the order of his list is not also the order of priority that he assigned each of these requirements, based on what he wrote elsewhere on the same subject, it appears that the fourth and fifth—a large population and an array of natural resources—were the ones on which all the others pivoted. In fact, such was the importance of these two variables that in his contribution to *Monthly Review* on the occasion of the twenty-fifth anniversary of the publication, he counseled "small states" not to follow the example of a Cuba, but to content themselves with the "limited growth and development" under colonial or neocolonial political-economic arrangements unless or until they become part of larger, regional socialist entities. In the same article he went on to add that the "areas intended for socialist growth must be large enough to make the use of science and technology in production self-generative."[55] Thus, on the subject of socialism's "take-off," Cox felt that size matters.

Cox neither quantified nor specified the population or natural resources necessary for the successful institutionalization of a socialist regime. Nevertheless, I think it safe to assume that, in the first instance, he had in mind a figure sufficient to encourage occupational differentiation or specialization,[56] and in the second, the presence, in adequate quantity, of fuel and of metal ores to form the basis of heavy industry. Although he never mentioned it, industrial developments such as these require corresponding changes in agriculture, particularly in the way of productivity increases. "For if productivity were not increasing faster than demand," observed W. Arthur Lewis, "agriculture would not be releasing the labor which was needed for expanding other industries," and the "increase in the cost of living which, by raising wages, would make it hard for the new manufacturing enterprises to pay their way."[57] Joseph Stalin's measure to increase agricultural productivity and to fund industrialization through savings on food costs was collectivization, or, as he benignly described it, the "transformation of small and scattered peasants' plots into large consolidated farms based on the joint cultivation of land using new superior techniques."[58]

Here is not the place to recount the story of Soviet collectivization in the 1930s which is richly chronicled elsewhere. Our concern is rather to know if Cox endorsed the Soviet model of industrialization. If he did, then it suggests that he was willing to compromise

democratic and racial/ethnic equality for the promise of a particular economic agenda.[59] It should be clear that this is a serious charge
since it was precisely these social achievements for which Cox lauded
the former Soviet Union. However, taking up these points, I would
like to say more about the implications of collectivization for the
socialist model of economic development.

As we will recall from chapter 4, Cox took Marx to task for having
made two claims: one, that the primary profit-generating relationship in the capitalist world economy is that between the owners of
the means of production and the proletariat in the leader nations;
and two, that as a result of its key position in the capitalist system, the
metropolitan proletariat will pioneer the societal transition to socialism. Cox's countercontention was that the larger portion of capitalist profits is drawn from the economic relationship between capitalists in the leader nations and the proletariat of the "backward"
areas and that, as a consequence, socialist revolutions are more likely
to take place in those backward areas than in capitalist leader nations. However, these plausible propositions complicate the prospects
for socialism in developing countries.

If, as Cox contends, socialist society requires the development of
"self-initiating technological and scientific growth,"[60] and if socialist
revolutions are most prone to happen in former colonial countries,
then the pressing question for the revolutionary leaders of these
countries is how to industrialize without colonies or neocolonies. Or
to rephrase the question: the state undertaking the socialist challenge must decide which segment of its domestic population it will
super-exploit in order to accumulate capital for industrialization.
The choices are ostensibly limited in countries characterized by huge
agricultural populations, miniscule industrial sectors, and equally
puny commercial classes. Yet, independent of the social composition
of the backward country in question, for most Marxists, the choice is
simple: given that they consider the industrial working class the basis
of the socialist revolution but are aware that backward countries lack
heavy industries, they naturally look to the agricultural sector to
finance industrialization. Thus, Stalin's decision to collectivize may
have been madness, but there was a method to it.

However, neither Marx nor Cox either seriously considered or
came to terms with the political-economic dilemmas of socialist
revolutions in largely nonindustrialized countries: Marx, because he

posited that the proletariat of the capitalist leader nations would spearhead the socialist transformation; and Cox, because he implicitly imagined socialist industrialization taking place in "backward" countries without recourse to the subjection of a sector of the population to assume the role of internal colony in that process.[61] Of the two sins of omission, I believe Cox's is greater. Not only did he fail to apply his own theory of capital accumulation to developing countries undertaking socialist projects, but he also avoided the related issue that, on the domestic front, these countries of necessity imitated the capitalist methods of economic exploitation to which they had hitherto been subjected as colonies or neo-colonies.[62] These omissions lead me to believe that he implicitly justified Stalin's political-economic prerogatives as the necessary courses of action for the achievement of industrialization in a backward country, the material and social basis of socialism. Having briefly considered the rationale behind socialist industrial strategy, we can now turn our attention to that strategy's effects on democracy and racial/ethnic relations in socialist society.

It hardly seems necessary to state that an economic development program such as this one per force compromises political democracy. Cox himself indirectly admitted as much when in *Race Relations* he ceased to vaunt socialism as the only authentic democratic political system, as he had in *Caste, Class, and Race*, concentrating instead in the later work on socialism's economic prospects.[63] But this type of intellectual evasion of the total social meaning of socialism not only abets, but ultimately, justifies the pseudo-dichotomy between political and economic socialism which, among other consequences, allows socialist leaders to suppress political participation while claiming that they do so in order to create the material foundations of socialist democracy. On the self-serving nature of this type of reasoning, Joseph Schumpeter commented, "it is obvious that any argument in favor of shelving democracy for the transitional period affords an excellent opportunity to evade all responsibility for it. Such provisional arrangements may well last for a century or more and means are available for a ruling group installed by a victorious revolution to prolong them indefinitely or to adopt the forms of democracy without substance."[64]

In short, there exists the strong possibility in societies that have undergone socialist revolutions that bureaucrats rather than work-

ers will govern in the short, intermediate, and long terms. Consequently, although nominally founded in the name of the industrial
working class, socialist governments are not beyond mandating the
adoption of management practices in industry even more competitive and coercive than those used in capitalist leader nations to increase productivity. Thus, it is not surprising to learn that Soviet
workers were paid "piece-rate" wages and that the Soviet government
enacted laws "providing sanctions against absenteeism, lateness, un-
authorized job mobility, and other breaches of labor discipline."[65]
Clearly, it is more likely that bureaucrats, rather than industrial workers, were the main proponents of these laws.

Socialist planners driven by the single-minded pursuit of industrialization would similarly find ethnic nationalism intolerable for
at least two reasons: it could mean the establishment of competing
centers of political-cultural power outside of the national capital's
jurisdiction; and it could overlay state-worker and management-
worker relations with an ethnic dimension which could prove potentially explosive. It appears, then, that when crash industrialization is the socialist state's explicit economic goal, the assimilation of
ethnic minorities is the implicit orientation of socialist social policy.
From our previous discussion of Cox's endorsement of assimilation
of racial minorities even in capitalist society, we know that socialist
policy on the "nationalities" question was certainly to his liking.

Assimilation, however, implies the presence of a dominant population or culture. Although this process is not necessarily a politically charged issue in capitalist society, it certainly is one in socialist
society for two reasons. First, it undermines the professed philosophy
of socialism which is equality in most, if not all, spheres of social life,
including a society's cultural life. Second, when the dominant ethnic
population is the same one that was dominant during the noncapitalist and capitalist eras, minority populations may interpret that
dominance as an uninterrupted historical pattern of imperialism,
regardless of the state's professed commitment to socialism.

However, the tension between socialist theory and practice on
matters of ethnic/racial equality only becomes problematic when
political muscle reveals it as such; without that force, the socialist
state, like the liberal capitalist state, can ignore its theoretical claim
of nondiscrimination on the basis of race or ethnicity while proceed-
ing to privilege particular ethnic/racial populations over others. In

a socialist society where the state bureaucracy both legislates and directs the economy, one crude measure of the degree to which particular ethnic populations are socially privileged is the percentage of posts held by representatives of those ethnicities. For example, in Stalin's Soviet Union and after, Great Russians were undoubtedly a privileged population in the state's governing bodies, in spite of the fact that Stalin himself was Georgian.[66] Great Russian numerical dominance in the state bureaucracy can be justified on the grounds that this population was the largest of all the nationalities;[67] that within its prerevolution borders were located the administrative capital and leading industrial centers; and that as a result of these two factors, the Russian language became the official language of the Soviet state. But these realities were hardly comforting to the other ethnic groups. In any event, Cox took on face value socialist theory on ethnic minorities and opted, therefore, not to test its practice by focusing his attention on the ethnic composition of the sites of socialist political power. We now know only too well the ethnic cauldron that only the Kremlin was able to contain.

As we saw in chapter 3, apart from fearing that other ethnic or racial minorities would benefit from a pluralist political program more than Blacks, Cox's reasons for rejecting black nationalism as a viable political project were ultimately based on a more revolutionary logic. Short of that, he rejected black nationalism on the grounds that it was an inappropriate platform in a bipartite situation of race relations where black Americans are already a small minority and where it can be manipulated by conservatives to further marginalize politically, economically, and socially those areas where poor Blacks and other people of color live. These immediate and practical reasons for denouncing black nationalism were more convincing than his final one: that it is a disservice to what I have termed his middle-class road to socialism. Like many of Cox's claims about socialist society, this theory of capitalist society's transition to socialism was short on empirical verification and blind to likely social obstacles, particularly those facing racial minorities as they seek to become members of their national middle class. Cox was on safer ground when he proceeded from the position that socialist revolutions are more likely to occur in "backward" than in leader capitalist nations. Nevertheless, as we have seen in the case of one of these larger nations whose leadership called itself socialist—the former Soviet Union—the goal of rapid industrialization led to the abandonment of the supposed socialist commitment to democracy as well as to ethnic/racial equality, the very political achievements with which Cox had credited socialist society.

Concluding Remarks

My greatest hope for this study is that the reader takes from it an appreciation and an admiration for a man whom I consider one of the most important thinkers of the twentieth century. In many respects, writing with that goal in mind has been the least difficult task; the sheer volume and breadth of Cox's work speaks for itself. Nevertheless, these characteristics of Cox's work are the very things that make writing about him so daunting; they demand of the student of his work a familiarity with a variety of subjects and schools of thought. Suffice it to say that to engage in work on Cox is a learning experience in itself.

And apart from even those intellectual requirements is the no less important one of grappling with his political positions. As I have remarked throughout this study, Cox wrote his politics into his social observations and theories. Consequently, the student of his work is forced to wonder if, where, and when he wrote as an undeclared policy maker in addition to social observer. I have raised this point in a number of places: as an aspect of his criticisms of both the caste school of race relations and of ethnic/racial nationalism in capitalist leader nations; as well as in his claims about the supposed cultural characteristics of Jews. Of course, it is probably a futile exercise to attempt to separate the two, for the case can be made that all social theorists engage simultaneously in observation and prescription. Still, it is a dimension of Cox's work to consider.

Another mixed blessing of Cox's work is the unyielding logic that guides it. As we saw in the cases of his critiques of the caste school of race relations and of capitalist definitions of freedom, Cox could devastate his opponents by demonstrating with consummate analytical skill the speciousness of their arguments. On the other hand, this same insistence on intellectual consistency from his opponents often came back to haunt him. For example, though a staunch supporter of the former Soviet Union's brand of socialism, he, like the caste theorists he took to task, never undertook a study of his "control" society. Similarly, he refused to concede to black nationalists that his own writings (particularly his description of the bipartite situation of race relations) supported some of their political positions.

Some of this impatience with inconsistency on the part of others I attribute to a feature of Cox's life: work in isolation. This should not be confused with the solitude that is a necessity of all academic work. Rather, I am referring to Cox's professional isolation. As we know, he spent virtually his entire academic career in small colleges and universities well removed from major urban centers. This relative isolation encouraged his intellectual independence, but it did not afford him the benefit of immediate feedback from colleagues working on related themes; even less as the years passed. Similarly, Cox's retreat from life with an intimate or intimates after (I am assuming) the onset of polio, deprived him of the opportunities to "sound out" his ideas with his partner and children. Such a forum of intimates, I believe, may have tempered some of his rigid formalism and added a palpably empathic element to his work, particularly on black nationalism.

Finally, I would like to conclude these brief remarks with another word on Cox's intellectual independence. I attribute most of it to his birth and rearing outside of the United States. That his "home" happened to be the Caribbean is important only to the degree that it provided Cox with a basis of comparison by which to isolate the key variables of the two themes that most preoccupied him: race relations and capitalism. As I said at the outset of this study, Cox was a "natural born" comparativist. Frankly, I see no other convincing way of explaining his marked departure from then mainstream understandings of either the social bases of race relations or the origins and reproduction of the capitalist world economy than by taking into account his Caribbean background. Still, whatever the exact proportions of Cox's intellectual inspirations, I believe they are the wellsprings of a truly pan–African American scholar. For this reason, as well as for a host of others, his reflections on some of the most pressing social problems of our time deserve the widest audience.

Notes

Introduction

1. For example, the late Guyanese scholar, Walter Rodney, mistakenly identified Cox as "African-American" in his classic *How Europe Underdeveloped Africa* (Washington, D.C: Howard University Press, 1982), 90.

2. See Oliver C. Cox, "Marxism: Looking Backward and Forward," *Monthly Review* 26 (June 1974): 53. One of those who considered Cox a Marxist, Paul M. Sweezy, long-time editor of *Monthly Review,* provided the most convincing reasons for doing so: "Was Oliver Cox, a Marxist? There is no right or wrong answer. Once again, I can only give my own: Yes, he certainly was a Marxist. He made no effort to minimize or disguise his intellectual debt to Marx. He thought like a Marxist. The revolutionary conclusions to which his work led, even if not always explicitly spelled out, were basically the same as Marx's. This last point for me is the decisive one. If I had my way, I would deny the honorific title of Marxist to anyone who denies or repudiates the rock-bottom revolutionary content of Marx's thought. By this standard, Oliver Cox clearly qualifies as a Marxist. If he often felt it necessary to deny that he was a Marxist, this was because what most

American social scientists, not to mention the public at large, understand by Marxism was (and unfortunately still remains) a vicious caricature of the real thing." "Foreword" to *Race, Class, and the World System: The Sociology of Oliver C. Cox,* ed. Herbert M. Hunter and Sameer Y. Abraham (New York: Monthly Review Press, 1987), xi.

3. Ernest Mandel, e.g., thought Cox a historian. See his *Late Capitalism* (London: Verso, 1978), 49.

4. In making this claim, I run the risk of denying the efforts of the pioneering Cox scholar, Herbert M. Hunter. My many references to his work should make it clear that this is the farthest intention from my mind; anyone who writes about Cox owes something to Herb Hunter. I refer the reader to his doctoral dissertation and to his numerous essays on Cox: "The Life and Work of Oliver C. Cox" Ph.D. diss., Department of Sociology, Boston University, 1981); "Oliver C. Cox: A Biographical Sketch of His Life and Work," *Phylon* 44, 4 (1983); "The World-System Theory of Oliver C. Cox," *Monthly Review* 37, 5 (October 1985); with Sameer Y. Abraham, "Introduction" to *Race, Class, and the World System;* and "The Political Economic Thought of Oliver C. Cox," in *A Different Vision: African American Economic Thought,* vol. 1, ed. Thomas D. Boston (London: Routledge, 1997), 270–89.

5. Some of the most notable works by C. L. R. James are: *The Life of Captain Cipriani: An Account of the British Government in the West Indies* (Nelson: Coulton, 1932); *The Black Jacobins: Toussaint L'Ouverture and the San Domingo Revolution* (New York: Vintage, 1989); *A History of Pan-African Revolt* (Chicago: Charles H. Kerr, 1995); *American Civilization* (Oxford: Blackwell, 1993); *Beyond a Boundary* (Durham, N.C.: Duke University Press, 1993); *The C. L. R. James Reader,* ed. Anna Grimshaw (Oxford: Blackwell, 1992); *C. L. R. James and Revolutionary Marxism: Selected Writings of C. L. R. James, 1939–1949,* ed. Scott McLemee and Paul Le Blanc (Atlantic Highlands, N.J.: Humanities Press, 1994); and *C. L. R. James on the "Negro Question,"* ed. Scott McLemee, (Jackson: University of Mississippi Press, 1996). Among the most relevant recent books about his life and thought are: Kent Worcester, *C. L. R. James: A Political Biography* (Albany, N.Y.: SUNY Press, 1996); Grant Farred, ed., *Rethinking C. L. R. James* (Cambridge: Blackwell, 1996); Selwyn Cudjoe and William E. Cain, eds., *C. L. R. James: His Intellectual Legacies,* (Amherst: University of Massachusetts Press, 1995); and Paget Henry and Paul Buhle, eds., *C. L. R. James' Caribbean,* (Durham, N.C.: Duke University Press, 1992). George Padmore's best known works are: *The Life and Struggles of Negro Toilers* (Hollywood, Calif.: Sun Dance Press, 1971); *How Britain Rules Africa* (New York: Negro Universities Press, 1969); *Africa and World Peace* (London: Frank Cass, 1972); and *Pan-Africanism or Communism* (Garden City, N.Y.:

Doubleday Anchor, 1972). To date, there remains only one biography of Padmore: James Hooker, *Black Revolutionary: George Padmore's Path from Communism to Pan-Africanism* (New York: Praeger, 1967).

Chapter 1.   The Molding of a Mind

1. Arno J. Mayer, *The Persistence of the Old Regime: Europe to the Great War* (New York: Pantheon, 1981), 84.

2. Walter Russell Mead, *Mortal Splendor: The American Empire in Transition* (Boston: Houghton Mifflin, 1987), 32.

3. Walter Rodney, *How Europe Underdeveloped Africa* (Washington, D.C.: Howard University Press, 1982), 89.

4. Hunter, "Life and Work of Oliver C. Cox," 15, 16.

5. Ibid., 16. In the context both of general Trinidadian and Cox's personal history, the family "estate" in Tabaquite was significant for at least three reasons: one, greater Montserrat, within whose boundaries Tabaquite is located, was one of the regions where Governor A. H. Gordon (1866–70) made Crown lands available to landless Trinidadians for the reasonable price of "£1 per acre" for a "minimum lot of 5 acres" in defiance of the island's sugar planters who wished to continue denying Trinidad's rural poor the means to leave plantation work; two, cocoa, the export of which superseded that of sugar by the turn of the century, was initially cultivated on small farms by "Creoles, peons, Africans, British West Indian immigrants and, from the 1870s, Indians," before these plots were consolidated by French Trinidadian planters; and three, the region was home to a far larger number of Trinidadians of East Indian descent than was the capital itself: some 8,000 versus 2,500 in 1911. As far as this last point is concerned, it seems fair to surmise that Cox's first contacts with Trinidad's East Indian community (about which we will have more to say in chapter 3) occurred in Tabaquite. On the first two points, see Bridget Brereton, *A History of Modern Trinidad, 1783–1962* (Oxford: Heinemann, 1981), 89, 90, and on the last, Walton Look Lai, *Indentured Labor, Caribbean Sugar: Chinese and Indian Migrants to the British West Indies, 1838–1918* (Baltimore: Johns Hopkins University Press, 1993), 280.

6. Hunter, "Life and Work of Oliver C. Cox," 16.

7. Interview with Aldwin Vidale, Petel Valley, Trinidad, 19 May 1978, as cited in Hunter, "Life and Work of Oliver C. Cox," 17.

8. Hunter, "Life and Work of Oliver C. Cox," 18.

9. Brereton, *History of Modern Trinidad,* 205, and Eric Williams, *History of the People of Trinidad and Tobago* (London: Andre Deutsch, 1964), 152.

10. Brereton, *History of Modern Trinidad*, 93, 201.

11. Bridget Brereton, *Race Relations in Colonial Trinidad, 1870–1900* (Cambridge: Cambridge University Press, 1979), 146.

12. Hooker, *Black Revolutionary*, 3.

13. The presentation and teaching of history could, of course, raise these thorny issues if particular care was not taken to separate, for example, Roman imperialism from that practiced by England.

14. See Eric Williams, *Inward Hunger: The Education of a Prime Minister* (Chicago: University of Chicago Press, 1971), 11–25.

15. Brereton, *History of Modern Trinidad*, 136.

16. Brereton, *Race Relations in Colonial Trinidad*, 78.

17. Williams, *Inward Hunger*, 23.

18. Bridget Brereton, "The Development of an Identity: The Black Middle Class of Trinidad in the Later Nineteenth Century," in *Caribbean Freedom: Economy and Society from Emancipation to the Present*, ed. Hilary Beckles and Verene Shepherd (Princeton: Markus Weiner, 1996), 274.

19. Brereton, *Race Relations in Colonial Trinidad*, 94.

20. James, *Beyond a Boundary*, 17.

21. Brereton, "Development of an Identity," 275.

22. Worcester, *C. L. R. James*, 11.

23. See C. L. R. James, "George Padmore: Black Marxist Revolutionary," in *At the Rendezvous of Victory: Selected Writings* (London: Allison & Busby, 1984), 251–63, 252 (quotation).

24. Brereton, "Development of an Identity," 275.

25. Gordon K. Lewis, *The Growth of the Modern West Indies* (New York: Monthly Review Press, 1968), 20.

26. Oliver C. Cox, *Caste, Class, and Race: A Study in Social Dynamics* (New York: Monthly Review Press, 1970), 361.

27. James, *Life of Captain Cipriani*, 15.

28. Winston James, *Holding Aloft the Banner of Ethiopia: Caribbean Radicalism in Early Twentieth-Century America* (London: Verso, 1998), 358, table 1.3.

29. Hunter, "Life and Work of Oliver C. Cox," 19.

30. James R. Grossman, *Land of Hope: Chicago, Black Southerners, and the Great Migration* (Chicago: University of Chicago Press, 1989),123, 127.

31. Allan H. Spear, *Black Chicago: The Making of a Negro Ghetto, 1890–1920* (Chicago: University of Chicago Press, 1967), 130.

32. Anywhere from 15% to 25% higher than what Whites paid for comparable housing. See William M. Tuttle Jr., *Race Riot: Chicago in the Red Summer of 1919* (Urbana: University of Illinois Press, 1996), 164.

33. Ibid., 162, 168, 164.

34. See Oliver C. Cox, *Race Relations: Elements and Social Dynamics* (Detroit: Wayne State University Press, 1976), 129, 148, 150.

35. As a result of white prejudice against black people at this point in time and its concrete denial of socioeconomic opportunities to them, the "Negro class structure," to borrow the words of Allan H. Spear, "[did] not always correspond with the white class structure. The Negro upper class, for instance, include[d] professional people, whose white counterparts [were] usually considered middle class. At the same time, postal clerks, Pullman porters, waiters, and other occupational groups that would belong to the upper lower class among whites ha[d] traditionally formed the core of the Negro middle class." Spear, *Black Chicago*, 23 n. 29.

36. Cox, *Race Relations*, 129.

37. Cox, *Caste, Class, and Race*, 427.

38. Cox, *Race Relations*, 133.

39. It was then called the Hyde Park Improvement Protective Club. See Spear, *Black Chicago*, 22.

40. Ibid., 23.

41. Tuttle, *Race Riot*, 159, 182. Tuttle later adds that as soon as restrictive covenants were employed (circa 1925) to maintain or to create residential segregation, the bombings were no longer necessary.

42. Ibid., 174. Tuttle provides circumstantial evidence that points to Hyde Park–Kenwood Property Owners' Association complicity in the bombings: "Whether or not the realtors of the Hyde Park–Kenwood Association conspired to bomb out the blacks, two facts were evident: that the bombings usually occurred shortly after the speakers at the association's meetings had denounced the blacks in vitriolic language (four bombs succeeded the organization's May 5 meeting); and that these denunciations were becoming decidedly more vitriolic in the summer of 1919" (p. 179).

43. Ibid., 178.

44. I have in mind what Cox approvingly wrote in his introduction to Nathan Hare's *Black Anglo-Saxons:* "In our dynamic culture, a minority of upper-middle and upper-class persons sets the norms and style of life which the great majority of the population copies and assimilates. These leaders of taste and practice are inevitably the leaders of Negroes as well. The latter's attitudes regarding occupational ideals or standards of consumption are similarly determined." Oliver C. Cox, "Introduction" to Nathan Hare, *The Black Anglo-Saxons* (New York: Marzani & Munsell, 1965), 11.

45. This is a theme that Elmer P. Martin underscores in his essay, "The Teaching Mission of Dr. Oliver C. Cox," in *The Sociology of Oliver C. Cox: New Perspectives,* ed. Herbert M. Hunter, 21–40 (Stamford, Conn.: JAI Press, 2000).

46. Grossman, *Land of Hope*, 129.

47. By and large, black Chicagoans who had settled in the city before the Great Migration were from the Upper South and border states. See Grossman, *Land of Hope*, 150.

48. Grossman, *Land of Hope,* 140, 144.

49. As cited in ibid., 145–46.

50. St. Clair Drake and Horace R. Cayton, *Black Metropolis: A Study of Negro Life in a Northern City* (New York: Harcourt, Brace, 1945), 562. As this reply [to the question of why "lower-class" people behave in the ways that they do] suggests, lower-class comportment in the eyes of many elite, middle class, and even working-class Blacks, was not defined by class position alone. "Rowdy or indecorous behavior in public," remarked Drake and Cayton, "seemed to be the one trait that in these expressions emerged most consistently as an index to lower-class status. Lower-class people are those who give free rein to their emotions, whether worshiping or fighting, who 'don't know how to act,' or dress correctly, or spend money wisely" (562–63).

51. Cox, *Race Relations,* 57.

52. W. E. B. DuBois, *The Autobiography of W. E. B. DuBois: A Soliloquy on Viewing My Life from the Last Decade of Its First Century* (New York: International Publishers, 1968), 80.

53. Oliver C. Cox, "Leadership Among Negroes in the United States," in *Studies in Leadership,* ed. Alvin W. Gouldner (New York: Harper & Bros., 1950), 228–71.

54. The most thorough treatment to date of West Indian involvement in black American radical politics is offered by Winston James, *Holding Aloft the Banner of Ethiopia.*

55. Hunter, "Life and Work of Oliver C. Cox," 20.

56. As cited in Harold Cruse, *The Crisis of the Negro Intellectual: From Its Origins to the Present Crisis* (New York: William Morrow, 1967), 121.

57. David Levering Lewis, *When Harlem Was in Vogue* (New York: Oxford University Press, 1989), 41.

58. The figures for Great Britain were drawn from Peter Fryer, *Staying Power: Black People in Britain Since 1504* (Atlantic Highlands: Humanities Press, 1984), 296, and A. J. P. Taylor, *English History, 1914–1945* (London: Oxford University Press, 1965), 164. Those for the United States were taken from Stuart Bruchey, *Enterprise: The Dynamic Economy of a Free People* (Cambridge: Harvard University Press, 1990), 264, and Lewis, *When Harlem was in Vogue,* 8.

59. For the disturbing details of these unprovoked assaults, see Fryer, *Staying Power,* 298–316.

60. James, *Holding Aloft the Banner of Ethiopia,* 52.

61. Taylor, *English History,* 120.

62. Fryer, *Staying Power,* 296.

63. Among others, see James, *Holding Aloft the Banner of Ethiopia,* 52–66.

64. Ibid., 64.

65. Tony Martin, "Marcus Garvey and Trinidad, 1912–1947," in *The Pan-African Connection: From Slavery to Garvey and Beyond* (Dover, Mass.: Majority Press, 1983), 76.

66. Cox, "Leadership Among Negroes in the United States," 263.

67. Cox gave 5905 Indiana Avenue as the return address in his 27 December 1931 letter to the dean of Northwestern University's School of Law, John Henry Wigmore. Northwestern University Archives. John H. Wigmore Papers (Series 17/20: General and Subject Correspondence Files, box 40, folder 9). I would like to thank Northwestern University archivist, Kevin B. Leonard, for finding and sending copies of this letter to me.

68. Cox recorded 2824 Walnut Street as the return address in his 3 January 1931 correspondence to Dean Wigmore.

69. Hunter has Cox graduating from high school in 1923 and attending Lewis Institute from 1923 to 1925 for an associate's degree. The "Northwestern University Bulletin: Annual Catalog, 1927–1928" also names Lewis Institute as one of the institutions that Cox attended, but it neither mentions the years nor the degree taken. However, according to Cox's "Personal Data Sheet for Teaching, Counseling, and Administrative Personnel" for Wayne State University, which I have no reason to doubt that he filled out himself, he graduated from Central YMCA in 1924 but never attended Lewis Institute.

70. I would like to thank Patricia Bartkowski, archivist at the Walter P. Reuther Library, Wayne State University, for sending me a copy of this document.

71. It is conceivable that Cox attended Lewis Institute for a stenographer's license.

72. He did not specify which art classes he took. However, the fruits of these classes, his own talent, and his practice of this craft can be seen in five of his originals in the Cole Library of Wiley College that Cox left to the school. I would like to thank librarian, Syd Myers, for bringing these Cox paintings to my attention.

73. Hunter, "Life and Work of Oliver C. Cox," 21.

74. In some respects, what I imagine to have been Cox's response to his illness parallels the black belt's response to the depression, at least as Horace Cayton saw it: "All the city suffered from the depression, but the black belt suffered more and differently. The first reaction was panic and a deep sense of frustration, followed by spontaneous, unorganized demonstrations. . . . Finally the community began to form some semblance of an organization to meet the impending crisis." Horace R. Cayton, *Long Old Road* (New York: Trident Press, 1965), 181.

75. Northwestern University Archives, John H. Wigmore Papers (Series 17/20: General and Subject Correspondence Files, box 40, folder 9).

76. Though Cox was awarded his master's degree in economics in 1932, he had completed his course work for the degree in the fall semester of 1931. The chronology suggest that he had some idea of his master's thesis topic in the course of 1931. Oliver C. Cox, "Workingmen's Compensation in the U.S., With Critical Observations and Suggestions" (Master's thesis, Department of Economics, University of Chicago, June 1932).

77. Hunter, "Life and Work of Oliver C. Cox," 23.

78. It is noteworthy that in his 10 August 1970 Personal Data Sheet for Teaching, Counseling, and Administrative Personnel Cox listed Millis as his second "Educational Reference." The first was Wigmore, and the third Ernest W. Burgess of the University of Chicago's sociology department.

79. Hunter, "Life and Work of Oliver C. Cox," 21–22.

80. Paul A. Samuelson, "Jacob Viner," in *Remembering the University of Chicago: Teachers, Scientists, and Scholars,* ed. Edward Shils (Chicago: University of Chicago Press, 1991), 538.

81. Hunter, "Life and Work of Oliver C. Cox," 22. For a perceptive discussion of Cox's comparative historical method, see Richard Williams' contribution, "O.C. Cox and the Historical Method," in Hunter, *Sociology of Oliver C. Cox,* 85–115.

82. Elmer P. Martin, "The Sociology of Oliver C. Cox: A Systematic Inquiry" (Master's thesis, Department of Sociology, Atlanta University, May 1971), 12, as cited in Hunter, "Life and Work of Oliver C. Cox," 23.

83. John Kenneth Galbraith, *American Capitalism: The Concept of Countervailing Power* (Boston: Houghton & Mifflin, 1956), 22.

84. Hunter, "Life and Work of Oliver C. Cox," 24.

85. William H. McNeill, *Hutchins' University: A Memoir of the University of Chicago, 1929–1950* (Chicago: University of Chicago Press, 1991), 46.

86. Ibid., 64.

87. See Cox, *Caste, Class, and Race,* 264–66.

88. In his letter dated 27 December 1931 from 5905 Indiana Avenue to Dean John Wigmore of Northwestern University's School of Law, Cox remarked that "[s]o far I must still use canes, but I am much more confident now than when I started just one year ago. I feel quite well, too, for the experience. When I started I had to take a taxi cab back and forth; now, however, I walk to the bus with comparative ease—yes, sometimes I walk to school, which is about twelve or fifteen blocks from my home." Northwestern University Archives, John H. Wigmore Papers, Series 17/20, box 40, folder 9.

89. Rick Halpern reports that "[I]n 1931 over 40 percent of [Chicago's] workforce was jobless, and those fortunate to have work found their hours drastically reduced." In the black belt, the number of unemployed was higher

than the city average—45 percent—"and certain sectors of the first and second wards reported a staggering jobless rate of 85 percent." Halpern adds that "[a]lthough the black population comprised only 7.7 percent of the [city's] population, black families accounted for over 30 percent of those on relief." Rick Halpern, *Down on the Killing Floor: Black and White Workers in Chicago's Packinghouses, 1904–1954* (Urbana: University of Illinois Press, 1997), 98, 105.

90. There is some dispute over whom or which organization(s) initiated the formation of Chicago's Unemployed Council, the Communist Party or independent grassroots activists. Horace R. Cayton was of the opinion that it was a spontaneous movement that was "eventually taken over by the Communists." Conversely, Harry Haywood contended that it was "[l]ed by communists." See Horace R. Cayton, *Long Old Road* (New York: Trident Press, 1965), 180, and Harry Haywood, *Black Bolsheviks: Autobiography of an Afro-American Communist* (Chicago: Liberator Press, 1978), 442.

91. See Halpern, *Down on the Killing Floor,* 109.

92. On this matter, too, there is some difference of opinion. Halpern suggests that the Communist Party was supportive of the campaign, but Cayton stated that it was critically against it. See Halpern, *Down on the Killing Floor,* 107–8 and Cayton, *Long Old Road,* 181. Cox's own investigation into the campaign (written originally in 1932 and revised though never published in the 1960s) led him to the conclusion that the American Communist Party was "not particularly enthusiastic about the movement." Conversely, he found that the Socialist Party of America was. "The Origins of Direct Action Protest among Negroes," microfiche copy, Kent State University Library, Kent, Ohio, 145.

93. Morton G. Wenger has addressed this theme in his "Are There Weberian Answers to the Puzzle of Oliver C. Cox's Marxism? A Theoretical Realignment and Its Analytical Consequences," in Hunter, *The Sociology of Oliver C. Cox,* 139–53.

94. It is conceivable that Cox began questioning the "caste school" of southern race relations while a graduate student, basing his objections on the fact that the manner in which his professors, fellow graduate students, and black belt denizens described southern race relations differed greatly from how he understood the Indian caste system as it had been reconstituted in the Trinidad of his youth. However, in the absence of documentation to support this hypothesis, I prefer to assume that Cox could only seriously call into question the caste school of southern race relations after having lived in the South himself, which was precisely when his first criticisms of the school appeared in print.

95. Cox, *Caste, Class, and Race,* 29.

96. *Gesammelte Aufsätze zur Religionssoziologie,* 3 vols. (Tubingen: J. C. B. Mohr [Paul Siebeck], 1920–21). Cox named this collection, among other Weber studies, in the bibliography of *Caste, Class, and Race.* See Max Weber, *Economy and Society: An Outline of Interpretive Sociology,* eds. Guenther Roth and Claus Wittich (Berkeley: University of California Press, 1978), xxv–xxviii.

97. Anthony M. Platt, *E. Franklin Frazier Reconsidered* (New Brunswick, N.J.: Rutgers University Press, 1991), 87.

98. Hare, *Black Anglo-Saxons.*

99. Cox, "Introduction," *Black Anglo-Saxons,* 11–12.

100. According to Frazier's widow, Marie Brown Frazier, Park frequently told Frazier that "[w]henever I want a damn good fight, I know right where to come." Platt, *E. Franklin Frazier Reconsidered,* 90, 166.

101. According to Frazier's biographer, Anthony M. Platt, more than professional strategy separated Frazier from Cox: "Throughout his life— and his years in Chicago were not an exception—Frazier was both fiercely independent and open to new ideas. He was not an original theorist, and he willingly drew on analytical constructs from an eclectic group of theorists. This flexibility was both a strength and a weakness in Frazier's intellectual development. On the one hand, he was not a dogmatist; he found and used ideas from several disciplines (especially sociology, history, psychology, and social work), even learning from people with whom he had profound political disagreements. On the other hand, he had difficulty speaking with a unique theoretical voice and, unlike DuBois and Oliver Cox, did not leave his distinctive mark on sociological theory." Platt, *E. Franklin Frazer Reconsidered,* 90.

102. Cox, *Caste, Class, and Race,* 262. However, a couple of pages earlier, Cox made the following remarks, indicating that he was not entirely certain of Roosevelt's ideological position on what he considered the "democratic" movement of the 1930s: "Apparently Roosevelt subconsciously feared the consequences of an achieved democracy. What he said and did contributed greatly to the final winding up of capitalism; but, like a true reformer, he sincerely believed that his mission was only to make the existing system work more felicitously." Then, contrary to these comments, Cox went on to say: "To be sure, he had little opportunity to become a proletarian dictator in the United States. He was probably more advanced in his thinking than any controlling member of his party or Cabinet, and the people as a whole had too little political education to support him effectively. Indeed, the great tragedy of Roosevelt's time is that it found him with a nation badly prepared intellectually for his plans of action in the interest of a democratic society. There was difficulty even in finding 'socially minded' personnel for the New Deal. He had to lead a people who emotionally and physically wanted economic democracy but who, at

the same time, had only a confused understanding of it. They were ide-ologically enslaved by a worshipful reliance upon the idea of the social indispensability of 'free busines enterprise,' and conditioned by capitalist propaganda to a mortal dread of 'communism.' Thus, in the very act of reducing the power of the bourgeoisie, Roosevelt had to pay lip service to his allegiance to the welfare of capitalism. And now that Roosevelt is gone it is as if the people do not know what he really stood for; they wish for him, for leadership of his type, but they have, on the whole, no ideologi-cal foundation sufficient to create a clear-cut demand" (260–61). By these words, Cox apparently wanted to suggest that had the American work-ing class been both more radical and more ideologically anticapitalist during the 1930s, Roosevelt would have been the American Lenin. Suf-fice it to say that most scholars of the era would find this interpretation groundless.

103. Cox, *Caste, Class, and Race*, 254 ff., 28.

104. Franklin Delano Roosevelt, address delivered at the Democratic state convention, Syracuse, 29 September 1936, as cited in Cox, *Caste, Class, and Race*, 264.

105. Richard Hofstadter, *The American Political Tradition and the Men Who Made It*, (New York: Vintage, 1973), 455.

106. Ibid., 440.

107. Cox, *Caste, Class, and Race*, 262 n. 43a.

108. See Steven J. Rosenthal, "Oliver C. Cox's Analysis of Fascism in *Caste, Class, and Race*," in Hunter, *Sociology of Oliver C. Cox*, 212–14.

109. See Cox, *Caste, Class, and Race*, xxxii–xxxv.

110. Ibid., xxxiii.

111. Elmer P. Martin maintains that there was undoubtedly a connec-tion between Cox's admiration for Roosevelt and their common disease and writes that "there is no doubt in my mind that he not only saw Presi-dent Roosevelt as a great symbol of democracy, but also as a role-model because Roosevelt also suffered from poliomyelitis. Roosevelt's ability to rise to the presidency despite his debilitating physical condition no doubt inspired Cox to cope with his own physical disability and become the great scholar he did." "Teaching Mission of Dr. Oliver C. Cox," 30.

112. Perhaps, as the following passage suggests, Cox believed that Roosevelt's record on aid to American workers generally more than com-pensated for his lack of specific concern for the civil rights of black Americans: "[W]ithout any considerable attention to the 'Negro prob-lem' particularly, President Franklin D. Roosevelt undoubtedly did more to elevate the status of Negroes in the United States than all other lead-ers, white and black together, over a period of decades before him." *Caste, Class, and Race*, 582.

113. Earl Ofari Hutchinson, *Betrayed: A History of Presidential Failure to Protect Black Lives* (Boulder, Colo.: Westview Press, 1996), 50, 38.

114. Hutchinson notes with due sarcasm that when Roosevelt first spoke out publicly against lynching, he "was not specifically talking about the lynching of black men . . . [but] [r]ather, Roosevelt was angry at California's Republican governor, James Rolph, who stupidly congratulated members of a mob 'for making a good job of it' after they had lynched two white men." Hutchinson, *Betrayed*, 32.

115. For details, see Harvard Sitkoff, *A New Deal for Blacks: The Emergence of Civil Rights as a National Issue: The Depression Decade* (New York: Oxford University Press, 1978), 34–57, quotation 45, 42. Or, even more cynically, attributing the president's silence to the fact that since Blacks voted overwhelmingly Republican in the 1932 presidential election, they could not make any claims on Roosevelt until 1936, when the majority of black Americans voted Democrat in that presidential election, marking the exodus from the "party of Lincoln."

116. John Salmond, "Aubrey Williams Remembers: A Note on Franklin D. Roosevelt's Attitude Toward Negro Rights," *Alabama Review*, 25 (January 1972): 68–69, as cited in Sitkoff, *New Deal for Blacks*, 45–46.

117. Cox, *Caste, Class, and Race*, 254.

118. On the broader and deeper meaning of democracy, Cox had this to say: "The mere fact of universal suffrage and representative institutions, however, need not indicate the exact extent to which democracy has attained maturity. To the extent that the questions put to the people concern the welfare of capitalism, to that extent also the ballot is not in the service of the proletariat . . . The focus of interest of democracy is in the well-being of the masses, and this interest cannot be made dependent upon the success or pleasure of businessmen" (*Caste, Class, and Race*, 226).

119. Cox, *Caste, Class, and Race*, 224.

120. Ibid., 225, 227.

121. Ibid., 232.

122. Ibid., 238.

123. Ibid., 239.

124. Ibid., 238. On this theme of personhood in a true or "attained" democracy, Cox added: "Democracy tends to confer upon every individual a priceless sense of being a recognized part of a supremely vital organization. By this means alone the individual is able to form a positive conception of himself as a responsible social object" (238–39).

125. Ibid., 239.

126. François Furet, *The Passing of an Illusion: The Idea of Communism in the Twentieth Century* (Chicago: University of Chicago Press, 1999), 273.

127. Cox, *Caste, Class, and Race*, 236.

128. Ibid., 243.

129. Furet, *Passing of an Illusion*, 233.

130. Cox, *Caste, Class, and Race*, 223. To his credit, nevertheless, Cox did note a page earlier that "modern democracy has not yet fully emerged in any part of the world."

131. Furet, *Passing of an Illusion*, 223–24.

132. Cox never quite made up his mind on the relationship between fascist and bourgeois capitalism. On the one hand, he stated that the fascism was a "degenerate" (*Caste, Class, and Race*, 198) form of the capitalism; on the other, he seemed to think of it as the ultimate form of capitalism. In other words, Cox never made it clear if fascism emerges when capitalism is at its weakest or strongest point. The best-known fascist cases—those of Italy, Germany, and Spain—point toward the first condition. For a discussion of this ambiguity in Marxist theory and its disastrous effects on Communist Party politics in the late 1920s and early 1930s, see Nicos Poulantzas, *Fascism and Dictatorship: The Third International and the Problem of Fascism* (London: Verso, 1979), 36–54.

133. Here, for example, is how he distinguished (and defended) fascist dictatorship from the dictatorship of the proletariat: "It should be emphasized that the distinguishing fact about fascist governments is not that they are dictatorships. There is a popular belief, sometimes purposely indoctrinated, that all dictatorships subsume an identity of economic organization. Nothing, however, is farther from the truth. When a people is at war, a degree of dictatorship becomes imperative, and the greater the intensity of the conflict, the more complete the dictatorship is likely to become. . . . Hence the presence of a dictatorship does not necessarily indicate the form of social organization. The proletarian government of Russia, for instance, is a dictatorship; all fascist governments are also dictatorships, but these two types of economic organization lie at opposite extremes of modern social systems." Cox, *Caste, Class, and Race*, 191.

134. Cox, *Caste, Class, and Race*, 189, 188, 192–97.

135. Denis Mack Smith, *Mussolini: A Biography* (New York: Vintage, 1983), 1. Smith warns, nevertheless, that "like Hitler," Mussolini "exaggerated in retrospect the privations of his youth. There were plenty of books in the house and his parents could afford domestic help. They had land from which they made their own wine, and the food—if simple—was abundant. The boys were able to remain at school until they were eighteen, something that must have been quite exceptional in such a neighborhood" (p. 2).

136. William L. Shirer, *The Rise and Fall of the Third Reich: A History of Nazi Germany* (New York: Simon & Schuster, 1960), 6.

137. Stanley G. Payne, *El Regimen de Franco, 1936–1975* (Madrid: Alianza Editorial, 1987), 79–80.

138. See Cox, *Caste, Class, and Race,* 192.

139. Eric Hobsbawm, *The Age of Extremes: A History of the World, 1914–1991* (New York: Vintage, 1996), 117.

140. Ibid., 129.

141. On this point, Peter Duignan and L. H. Gann tellingly note that "Hitler's conservative allies understood as little about the realities of power as his Marxist opponents. The industrialists could not control the monster they had helped to create. Once Hitler was firmly in office, he was free from control by any specific class. The workers could not constrain him — but neither could the capitalists. For instance, once in power Hitler increased corporate taxes, and enforced a sweeping reduction of interest on mortgages, municipal and Reich bonds. He introduced strict controls on wages, prices, and foreign currency transactions. Titled profiteers, such as Hermann Goering, learned the art of transmuting political control over the means of production into ownership of the means of production; thus they built for their own benefit great state enterprises that spread their control over the whole of Europe, with interests in steel, arms of every kind, oil, machinery, transport equipment, and so on." Peter Duignan and L. H. Gann, *The Rebirth of the West: The Americanization of the Democratic World, 1945–1958* (Cambridge: Blackwell, 1992), 145–46.

142. For an insightful discussion of the elements of aristocratic thought, I strongly recommend the fifth chapter of Mayer's *Persistence of the Old Regime.* For the constituents of fascism, see the first chapter of Stanley G. Payne's *Fascism: Comparison and Definition* (Madison: University of Wisconsin Press, 1980).

143. The most noteworthy finding in Cox's dissertation is that "[a]mong Negro women gainful employment is a very significant factor [in marital status]. Negro women are more highly employed than any other population class in the United States, and the difference is most evident among married women. Whereas the relationship of employment and marriage for native white women is negative, it is positive for Negro women. Negro women seem to go into gainful employment after marriage faster than they are withdrawn, a fact which is probably true for no other racial or nationality group in the United States." Oliver C. Cox, "Factors Affecting the Marital Status of Negroes in the United States" (Ph.D. diss., Department of Sociology, University of Chicago, 1938), 10.

144. Actually, before accepting the position at Wiley, Cox taught for five months in 1937 at Louisville Municipal College in Louisville, Kentucky. This appears on his "Personal Data Sheet For Teaching, Counseling, And Administrative Personnel," dated 10 August 1970 for his post at Wayne State University.

145. Oliver C. Cox, "Provisions for Graduate Education Among Ne-groes," *Journal of Negro Education* 9 (January 1940): 22–31; "Farm Tenancy and Marital Status," *Social Forces* 19 (October 1940): 81–84; "Sex Ratio and Marital Status Among Negroes," *American Sociological Review* 5 (December 1940): 937–47; "Marital Status and Employment of Women," *Sociology and Social Research* 25 (December 1940): 157–65; "Sex Ratio and Marriage in Rural Communities," *Rural Sociology* 5 (June 1940): 222–27; and "Employ-ment, Education, and Marriage," *Journal of Negro Education* 10 (January 1941): 39–42.

146. Oliver C. Cox, "The Modern Caste School of Race Relations," *Social Forces* 21 (December 1942): 218–26.

147. Richard Williams suggests that Cox's critique of the caste school developed after graduate school. See his, "O.C. Cox and the Historical Method," 107–8.

148. Cox, *Caste, Class, and Race*, xvi.

149. V.O. Key Jr. and Alexander Heard, *Southern Politics in State and Na-tion* (New York: Alfred A. Knopf, 1950), 9.

150. As Key and Heard explained, East Texas, home to both the majority of the state's black residents and Wiley College, was not black belt country for several reasons: "East Texas is no solid bloc of counties with high proportions of Negroes. The area of Negro residence is broken up by numerous counties in which blacks are outnumbered by whites more than three to one. More-over, the usual black-belt economy of multiple-unit plantation agriculture has been diluted by other forms of economic activity. The odor from oil re-fineries settles over the cotton fields and makes scarcely perceptible the mag-nolia scent of the Old South. Further, the settlement of West Texas, largely since 1900, created a huge territory with few Negroes and thereby reduced the significance in the state as a whole of those counties immediately and in-tensely concerned with the race question. In addition, the urbanization of the state, which by 1940 had made it the second most urban southern state, has had its effects on attitudes towards the Negro. By 1940, too, the state's population was only 14.4 per cent Negro (compared with 11.7 per cent Mexican-American in 1930), and the black belt, such as it was, had come to be overshadowed politically." Key and Heard, *Southern Politics*, 260.

151. See Cox, *Caste, Class, and Race*, 342–44; "The New Crisis in Leader-ship Among Negroes," *Journal of Negro Education* 19 (fall 1950): 459–65; "Leadership Among Negroes in the United States," 235–39; and "The Lead-ership of Booker T. Washington," *Social Forces* 30 (October 1951): 91–97.

152. And intellectual philanthropy as well. I have in mind Robert Park's relationship with Booker T. Washington between 1905 and 1912, some years before his first academic appointment. During that period, Park, in

the words of Washinton biographer, Louis R. Harlan, "researched, drafted, or revised most of Washington's writings for publication . . . including his principal magazine articles and even many of his letters, particularly to foreigners. More importantly, Park took the book manuscripts that other ghostwriters had bungled and brought them into more sophisticated condition, while retaining the distinctive Washingtonian plainness of style." Louis R. Harlan, *Booker T. Washington: The Wizard of Tuskegee, 1901–1915* (New York: Oxford University Press, 1986), 291. Of the many relationships that Cox found intolerable, that of a black person's dependence on the ideas of white men ranked high on his list. Furthermore, in Cox's mind, this relationship would have directly implicated Park in Washington's conservative agenda. Consequently, I cannot help but wonder to what degree Cox's interest in Tuskegee was stimulated by the desire both to see for himself and to test Park's ideas on southern race relations in the milieu where he largely formed them, even some forty years afterward. Perhaps Cox felt, on some level, that he needed to "know" Tuskegee before he could really call into question the ideas of Park et al. at the University of Chicago.

153. Cox, "Leadership of Booker T. Washington," 93. Later in the same article, Cox questioned the wisdom in calling Washington a black "leader": "He was not a leader of the masses in the Garvian sense; his function was rather that of controlling the masses. He deflated and abandoned their common cause. He demanded less for the Negro people than that which the ruling class had already conceded. And because he was in reality sent with a mission to subdue the spirit of protest in the masses instead of his arising among them as a champion of their cause, he was frequently insulting and 'harsh' toward them" (95).

154. Note Cayton's musings while meeting with then Tuskegee president Robert Russa Moten to request permission to leave the school before the end of his contract: "Did Robert Russa Moten realize that the Tuskegee dream had died perhaps even before Mr. Washington, that the experiment had been doomed by history? The industrialization and urbanization of the South left no room for the hard-working small farmer, black or white, and the boom in mass production industries had made obsolete the black craftsmen the institute was turning out. Was Moten aware that he had inherited a monument erected on a sinking foundation? Or did he feel that it was only that he himself had failed to measure up to the standards and achievements of Washington?" Cayton, *Long Old Road*, 204.

155. In two senses: one, that, because of the chronic underfunding of the education of black children generally at the state and county levels throughout the South, many entering Tuskegee undergraduates were ill-prepared for college-level work; and two, that Cox was the "only person in

the School of Education to have a Ph.D. in any of the social sciences."
Hunter, "Life and Work of Oliver C. Cox," 30.

156. Most of Cox's articles published between 1944 and 1947 became
chapters of *Caste, Class, and Race.*

157. These articles originally appeared as: "Racial Theories of Robert E.
Park, et al.," *Journal of Negro Education* 13 (fall 1944): 452–63; "Class and
Caste," *Journal of Negro Education* 13 (spring 1944): 139–49; "Race, Prejudice,
and Intolerance," *Social Forces* 24 (fall 1945): 216–19; "Race and Caste: A
Definition and a Distinction," *American Journal of Sociology* 50 (March 1945):
360–68; "Lynchings and the Status Quo," *Journal of Negro Education* 14
(spring 1945): 576–88; "An American Dilemma," *Journal of Negro Education*
14 (spring 1945): 132–48; "Estates, Social Classes, and Political Classes,"
American Sociological Review 10 (August 1945): 464–69; "The Nature of the
Anti-Asiatic Movement on the Pacific Coast," *Journal of Negro Education* 15
(fall 1946): 603–14; "The Nature of Race Relations: A Critique," *Journal of
Negro Education* 16 (fall 1947): 506–10; and "Modern Democracy and the
Class Struggle," *Journal of Negro Education* 16 (spring 1947): 155–64.

158. Hunter, "Life and Work of Oliver C. Cox," 31.

159. In writing about HUAC in *Caste, Class, and Race* (pp. 269–75), Cox
had all but guaranteed his academic blacklisting as he himself said was the
indirect effect of the committee's allegations against specific university professors: "The value of these witch hunts is to elicit a public denial of any com-
munistic tendencies on the part of the faculty and to condition it to shy away
from any investigation of vital social problems unless it is apparent that its conclusions will be in glorification or in resigned acceptance of the status quo.

"It is fairly certain that the social sciences, having experienced such
panic and warning, will thereafter tend toward scholastic ruminations and
statistical refinements of inconsequential details" (266). Again, in having
chosen not to pursue the above lines of investigation, Cox suffered the consequences of his political position.

160. Cox, *Caste, Class, and Race,* 574.

161. Elmer P. Martin notes that in eight of the ten book reviews that he
examined in the early 1970s, Cox was described by the authors as a Marxist.
See Martin, "Teaching Mission of Cox," 38.

162. For a critical analysis of the Fair Deal, see George Lipsitz, *Rainbow
at Midnight: Labor and Culture in the 1940s* (Urbana: University of Illinois
Press, 1994).

163. Cox, *Capitalism and American Leadership* (New York: Philosophical
Library, 1962), 186, 187–88, 189.

164. David Caute, *The Great Fear: The Anti-Communist Purge Under Truman
and Eisenhower* (New York: Simon & Schuster, 1978), 27.

165. This formulation is drawn from Gerald Horne's thesis that the federal government only promoted the civil rights of black Americans so as to deny the Communist Party the claim that it was the consistent advocate of black causes. The attempt to alter the historical record, however, required the abrogation of the civil liberties of communists and progressive liberals. These included, with some irony, their black members as well. See Gerald Horne, *Black Liberation/Red Scare: Ben Davis and the Communist Party* (Newark: University of Delaware Press, 1994). For his part, Cox noted that the foreign policy ideologies of the two political parties were transformed by Truman's actions in that domain: "What happened at this juncture was that, paradoxically, the Republican Party moved to the Left of the Democrats in the crucial political area: foreign policy. Moreover, it succeeded in keeping the Democrats pinned in that unenviable position; so much so indeed that the latter have since become recognized as champions of militarization and of high taxes for that purpose. Significantly, also, this inversion voided American politics of its vital issue, the question of the soundness of its foreign program. Since the leadership of the traditional opposition Party had succeeded, principally by its own post-Rooseveltian efforts, in checkmating itself at the Right of the Republicans, it could have no decisive argument with them. The leadership, furthermore, was safely kept on the sterile Right by periodic Republican charges that it is in sympathy with communism. In the political doldrums thus created, the policies of President Eisenhower came to symbolize 'constructive moderation.'" *Capitalism and American Leadership*, 201.

166. See Martin, "Teaching Mission of Cox," 30.

167. Monthly Review Press reissued the work in 1959 and has kept it in print ever since.

168. Martin, "Teaching Mission of Cox," 36.

169. Ibid., 35–36, for his former students' reflections on this theme.

170. Martin, "Teaching Mission of Cox," 22.

171. Personal communication of Dr. Frederick E. Smith with Elmer P. Martin, March 1997, as cited in Martin, "Teaching Mission of Cox," 22.

172. Martin, "Teaching Mission of Cox," 22.

173. Initially, Cox may not have had a choice in the matter since he "found it impossible to obtain suitable housing because of the city's [Jefferson City's] segregationist practices." Lorenzo J. Greene, Gary Kremer, and Antonio F. Holland, *Missouri's Black Heritage* (Columbia: University of Missouri Press, 1993), 162.

174. Oliver C. Cox, "New Crisis in Leadership," 459–65; "Leadership Among Negroes in the United States," in *Studies in Leadership*, ed. Alvin W. Gouldner (New York: Harper and Brothers, 1950), 228–71; "Leadership of Booker T. Washington," 91–97; "Vested Interests Involved in the In-

tegration of Schools for Negroes," *Journal of Negro Education* 20 (1951): 112–14; "The Program of Negro Civil Rights Organizations," *Journal of Negro Education* (summer 1951): 354–66; "The Medieval City: Its Relationship to Modern Culture," *Mid-West Journal* 7 (summer 1955): 165–75; and "The Preindustrial City Reconsidered," *Sociological Quarterly* 5 (spring 1964): 133–44.

175. The only indication that I have seen of Cox's intention of writing a history of capitalism in the 1950s was his 1950 travel itinerary. In the resume dated 27 February 1970 that Cox sent along with other material to Wayne State University, Cox reported that he had traveled to Venice, Rome, London, and Paris in 1950 for "scientific orientation." That resume is in the Collections of Archives of Labor and Urban Affairs at Wayne State University. I thank archivist Patricia Bartkowski for sending a copy of it to me.

176. Where Cox provided the most information on this theme (albeit in a dispassionate way) was in the preface of *The Foundations of Capitalism*: "The capitalist system is indubitably the most powerful and dynamic form of social organization ever created by man. And yet, it is currently undergoing such vital changes that an understanding of its nature becomes an immediate prerequisite to any meaningful interpretation of the subordinate though critical social issues involved. Major social problems of contemporary society are essentially problems of capitalism. There is available, however, surprisingly little transmissible knowledge about its characteristics." Then he specified a couple of themes that a study of the capitalism could clarify: "Suppose, for example, it becomes necessary to distinguish between the caste system and modern race relations and the conclusion was reached that race relations are a feature exclusively of capitalism, where can the student find a discussion of capitalism sufficiently definitive to verify this assertion? And if indeed we say that the business cycle has developed as a peculiar trait of the capitalist system, it would seem that an understanding of the nature of that system becomes a pre-condition to any full comprehension of cyclical movements. Repeated frustrations of efforts to find such support in existing materials partly led me to the present study." Oliver C. Cox, *The Foundations of Capitalism* (New York: Philosophical Library, 1959), 1. Ironically, Cox said little about either theme in the body of the study.

177. Paul M. Sweezy, "Foreword," in *Race, Class, and the World System: The Sociology of Oliver C. Cox*, x.

178. As I will have reason to mention again, Cox's reaction to the Black Power Movement was based, in part, on his rather rigid ideas on what is appropriate behavior for young adults. What, then, may have first been a matter of "home training," ultimately had political consequences.

179. Interview with Valentino Toppin, Jefferson City, Missouri, 9 March 1978, as cited in Hunter, "Life and Work of Oliver C. Cox," 45.

180. Martin, "Teaching Mission of Cox," 25. Some students were not above paying janitors to search out his examinations in Cox's apartment.

181. Hunter, "Life and Work of Oliver C. Cox," 45, 46.

182. See Martin, "Teaching Mission of Cox," 24, 28.

183. William L. Van DeBurg, for example, contends that the Black Power movement was first and foremost a cultural movement. See his *New Day in Babylon: The Black Power Movement and American Culture, 1965–1975* (Chicago: University of Chicago Press, 1992).

184. Elmer P. Martin makes a somewhat similar point in his "Teaching Mission of Cox," 38.

185. Oliver C. Cox, "The Question of Pluralism," *Race* 7 (April 1971): 386–99, and "Jewish Self-interest in Black Pluralism," *Sociological Quarterly* 14 (spring 1974): 183–98.

186. Martin, "Teaching Mission of Cox," 39.

187. See "Comments on Cox," *Sociological Quarterly* 16 (winter 1975): 131–34. Unfortunately, Cox had already died before these responses to his article appeared.

188. Cox, "Introduction" to Hare's *Black Anglo-Saxons,* 14 n. 1.

189. See, inter alia, Alec Nove, *The Soviet Economic System* (London: Unwin Hyman, 1987).

190. Hunter, "Life and Work of Oliver C. Cox," 51.

Chapter 2.   A Typology of Race Relations

1. See Cox, *Caste, Class, and Race,* 352–76.

2. Harmannus Hoetink also believes that five of Cox's situations of race relations are *phases* of the remaining two. I differ with him, however, on the choice of which situations of race relations are the dominant ones. See Harmannus Hoetink, *Slavery and Race Relations in the Americas: An Inquiry into Their Nature and Nexus* (New York: Harper & Row, 1973), 177. The first four named situations of race relations tend to be phases of the remaining three, and of these the last two are frequently products of the ruling-class and bipartite situation of race relations. It can be argued that Cox himself suggested as much when in a public address he reduced his seven situations of race relations to three: slavery, ruling-class, and bipartite. See Cox, "Patterns of Race Relations," 34–35.

3. Cox, *Caste, Class, and Race,* 320, 319.

4. Ibid., 319–20.

5. Ibid., 317.

6. Pierre van den Berghe estimated that in the social setting of what he termed the *paternalistic* type of race relations (roughly the equivalent of Cox's ruling-class situation of race relations), the "dominant group" should be no more than "ten per cent of the total population." See Pierre van den Berghe, *Race and Racism: A Comparative Perspective* (New York: John Wiley & Sons, 1967), 25. Recently, Peter Wade suggested the use of a similar social index to explain the foundations of race relations in the Americas. See his *Blackness and Race Mixture: The Dynamics of Racial Identity in Columbia* (Baltimore: Johns Hopkins University Press, 1993), 25–26. Curiously, Wade makes no reference here to the work of those scholars (including Cox's) which anticipated his own findings.

7. Cox described this population as "mainly sojourning rulers" for whom "[o]rdinarily 'home' is in Europe or America, and they seldom set their roots in the area." *Caste, Class, and Race,* 360. Hoetink counters (I believe, correctly) that "[I]n the British West Indies . . . there does exist a considerable group of native whites who consider Trinidad, Barbados, and Jamaica as their respective homelands." *Slavery and Race Relations in the Americas,* 176.

8. Cox, *Caste, Class, and Race,* 360.

9. Ibid., 360, 366.

10. Eric Williams, *History of the People of Trinidad and Tobago* (London: Andre Deutsch, 1964), 67–68.

11. Ralph Davis, *The Rise of the Atlantic Economies* (Ithaca, N.Y.: Cornell University Press, 1973), 126. The number of European Barbadians recorded here, however, should not lead us to believe that this figure represents their demographic peak in the seventeenth century. It was not. It is possible, for example, that in 1667 Barbados's total white population had attained the 30,000 mark. See Hilary McD. Beckles, *White Servitude and Black Slavery in Barbados, 1627–1715* (Knoxville: University of Tennessee Press, 1989), 18. While high mortality rates certainly took their share of white Barbadians in the seventeenth century, their lower numbers in subsequent decades were due in larger measure to flight to other Caribbean islands as the land monopolization that typically accompanied the extension and intensification of sugar production made it harder for them to secure plots in Barbados.

12. Jerome S. Handler and Arnold A. Sio, "Barbados," in *Neither Slave Nor Free: The Freedmen of African Descent in the Slave Societies of the New World,* ed. David W. Cohen and Jack P. Greene (Baltimore: Johns Hopkins University Press, 1972), 218.

13. Davis, *Rise of the Atlantic Economies,* 126.

14. Douglas Hall, "Jamaica," in Cohen and Greene, *Neither Slave Nor Free,* 194.

15. Alex Dupuy, *Haiti in the World Economy: Class, Race, and Underdevelopment Since 1700* (Boulder, Colo.: Westview, 1989), 21.

16. The expression is taken from the title that Eric Williams gave to the seventh chapter of his *History of the People of Trinidad and Tobago.*

17. This, too, was Williams's conclusion: "But Trinidad in 1833 was not a plantation society. Rather it was a society of small estates operated by a few slaves. . . . Eighty per cent of the slave owners in Trinidad in 1833 owned less than ten slaves each. One percent owned more than 100 slaves." Ibid., 84.

18. Ibid., 69.

19. Brereton, *History of Modern Trinidad,* 25.

20. James Millette, *Society and Politics in Colonial Trinidad* (London: Zed Books, 1985),16.

21. Ibid., 34.

22. Cox, *Caste, Class, and Race,* 360.

23. Ibid., 361–62.

24. Winston James underscores the same point for a different purpose. See *Holding Aloft the Banner of Ethiopia,* 110, 114.

25. Cox, *Caste, Class, and Race,* 380. It should be clear from this passage that in the debate over the primacy of consensus or conflict between social strata in Anglophone Caribbean society, Cox aligned himself with the consensus group. Years later, Cox would call into question the central tenet of the conflict group—pluralism—on the grounds that a term which was originally employed to describe twentieth-century colonial society in Southeast Asia, was later generalized to "conceive of virtually any cultural difference in social groups as a basis of pluralism." Oliver C. Cox, "The Question of Pluralism," *Race* 12, 4 (1971): 392. For the "classic" exposition of pluralism, see John S. Furnivall's, *Colonial Policy and Practice: A Comparative Study of Burma and Netherlands India* (London: Cambridge University Press 1948). For the "classic" application of the concept of pluralism to Anglophone Caribbean society, see M. G. Smith's articles collected in *The Plural Society in the British West Indies* (Berkeley: University of California Press, 1965).

26. Cox, *Caste, Class, and Race,* 368.

27. Even friendly critics of Cox's theory of race relations overlook this variable. See, for example, John Rex, "The Problem of the Sociology of Race Relations," in *Race, Colonialism, and the City* (London: Routledge & Kegan Paul, 1973), 196.

28. In time, this second-tier population may become the numerically dominant one and subsequently the new standard of social comparison.

29. Cox, *Caste, Class, and Race,* 363.

30. The smaller figure is Douglas H. Ubelaker's from his article, "Prehistoric New World Population Size: Historical Review and Appraisal of North American Estimates," *American Journal of Physical Anthropology* 45

(1976): 664, as cited in Russell Thornton, *American Indian Holocaust and Survival: A Population History Since 1492* (Norman: University of Oklahoma Press, 1990), 29. The larger estimate is William M. Denevan's based on the doubling of Ubelaker's revised 1988 estimate of the total precontact Amerindian population of North America. See Denevan's article, "Native American Populations in 1492: Recent Research and a Revised Hemispheric Estimate," xvii–xxxviii, in William N. Denevan, ed. *The Native Population of the Americas in 1492* (Madison: University of Wisconsin Press, 1992), xxviii. The Ubelaker estimate on which Denevan's is based can be found in his article, "North American Indian Population Size, A.D. 1500 to 1985," *American Journal of Physical Anthropology* 77 (1988): 291.

31. Francis Jennings, *The Founders of America: How Indians Discovered the Land, Pioneered in it, How They Were Plunged into a Dark Age by Invasion and Conquest, and How They Are Reviving* (New York: W.W. Norton, 1993), 211.

32. John J. McCusker, "The Rum Trade and the Balance of Payments of the Thirteen Continental Colonies" (Ph.D. diss., University of Pittsburgh, 1970), 584, 586, 703, 704, 712 (and appendix B), as cited in John J. McCusker and Russell R. Menard, *The Economy of British North America, 1607–1789* (Chapel Hill: University of North Carolina Press, 1985), 54.

33. Jennings, *Founders of America,* 209.

34. McCusher and Menaud, *Economy of British North America,* p. 54.

35. Bernard Bailyn, *Voyagers to the West: A Passage in the Peopling of America on the Eve of the Revolution* (New York: Vintage, 1988), 26.

36. Jennings, *Founders of America,* 199.

37. We must be sure to note that Amerindians often willingly entered into alliances with Europeans in order to subdue fellow Amerindians. Neither Amerindians nor Europeans were wont to act as unified peoples. However, even those Amerindian nations on the winning side of these contests fared no better than their brethren on the losing side. "When Europeans formed one of the contracting parties, one must remember that the parties understood a treaty from the viewpoints of their different societies. Indians regarded such bicultural negotiations as agreements between sovereign peers, but most Europeans clearly regarded them as arrangements of necessity and convenience, to be dispensed with when circumstances would permit." Jennings, *Founders of America,* 197.

38. Gary B. Nash, *Red, White, and Black: The Peoples of Early America* (Englewood Cliffs, N.J.: Prentice-Hall, 1982), 94.

39. Even when the African population attained its highest percentage of the total American population (20%) in the 1770s, northern blacks constituted only 10% of the total number of African Americans. See Harry A. Ploski and James Williams, eds., *The Negro Almanac: A Reference Work on the Afro-American* (New York: John Wiley & Sons, 1983), 457.

40. John Chester Miller, *The Wolf By the Ears: Thomas Jefferson and Slavery* (Charlottesville: University Press of Virginia, 1991), 2.

41. Edmund S. Morgan, *American Slavery, American Freedom: The Ordeal of Colonial Virginia* (New York: W.W. Norton, 1975), 297–98.

42. A. Leon Higginbotham Jr., *In the Matter of Color: Race and the American Legal Process, The Colonial Period* (New York: Oxford University Press, 1978), 38, 37.

43. Allan Kulikoff, *Tobacco and Slaves: The Development of Southern Cultures in the Chesapeake, 1680–1800* (Chapel Hill: University of North Carolina Press, 1986), 38, 39.

44. Michael Goldfield, *The Color of Politics: Race and the Mainsprings of American Politics* (New York: New Press, 1997), 46.

45. Ibid., 43.

46. Cox, *Caste, Class, and Race*, 365.

47. Ibid., 380.

48. Ibid., 366–367.

49. Ibid., 368–69.

50. See ibid., 548–67, for Cox's extensive discussion of "Judge Lynch." Cox was at pains to stress that contrary to the claim that lynchings frequently occurred in response to reputed sexual violations of white women by black men, the *real* or material reasons for these ritualized murders was to "suppress" in black people the attempt to "rise from an accommodated position of subordination or [to] subjugate them further to some lower social status" (p. 549). It was toward these ends that Blacks, as Cox noted, "have been lynched for such apparent trivialities as 'using offensive language,' 'bringing suit against white men,' 'trying to act like white men,' 'frightening women and children,' 'being a witness,' 'gambling,' 'making boastful remarks,' and 'attempting to vote' (p. 558). Nonetheless, for more than merely symbolic reasons was the cry of rape frequently used to justify lynchings. Given that "[r]ace prejudice rests upon physical identifiability. . . .[a] 'mongrelized' South will ultimately mean not only a non-segregated South but also a non-aristocratic South, the perennial nightmare of the Southern oligarchy" (pp. 558, 559). In conclusion, Cox maintained that the "shibboleth of white womanhood provides the most effective rationale of the interests of the Southern aristocracy" (p. 560).

51. Ibid., 561.

52. Ibid., 549, 553.

53. Ibid., 545. Earlier, in the same work (p. 452), Cox explained the social basis of the desire to assimilate on the part of black Americans: "This is particularly powerful among Negroes because their parent culture was not only designedly extirpated, but it also lost virtually all prestige on the American scene. Colored people, then, are oriented toward the broader

culture of the country; only through social rebuffs are they turned back upon themselves."

54. Ibid., 546, 581, n. 79.

55. Ibid., 371.

56. Ibid., 372, 373, 371. Given that Cox drew a distinction between "settlement" and "exploitation" colonies, and that he placed Spanish and Portuguese colonial possessions into the latter camp, it would have been less confusing had he used another verb in place of "settled."

57. Ibid., 374, 375.

58. Ibid., 375.

59. Cox was undecided about the social consequences of commercial exploitation in colonial settings, particularly their manifestations in Spanish and Portuguese colonies. On the one hand, he argued that commercial exploitation promoted meaningful cross-racial interaction; on the other, he maintained that it was precisely the absence of commercial exploitation in Spanish and Portuguese colonies that explained why race relations there were better than those in English, French, and Dutch colonies. For example, elsewhere in *Caste, Class, and Race* (p. 328), Cox wrote: "For the full profitable exploitation of a people, the dominant group must devise ways and means of limiting that people's cultural assimilation. So long as the Portuguese and Spaniards continued to accept the religious definition of human equality, so long also the development of race prejudice was inhibited."

60. Ibid., 371.

61. "The most generous estimate," according to Bernard Bailyn, doubles or triples that figure. See Bailyn, *Voyagers to the West*, 24.

62. Robin Blackburn claims that in spite of its size relative to Spain, Portugal "sent a larger stream of emigrants to its colonies: some 3,000–4,000." Blackburn, *Making of New World Slavery*, 173. Although one may assume that Blackburn is referring to Portuguese emigration to Brazil in the seventeenth century, since he specified neither period nor destination, this must remain an assumption. It may be safer, therefore, to go with Bailyn's "reasonable" though conservative estimate of a "maximum yearly average of only 500 departures over two centuries of colonial rule" to Brazil. See Bailyn, *Voyagers to the West*, 24.

63. John Hemming, *Red Gold: The Conquest of Brazilian Indians* (Cambridge: Harvard University Press, 1978), 36.

64. One student of Brazil's indigenous peoples estimates that the precontact population of those Amerindians living within the current borders of the country was "at least two and a half million." John Hemming, "Indians and the Frontier," in *Colonial Brazil*, ed. Leslie Bethell (Cambridge: Cambridge University Press, 1987), 189.

65. See Ann M. Pescatello, *Power and Pawn: The Female in Iberian Families, Societies, and Cultures* (Westport, Conn.: Greenwood, 1976), 34.

66. Abdias do Nascimento and Elisa Larkin Nascimento, *Africans in Brazil: A Pan-African Perspective* (Trenton, N.J.: Africa World Press, 1992), 91.

67. Herbert S. Klein, *African Slavery in Latin America and the Caribbean* (Oxford: Oxford University Press, 1986), 42. We should be sure to note as does Klein (p. 41) that "[f]rom 1540 to 1570, Indian slaves were the primary producers of sugar in Brazil and accounted for four-fifths or more of the labor component in the southern sugar mills developing in the Rio de Janeiro region."

68. Schwartz, *Sugar Plantations in the Formation of Brazilian Society,* 87.

69. Van den Berghe, *Race and Racism,* 61.

70. Celso Furtado, *Formación Económica del Brasil* (Mexico, D.F: Fondo de Cultura Económica, 1962), 82.

71. A.J.R. Russell-Wood, "Colonial Brazil," in Cohen and Greene, *Neither Slave Nor Free,* 97.

72. Ibid.

73. Nascimento and Nascimento, *Africans in Brazil,* 91.

74. Furtado, *Formación Económica del Brasil,* 82.

75. Herbert S. Klein, "Nineteenth-Century Brazil," in Cohen and Greene, *Neither Slave Nor Free,* 320.

76. Ibid.

77. George Reid Andrews, *Blacks and Whites in Sao Paulo, Brazil, 1888–1988* (Madison: University of Wisconsin Press, 1991), 34.

78. Ibid., 35.

79. Ibid., 54, 53.

80. See France Winddance Twine, *Racism in a Racial Democracy: The Maintenance of White Supremacy in Brazil* (New Brunswick, N.J.: Rutgers University Press, 1998), 98–107.

81. Ibid., 103, 71. Yet, as Twine correctly underscores (pp. 71, 72) there is an ideological-political danger for Afro-Brazilians in how working-class and poor Euro-Brazilians self-identify: "The social segregation between Euro-Brazilians of different socioeconomic classes is interpreted by working-class Euro-Brazilians to mean that Afro-Brazilians are also rejected on the basis of their subordinate class position. . . . Thus, the logic is that if race were a primary axis of power and privilege, there would be no class of poor whites. Since substantial white poverty exists, Vasalians [the fictitious name of the residents of her field site] conclude that Afro- and Euro-Brazilians encounter the *same* forms of social discrimination."

82. Ibid., 100.

83. Ibid., 85, 31.

84. As evidenced in the following passage, even until the time of his death, Cox was disposed to employ cultural arguments to explain differences in race relations across societies: "Had the Dutch or English colonized Brazil, the racial situation there would most likely have been similar to that of the southern United States or of South Africa." Oliver C. Cox, *Race Relations: Elements and Social Dynamics* (Detroit: Wayne State University Press, 1976), 12.

85. Frank Tannenbaum, *Slave and Citizen: The Negro in the Americas* (New York: Vintage, 1946), 48.

86. Among the widest known are: Herbert S. Klein, *Slavery in the Americas: A Comparative Study of Virginia and Cuba* (Chicago: University of Chicago Press, 1967); Carl N. Degler, *Neither Black Nor White: Slavery and Race Relations in Brazil and the United States* (Madison: University of Wisconsin Press, 1971); and Harmannus Hoetink, *Slavery and Race Relations in the Americas: An Inquiry into Their Nature and Nexus* (New York: Harper & Row, 1973). Related studies published in the same period include: Harmannus Hoetink, *The Two Variants in Caribbean Race Relations: A Contribution to the Sociology of Segmented Societies* (London: Oxford University Press, 1967); Pierre L. Van den Berghe, *Race and Racism: A Comparative Perspective* (New York: Wiley & Son, 1967); and Franklin W. Knight, *Slave Society in Cuba during the Nineteenth Century* (Madison: University of Wisconsin Press, 1970).

87. Without naming types of race relations, Herbert Klein said the following about the relevance of the free black in American slave society: "In attempting to analyze the structure of Negro slavery and the development of race relations in any New World society, it is essential to understand the condition of the free colored class. For the occupations, status, and degree of acceptance of the freedmen during slavery foreshadow the pattern of post-emancipation assimilation for the entire slave class. Even more crucially, the role of the free colored is an important indicator of the closed or open nature of a given slave regime. For the colored masses, free men of color offer alternative models to the slave role, and as a group they can also serve as intermediaries between the extremes of freedom and slavery and provide opportunites for non-master contact for the colored slaves." Klein, "Nineteenth-Century Brazil," 309.

88. See, for example, C. L. R. James, *The Life of Captain Cipriani* and Eric Williams, *The Negro in the Caribbean* (Brooklyn: A & B Books, 1994). On the subject of race relations, however, Williams's work relies heavily on James's observations.

89. Among the many contributions, we might name: Lloyd Braithwaite, "Social Stratification in Trinidad," *Social and Economic Studies* 2, 2–3 (October 1953); Raymond T. Smith, *The Negro Family in British Guiana: Family*

Structure and Social Status in the Villages (London: Routledge & Kegan Paul, 1956); Fernando Henriques, *Jamaica: Land of Wood and Water* (New York: London House & Maxwell, 1964); M.G. Smith, *The Plural Society in the British West Indies* (Berkeley: University of California Press, 1965); and Stuart Hall, "Pluralism, Race, and Class in Caribbean Society," in *Race and Class in Post-Colonial Society: A Study of Ethnic Group Relations in the English-Speaking Caribbean, Bolivia, Chile and Mexico,* ed. John Rex (Paris: UNESCO, 1977), 150–82.

90. Franklin Knight said as much when he remarked that the "real problem [for the Tannenbaum thesis] was the refusal of the Anglo-Saxon Protestants of the Caribbean to follow the pattern of their continental companions. Slavery and post-emancipation race relations differed significantly between any of the slaveholding states of the continental United States, and any island in the Caribbean, regardless of the cultural and religious inheritance derived from their separate metropolitan powers." Knight, *Slave Society in Cuba,* xiv–xv.

91. E. Franklin Frazier, "Sociological Theory and Race Relations," *American Sociological Review* 12, 3 (June 1947). Reprinted in *E. Franklin Frazier on Race Relations: Selected Writings,* ed. G. Franklin Edwards (Chicago: University of Chicago Press, 1968), 37.

92. Cox, *Caste, Class, and Race,* 474.

93. Van den Berghe, *Race and Racism,* 34.

94. Norman Girvan, "Aspects of the Political Economy of Race in the Caribbean and the Americas," *Working Paper* no. 7 (Institute of Social and Economic Research, University of the West Indies, 1975), 30.

Chapter 3. Outcasting the Caste School of Race Relations

1. W. Lloyd Warner and Allison Davis, "A Comparative Study of American Caste," in *Race Relations and the Race Problem: A Definition and an Analysis,* ed. Edgar T. Thompson (Durham: Duke University Press, 1939), 232–33.

2. Ibid., 229.

3. Ibid.

4. Cox, *Caste, Class, and Race,* 54.

5. Ibid., 56.

6. Ibid., 56–57, 55.

7. Ibid., 5, 12–13, 18, 19.

8. Ibid., 14 n. 43, 23–24, 37.

9. Ibid., 22.

10. Warner and Davis, "Comparative Study of American Caste," 236–37.

11. Cox, *Caste, Class, and Race,* 492.

12. Ibid., 495–96.

13. Ibid., 503, 475.

14. Ibid., 480.

15. Ibid., 472.

16. When asked in 1970 if he thought that his left perspective was most responsible for his marginalization in the American community of scholars, Cox replied: "No, I think my . . . tendency to be profoundly critical of previous writers. . . . has been the principle reason my work tends to get ignored in America." As cited in Martin, "The Teaching Mission of Dr. Oliver C. Cox," 39, 40. So much for scholarly exchange! On this strategy of naming names, Cox remarked in a footnote to *Caste, Class, and Race:* "Social theories gain in meaning and significance if their authors are known; and this fact, we shall hope, is the justification for our personal approach" (462, ff.1).

17. Everett C. Hughes, review of *Caste, Class, and Race, Phylon* 9 (9 March 1948): 66–68.

18. Oliver C. Cox, rejoinder to Everett C. Hughes's review of *Caste, Class, and Race, Phylon* 9 (June 1948), 171–72.

19. Cox, *Caste, Class, and Race,* 480.

20. Ibid., xv–xvi. Later in the same work (p. 509), Cox would add the following remarks about Myrdal's *An American Dilemma:* "As a source of information and brilliant interpretation of information on race relations in the United States, it is probably unsurpassed."

21. Ibid., 494–95.

22. Ibid., 472, 504.

23. Ibid., 577.

24. Ibid., 473.

25. Ibid., 93. A few pages earlier Cox made the related remark: "Almost without exception these authorities refer to the social situation which has developed between whites and Negroes in South Africa and in the Southern states of the United States in support of their theories. Always the African and American citations are more cogent than the point which they propose to establish about caste in India." Ibid., 84, ff.7.

26. Ibid., 97, 113,116, 104.

27. Louis Dumont, "Caste, Racism and 'Stratification': Reflections of a Social Anthropologist," in *Homo Hierarchicus: The Caste System and Its Implications* (Chicago: University of Chicago Press, 1980), 254, 255.

28. Ibid., 255. This claim may not be entirely true. Elmer P. Martin states that Cox once alluded to having visited India with one of his brothers. However, he specifies neither when Cox made that remark nor when he made the supposed trip. See "The Teaching Mission of Dr. Oliver C. Cox,"

31. In addition, Cox could also be taken to task for having idealized the caste system. This is the criticism that Irfan Habib leveled at Dumont himself: "It is obviously tempting to take the caste system's surviving elements (mainly religious) as the sole or crucial elements, and the declining aspects (economic) as secondary and even superfluous. Dumont not only falls to the temptation, he builds a whole theoretical structure on a false premise to explain what India is." In Habib's view, the caste system should be understood as a system of "class exploitation." "Caste in Indian History," in *Essays in Indian History: Towards a Marxist Perception* (New Delhi: Tulika, 1995), 164, 176.

29. Eric Williams, *Inward Hunger: The Education of a Prime Minister,* 19.

30. Cox, *Caste, Class, and Race,* xvii.

31. For a description of how the Indian caste system was transformed in a Caribbean society, see Raymond T. Smith, "Caste and Social Status Among the Indians of Guyana," in *The Matrifocal Family: Power, Pluralism, and Politics* (New York: Routledge, 1996), 111–41.

32. William Julius Wilson, *The Declining Significance of Race: Blacks and Changing American Institutions* (Chicago: University of Chicago Press, 1978), 4. In a similar vein, Stuart Hall remarked that "it does not follow that because developed capitalism here functions predominantly on the basis of 'free labour' that the racial aspects of social relations can be assimilated, for all practical purposes, to its typical class relations (as does Cox (1970), despite his many pertinent observations)." Stuart Hall, "Race, Articulation and Societies Structured in Dominance," in *Sociological Theories: Race and Colonialism* (Paris: UNESCO, 1980), 339.

33. See, for example, Robert Miles, "Class, Race, and Ethnicity: A Critique of Cox's Theory," *Ethnic and Racial Studies* 3, 2 (1980). Miles's critique of Cox's theory of race relations is ambivalent at best and is furthermore based on a selective reading of Cox's work. For example, although he acknowledges in one instance that Cox's effort in *Caste, Class, and Race* was the "first attempt by a 'Marxist' to systematically theorize a relationship between class structure and what Cox called ethnic systems" (p. 183), he maintains elsewhere that the "failure of Cox's attempt was due . . . to his attempt to conceptualize 'ethnic systems' independently or outside of class relations" (p. 184). If we assume that Miles is more inclined to believe the second of these two statements, we may also assume that, in his opinion, Cox's situations of race relations have no bearing on the "relationship between capitalism, class structure and racial categorization" (p. 178). However, this point of departure is an adulteration of Cox's position. For Cox, political class consciousness is informed by the range of ethnic/racial identities to which specific situations of race relations give rise. In a ruling-class situation of race relations, for example, it is, to borrow Miles's own words,

"possible for political class action to obstruct ethnic group solidarity" (p. 175) since there the social tendency is to rate class (and color) membership over racial identification in a racially mixed population. Conversely, in a bipartite situation of race relations, it is typical for "ethnic group solidarity to obstruct political class solidarity" (p. 175), for in this setting the social tendency is to identify oneself as a member of a ethnic/racial group before identifying oneself as a member of a political class. Thus, in the American bipartite situation in which the majority of people of color are workers, "racial antagonism is essentially political class conflict" from their point of view since their implicit, if not explicit, goal is to force white workers to commit ethnic/racial suicide. See Cox, *Caste, Class, and Race*, 333. The revolutionary implications of this battle within the ranks of labor should be obvious to everyone.

Yet, given that Miles has elected to disregard Cox's situations of race relations, he can make the unjustified claim that Cox's use of terms like "Negro" and "black" instead of "black working class" or "black bourgeoisie" is proof that in his theory of race relations the "class structure is presented as being distinct and separate from race relations" (p. 185), and that Cox "accord[ed] equal status to political class and national and racial ethnics as initiators of socio-economic change" (p. 184). Criticisms of this sort miss the crux of Cox's point, which was simply that given the class composition of African-American society, any gain or loss suffered by black Americans as a socially recognized racial group, necessarily impacts the class structure of the larger American society of which they are inextricably a part. In the final analysis, I believe that Miles is on much safer ground when he remarks that "Cox's emphasis remains very much upon the role of the contemporary white capitalist in re-producing race prejudice" (p. 176) and that Cox "either plays down or fails to confront that evidence which suggests that race prejudice has been forcefully articulated by the white working class in the USA" (p. 178).

34. Cox, *Caste, Class, and Race*, 332, 336.

35. Edward P. Thompson, *The Making of the English Working Class* (New York: Vintage, 1966), 10.

36. See Cox, *Caste, Class, and Race*, 283–97.

37. Oliver C. Cox, "Class and Caste: A Definition and a Distinction," *Journal of Negro Education* 13 (spring 1944).

38. Thompson, *Making of the English Working Class*, 9.

39. See Cox, *Caste, Class, and Race*, 285–86. Here Cox points out that his social class is Sombart's *Stande* (estate) and that this last's *Klassen* corresponds to his political class. Ralf Dahrendorf, incidentally, saw fit to make the same distinction, labeling as "stratum" what Cox termed social class,

and "class" Cox's political class. Ralf Dahrendorf, *Class and Class Conflict in Industrial Society* (Stanford, Calif.: Stanford University Press, 1959), ix.

40. Oliver C. Cox, "Estates, Social Classes, and Political Classes," *American Sociological Review* 10 (August 1945): 467.

41. Cox, "Class and Caste," 140, 144.

42. Ibid., 148.

43. Michel-Rolph Trouillot, *Haiti, State Against Nation: The Origins and Legacy of Duvalierism* (New York: Monthly Review Press, 1990), 121.

44. Cox, "Class and Caste," 146.

45. Ibid., 147. A few pages later (p. 155), Cox added that "[s]ocial solidarity is not a characteristic of social classes, for it is expected that persons are constantly attracted upward and away from their social position, while those who fall may be allowed to sink even farther."

46. Ibid., 149.

47. Ibid., 144, 180.

48. Ibid., 338–39. Earlier in the work (p. 184), Cox noted the effects of this social calculus on the psyche of the worker: "In capitalistic production labor is included in the same impersonal accounting as natural resources and capital, a fact which ordinarily brings home to the worker a fearful sense of being cut adrift in a sea of anonymity to eat and especially to be eaten as opportunity arises."

49. For one solid example of this perspective by a reputable Marxist scholar, see Eric Hobsbawm, "Notes on Class Consciousness," in *Workers: Worlds of Labour* (New York: Pantheon Books, 1984), 15–32.

50. Cox, *Caste, Class, and Race*, 187. Sadly, even Mario Barrera, who commends Cox for having provided in *Caste, Class, and Race* the "only really substantial Marxist theoretical work to date on race in the United States" (p. 208), still concludes that "[p]erhaps in part because of this confusion over the notion of class, Cox nowhere works out a systematic relationship between class and racial divisions in American society" (p. 209).

Yet the principal reason why Cox saw fit to entertain "non-Marxist" influences on social class identity was due to his discomfort with, in Barrera's own words, the assumption that "class divisions in capitalist society . . . will supersede other kinds of divisions including those based on race and ethnicity" (p. 206). However, an uncompromising economistic definition of social class will not be able to explain why in American society, for example, Blacks and Chicanos continue to be viewed by most white Americans as populations beyond the pale of "mainstream" American society irrespective of the social class positions of individual members of those populations. To repeat, Cox's perspective on social class was not due to "confusion over the notion of class," but to the inadequacy of an economistic definition of social class to account for the global persistence of ethnic and racial divsions within and between social classes. Mario Barrera, *Race and Class in the Southwest: A Theory of Racial Inequality* (Notre Dame: University of Notre Dame Press, 1979).

51. Cox, *Caste, Class, and Race,* 155, 160.

52. It appears that Cox's standard of what is political in the capitalist era was based, in part at least, on the definition of an estate in the feudal era which was, in his own words, customary participation in the "burdens and privileges of government as an organized group." Cox, *Caste, Class, and Race,* 139, 155.

53. Ibid., 160.

54. On this point Cox elaborated: "A revolutionary group, a political class, cannot become a political party—in fact, a political faction—of the existing government without defeating its purpose. Political party factions tend to feel responsibility for the existing government. Labor 'parties' tend to be reformist, whereas a true proletarian movement never loses sight of the fact that it can never adopt the fundamental political assumptions of the government; it does not, moreover, expect the capitalist state to die merely of inanition." Cox, *Caste, Class, and Race,* 199. About American political parties, Cox commented: "In the United States there is only one effective political party with two factions: Republicans and Democrats. There is no effective Socialist party, the organized leadership of the opposite political class" (p. 155 n. 9).

55. Ibid., 160.

56. Ibid., 158, 160.

57. On this subject Cox observed that "[I]ndeed the leadership of the aggressor class may arise from the ruling class itself." (ibid., 158).

58. Ibid., 155, 161.

59. Ibid., 158, 156, 157. Several pages later (p. 177) Cox added the following statement on the relationship between social and political classes: "The material interests of the individual in the system of production gives him his potential class affiliation, and his conscious sympathies born of class antagonism complete him as an active affiliate."

60. Ibid., 175, 189. Later (p. 199), he added that "[a]lthough the fascists are in fact a counterrevolutionary group, their methods must nevertheless be revolutionary."

61. Ibid., 166, 164, 167.

62. Ibid., 164.

63. Ibid., 168–69.

64. Ibid., 159, 183, 166 n. 43. It is interesting to note that just prior to proposing the social conditions under which revolutions are likely to occur, Cox felt it necessary to caution that "[I]n this discussion we should not be thought of as advocating violence or revolution."

65. Ibid., 187, 182.
66. Ibid., 185, 186.
67. Ibid., 185–86.
68. Ibid., 184, 186, 187.
69. Ibid., 187.
70. Oliver C. Cox, "The Nature of the Anti-Asiatic Movement on the Pacific Coast," *Journal of Negro Education* 15 (fall 1946): 603–14, which, like many of his articles published between 1940 and 1947, reappeared in *Caste, Class, and Race* under the section heading of "Race Prejudice, Class Conflict, and Nationalism," 408–22.
71. Cox, *Caste, Class, and Race,* 410.
72. Ibid., 408.
73. Sucheng Chan, *This Bitter Sweet Soil: The Chinese in California Agriculture, 1860–1910* (Berkeley: University of California Press, 1986), 26. See same source for details of the "credit-ticket system," which enabled many Chinese voyagers to make their way to California.
74. Ibid., 21.
75. Carey McWilliams, *California: The Great Exception* (Berkeley: University of California Press, 1999), 42.
76. Chan, *This Bitter Sweet Soil,* 26, 70.
77. Ibid., 58.
78. Leonard Pitt, *The Decline of the Californios: A Social History of the Spanish-Speaking Californians, 1846–1890* (Berkeley: University of California Press, 1966), 64.
79. Alexander Saxton, *The Indispensable Enemy: Labor and the Anti-Chinese Movement in California* (Berkeley: University of California Press, 1975), 33.
80. Chan, *This Bitter Sweet Soil,* 56.
81. For a synopsis and critique of these myths, see Saxton, *The Indispensable Enemy,* 46–52.
82. Ibid., 63, 62.
83. Here we must heed Chan's admonitions on the imprecision of these labor regime labels: "The inconsistent manner in which occupations were listed in the manuscript census makes it difficult to state exactly how many Chinese were factory workers and how many were independent producers. While all those listed as working in a factory were counted as factory workers, there were also others, listed as 'makers' of cigars, shoes, slippers, boots, candles, or matches, who might have worked in factories, but who could also have been independent artisans. Moreover, it is not certain whether persons listed as 'manufacturers' were owners of factories or workers in them." *This Bitter Sweet Soil,* 70–71.
84. Saxton, *Indispensable Enemy,* 6.

85. Herbert Hill, "Anti-Oriental Agitation and the Rise of Working-Class Racism," *Society* 10 (November 1972–October 1973): 50.

86. Ibid., 50.

87. Chan, *This Bitter Sweet Soil*, 76.

88. Hill, "Anti-Oriental Agitation," 50.

89. This is not to say that Cox was unaware of the fact that class conflict can express itself in racial/cultural terms. In the Trinidad of his youth, for example, Blacks generally questioned the religion, customs, dress, language, and conduct of East Indians, who in turn continued to believe a "myth about the origins of blacks which identified them with the ungodly and the polluted." Brereton, *Race Relations in Colonial Trinidad*, 188.

90. Cox, *Caste, Class, and Race*, 411–12.

91. Ibid., 410.

92. Ibid., 416.

93. Ibid., 417.

94. Carey McWilliams, *Brothers Under the Skin* (Boston: Little, Brown, 1964), 99.

95. According to Saxton's estimates for 1870, nearly one-quarter of California's inhabitants were born in Europe. Of these, the largest number were born in Ireland. *The Indispensable Enemy*, 10–11. It should be noted as well that of the "native" white Americans who constituted 40 percent of the state's population at the time, one-third of these hailed from the South. See McWilliams, *Brothers Under the Skin*, 99–100.

96. McWilliams, *Brothers Under the Skin*, 101.

97. Cox, *Caste, Class, and Race*, 413.

98. Ibid., 412. As will become clearer in the pages to come, it is likely that Cox meant this remark in *his* literal sense that working-class people can be intolerant of, but not racist toward, other ethnic/racial groups because they do not hire them. In light of the fact that Blacks and Indians were (at the time that Cox wrote these words) and are still overwhelmingly members of Trinidad's working class, Cox's words largely remain true. However, anyone who is familiar with that country's social history from circa 1850 to the present knows that mutual intolerance between the two groups has been more the rule than the exception.

99. Ibid., 417–18.

100. Ibid., 418.

101. Ibid., 422.

102. Miles, "Class, Race, and Ethnicity: A Critique of Cox's Theory," 177.

103. David Roediger, *The Wages of Whiteness: Race and the Making of the American Working Class* (London: Verso, 1991), 19.

104. Cox, *Caste, Class, and Race*, 417.

105. Cox expressed a similar point like this: "We may take it as axiomatic that never in the history of the world have poor people set and maintained the dominant social policy in a society." Ibid., 575–76.

106. Ibid., 393.

107. Ibid.

108. Ibid., 394, 393, 401.

109. Paul Johnson, *A History of the Jews* (New York: Harper & Row, 1987), 312.

110. For a synopsis of these restrictions, see ibid., 357–65.

111. For a synopsis of these codes, see Leon F. Litwack, *North of Slavery*, 66–74.

112. For variations on this theme, see Hannah Arendt, *The Origins of Totalitarianism* (San Diego: Harcourt, Brace, and Jovanovich, 1973), 11–68; Fritz Stern, *Gold and Iron: Bismarck, Bleichroder, and the Building of the German Empire* (New York: Vintage, 1979), 469; and Daniel Jonah Goldhagen, *Hitler's Willing Executioners: Ordinary Germans and the Holocaust* (New York: Vintage, 1997), 54, 65, 71.

113. Arendt, *Origins of Totalitarianism*, 22.

114. Cox, *Caste, Class, and Race*, 396.

115. We must bear in mind that at the time Cox wrote these words, the majority of Jewish Americans had already joined the ranks of the country's middle class. In fact, even a decade earlier, the record of their social mobility was impressive: "In 1900, 59.6 percent of all American Jews were employed in industry. Thirty years later that number had fallen to 13.7 percent. In 1900 only about 20 percent of the Jews in the United States were in business, but by 1930 over half were. A similar rise occurred in the numbers of Jews in professional positions." Hasia Diner, *In the Almost Promised Land: American Jews and Blacks, 1915–1933* (Baltimore: Johns Hopkins University Press, 1995), 15.

116. Cox, *Caste, Class, and Race*, 397.

117. Ibid., 397. Some years later, Cox made the same point with regard to George Wallace's platform in his 1972 presidential campaign. See Oliver C. Cox, "Jewish Self-interest in 'Black Pluralism,'" *Sociological Quarterly* 15 (spring 1974): 196.

118. Ibid., 183, 190.

119. Ibid., 183, 184.

120. Cox, "Jewish Self-interest in 'Black Pluralism,'" 190.

121. The tone of Cox's remarks in these passages makes it difficult for me to agree with Rutledge M. Dennis that they reflect more his "philo-Semitism" than anti-Semitism. See his, "Cox and Cultural Pluralism," in Hunter, *The Sociology of Oliver C. Cox: New Perspectives*, 168.

122. Cox, "Jewish Self-interest in 'Black Pluralism,'" 189.

123. Cox, "Question of Pluralism," 396.

124. Because the basis of his critique of the use of the term "pluralism" was that it had as many meanings as the different people who employed it, Cox never provided a definition of the term. Nevertheless, as a useful working definition and one with which Cox was familiar, we might borrow Van Deburg's: the "view [of] society as being composed of various ethnic groups, all of whom are competing with one another for goods and services." *New Day in Babylon*, 25.

125. Cox, "Jewish Self-interest in 'Black Pluralism,'" 186.

126. Another way of interpreting Cox's position on the weaknesses of black American culture in light of his views on nationalism, is that black Americans, on the whole, are not sufficiently middle-class either to sustain or to profit from a black nationalist or pluralist program.

127. Contrary to Cox's assertion that Jewish Americans could benefit from the advancement of a black nationalist agenda, Harold Cruse posited that Jewish nationalists lent their support to the black integrationist platform for a different reason: "A study of Jewish Zionist organizational and propaganda techniques reveals that influential Zionist thought sees Anglo-Saxon nationalism in the United States as its main potential political threat. Zionist thought also correctly sees the Negro civil rights drive for social equality and racial integration as a possible indirect threat to Jewish status, in the event that Negroes drive Anglo-Saxon nationalists into the radical rightist political camp. Hence, Jewish trends that are pro-Zionist and anti-Jewish-integration-assimilation, are forced to take a pro-Negro integration position and an anti-black nationalist position. *Thus, pro-Zionist influences within Negro civil rights organizations are strategically aiding and abetting Negro integration (assimilation), albeit Zionists, themselves, do not believe in integration (assimilation) for Jews.*" Harold Cruse, *The Crisis of the Negro Intellectual: From Its Origins to the Present* (New York: William Morrow, 1967), 484.

128. Cox, "Jewish Self-interest in 'Black Pluralism,'" 187.

129. Ibid., 194.

130. Ibid., 196.

131. Harold Cruse, *Plural but Equal: A Critical Study of Blacks and Minorities and America's Plural Society* (New York: William Morrow, 1987), 211.

Chapter 4.   The Foundations of Capitalism

1. Oliver C. Cox, *The Foundations of Capitalism* (New York: Philosophical Library, 1959), 73.

2. Ibid., 9.

3. Frederic C. Lane, *Venice: A Maritime Republic* (Baltimore: Johns Hopkins University Press, 1973), 7.

4. Ibid., 5.

5. Donald M. Nicol, *Byzantium and Venice: A Study in Diplomatic and Cultural Relations* (Cambridge: Cambridge University Press, 1992), 61.

6. See Cox, *Foundations of Capitalism*, 36–37.

7. Lane, *Venice*, 34.

8. Cox, *Foundations of Capitalism*, 15, 76, 77, 91.

9. Ibid., 356, 72.

10. Oliver C. Cox, *Capitalism and American Leadership* (New York: Philosophical Library, 1962), 63.

11. Philip D. Curtin, *The Rise and Fall of the Plantation Complex: Essays in Atlantic History* (Cambridge: Cambridge University Press, 1990), 5.

12. Charles Verlinden, "The Transfer of Colonial Techniques from the Mediterranean to the Atlantic," in *The Beginnings of Modern Colonization: Eleven Essays with an Introduction* (Ithaca, N.Y.: Cornell University Press, 1970), 20.

13. Immanuel Wallerstein, "Three Paths of National Development in Sixteenth-Century Europe," in *The Capitalist World-Economy: Essays by Immanuel Wallerstein* (Cambridge: Cambridge University Press, 1979), 42.

14. See Celso Furtado, *Formación Económica del Brasil* (Mexico City: Fondo de Cultura Economica, 1962), 17 n. 1.

15. Roger G. Kennedy, *Architecture, Men, Women, and Money in America, 1600–1800* (New York: Random House, 1985), 26. In any event, Cox was not of the opinion that "slave labor formed the basis of Venetian wealth." See *Foundations of Capitalism*, 87–88 n. 56.

16. Oliver C. Cox, "Patterns of Race Relations," 31–38. An address delivered at the Golden Jubilee Meeting of the Missouri Association for Social Welfare in St. Louis, Missouri, on October 20, 1950 and reprinted in *Midwest Journal* 3 (winter 1950–51): 33.

17. Oliver C. Cox, *Capitalism as a System* (New York: Monthly Review Press, 1964), 150.

18. Ibid., 138, 140.

19. Cox, *Foundations of Capitalism*, 76.

20. Ibid., 69.

21. Ibid., 110 n. 23.

22. Lane, *Venice*, 69.

23. Ibid., 69.

24. Janet Abu-Lughod, *Before European Hegemony: The World System, A.D. 1250–1350* (New York: Oxford University Press, 1989), 213.

25. Lane, *Venice*, 63, 64.

26. Ibid., 64.

27. Ibid., 60.

28. Cox, *Capitalism as a System*, 4.

29. Ibid., 5, 6.

30. Cox, *Foundations of Capitalism*, 38.

31. Ibid., 45, 42.

32. Frederic C. Lane, "Medieval Political Ideas and the Venetian Constitution," in *Venice and History: The Collected Papers of Frederic C. Lane* (Baltimore: Johns Hopkins University Press, 1966), 286.

33. Lane, *Venice*, 90.

34. Ibid., 91.

35. Cox, *Foundations of Capitalism*, 40.

36. See Lane, *Venice*, 92.

37. Ibid., 95.

38. Lane, "Medieval Political Ideas," 297.

39. Lane, *Venice*, 97.

40. Lane, "Medieval Political Ideas," 293, 290.

41. Lane, *Venice*, 96.

42. Lane, "Medieval Political Ideas," 286.

43. See Cox, *Capitalism as a System*, 18.

44. Cox, *Foundations of Capitalism*, 94.

45. Philippe Dollinger, *La Hanse* (Paris: Aubier, 1988), 11.

46. Cox, *Foundations of Capitalism*, 193.

47. Ian D. Colvin, *The Germans in England, 1066–1598* (Port Washington, N.Y.: Kennikat Press, 1971), xvii, as cited in Cox, *Foundations of Capitalism*, 201–2.

48. M.M. Postan, "The Trade of Medieval Europe: the North," in *The Cambridge Economic History of Europe*, vol. 2, *Trade and Industry in the Middle Ages*, ed. M.M. Postan and Edward Miller (Cambridge: Cambridge University Press, 1987), 292.

49. *Economic and Social History of Medieval Europe* (San Diego: Harcourt, Brace, & Jovanovich, 1937), 187.

50. Cox, *Foundations of Capitalism*, 194.

51. See Fernand Braudel, *L'Identité de la France*, vol. 2, *Les Hommes et Les Choses* (Paris: Flammarion, 1990), 316. Samir Amin describes it as "subcontracting" in *Capitalism in the Age of Globalization: The Management of Contemporary Society* (London: Zed Books, 1997), 5.

52. We should not conclude from this, however, that before the fourteenth century England's woolens industry had entirely dried up in the face of Hanseatic and Flemish pressures. On the contrary, the "high-priced cloths" from Lincoln and Stamford, for example, "were much in demand for the royal wardrobe and for presents to overseas sovereigns, and they were constantly exported. Lincoln cloths were singled out for

special mention in foreign tariffs, as in the Venetian tariff of 1265." Elea-
nora Carus-Wilson, "The Woolen Industry," in Postan and Miller, *Cambridge Economic History of Europe,* 2:633. It is for this reason that even before
England's dispute with Flanders in 1272 led to a wool embargo against
this last, "it had become clear, at least by 1258, that England was at a disadvantage in exporting wool to the Netherlands and importing finished
textiles." Cox, *Foundations of Capitalism,* 314.

53. Maurice Dobb, *Studies in the Development of Capitalism* (New York: International Publishers, 1963), 113.

54. Cox, *Foundations of Capitalism,* 196.

55. Ibid., 191.

56. Ibid., 2, 20.

57. Ibid., 124.

58. Ibid., 27.

59. Robert S. Lopez, "The Trade of Medieval Europe: the South," in
Postan and Miller, *Cambridge Economic History of Europe,* 2:306–401, 337.

60. Cox, *Caste, Class, and Race,* 143.

61. Cox, *Foundations of Capitalism,* 48.

62. Cox, *Caste, Class, and Race,* 143.

63. Cox, "Patterns of Race Relations," 31.

64. Cox, *Foundations of Capitalism,* 126.

65. Pirenne, *Economic and Social History of Medieval Europe,* 140–41.

66. Cox, *Foundations of Capitalism,* 16.

67. Ibid., 126–27.

68. See Karl Marx, *Capital,* vol. 1, *A Critical Analysis of Capitalist Production* (New York: International Publishers, 1967), 670 n.1, 672.

69. For a list of additional challenges that Cox posed to Marxist theory,
see Cedric J. Robinson, "C. L. R. James and the World System," in *C. L. R. James:
His Intellectual Legacies,* ed. Selwyn R. Cudjoe and William E. Cain, (Amherst:
University of Massachusetts Press, 1995), 246.

70. Curiously, Cox did not press the point when he had the opportunity. See Cox, *Foundations of Capitalism,* 440.

71. Charles Tilly, *American Sociological Review* 30, 6, (December 1965): 959.

72. Fernand Braudel, *Afterthoughts on Material Civilization and Capitalism*
(Baltimore: Johns Hopkins University Press, 1977), 66–67.

73. Wallerstein, "Three Paths of National Development," 42–43.

74. See Karl Marx, *Capital,* vol. 3, *The Process of Capitalist Production as a
Whole* (New York: International Publishers, 1967), 323–37.

75. Robert Brenner, *Merchants and Revolution: Commercial Change, Political
Conflict, and London's Overseas Traders, 1550–1653* (Princeton: Princeton University Press, 1993), 17.

76. Cox, *Foundations of Capitalism,* 130.

77. Braudel, *Afterthoughts on Material Civilization and Capitalism,* 88. This is a summary of Richard T. Rapp's article, "The Unmaking of the Mediterranean Trade Hegemony: International Trade Rivalry and the Commercial Revolution," *Journal of Economic History* 35 (September 1975): 499–575. On this subject, Cox only made mention of Dutch and English commercial interventions in the eastern Mediterranean and not of their equally important industrial incursions there: "In fact, Dutch and English ships began to invade Venetian commercial preserves by going directly to the Levant for what was left of the Eastern trade." *Foundations of Capitalism,* 130.

78. David Abulafia, "Asia, Africa, and the Trade of Medieval Europe," in Postan and Miller, *Cambridge Economic History of Europe,* 2:433.

79. See E. Ashtor, *A Social and Economic History of the Near East in the Middle Ages* (Berkeley: University of California Press, 1976), 308–10.

80. Carlo M. Cipolla, *Before the Industrial Revolution: European Society and Economy, 1000–1700* (New York: W.W. Norton, 1980), 261.

81. Wallerstein, "Three Paths of National Development," 43–44.

82. Cox, *Foundations of Capitalism,* 131.

83. Ibid., 220.

84. C. R. Boxer, *The Dutch Seaborne Empire, 1600–1800* (London: Penguin, 1973), 18.

85. Cox, *Foundations of Capitalism,* 211.

86. Ibid., 207, 213.

87. Boxer, *Dutch Seaborne Empire,* 14.

88. Cox, *Foundations of Capitalism,* 217.

89. Ibid., 217–18, 204.

90. Ibid., 220.

91. Ibid.

92. Boxer, *Dutch Seaborne Empire,* 18–19.

93. Ibid., 19–20.

94. Fernand Braudel, *Civilization and Capitalism, Fifteenth to Eighteenth Century,* vol. 3: *The Perspective of the World* (Berkeley: University of California Press, 1992), 187.

95. Cox, *Foundations of Capitalism,* 223.

96. Fernand Braudel, "Venise," in *La Mediterranée: Les Hommes et L'Héritage,* ed. Fernand Braudel (Paris: Flammarion, 1986), 160.

97. Pierre Goubert, *Louis XIV and Twenty Million Frenchmen* (New York: Vintage, 1972), 23.

98. Cox, *Foundations of Capitalism,* 230.

99. Immanuel Wallerstein, *The Modern World System II: Mercantilism and the Consolidation of the European World-Economy, 1600–1750* (San Diego: Academic Press, 1980), 43.

100. Boxer, *Dutch Seaborne Empire,* 22.

101. Cipolla, *Before the Industrial Revolution*, 274.

102. Boxer, *Dutch Seaborne Empire*, 76.

103. Cox, *Foundations of Capitalism*, 236.

104. Joyce Oldham Appleby, *Economic Thought and Ideology in Seventeenth-Century England* (Princeton: Princeton University Press, 1978), 77.

105. Daniel Defoe, *A Plan of the English Commerce* (London, 1728), 192, as cited in Cipolla, *Before the Industrial Revolution*, 270.

106. Goubert, *Louis XIV and Twenty Million Frenchmen*, 27–28.

107. Cox, *Foundations of Capitalism*, 229.

108. Wallerstein, *Modern World-System* 2:43.

109. Cipolla, *Before the Industrial Revolution*, 271.

110. Artur Attman, *Dutch Enterprise in the World Bullion Trade, 1550–1800* (Goteborg: Kungl. Vetenskaps-och Vitterhets-Samhallet, 1983), 31.

111. Braudel, *Civilization and Capitalism*, 3:209.

112. Wallerstein, *Modern World-System* 2:44.

113. "The average rate of interest in Amsterdam was about 3 percent when it was 6 percent in London." Cipolla, *Before the Industrial Revolution*, 274.

114. See Appleby, *Economic Thought and Ideology in Seventeenth-Century England*, 87–94.

115. Wallerstein, *Modern World-System* 2:49.

116. Ibid., 2:46.

117. Cox, *Foundations of Capitalism*, 230.

118. The republic's economic objective in entering Indian Ocean trade was naturally related to its military one: "But the union of 1602 had a wider aim than the giving of central direction to dispersed commercial effort: it was to create a military instrument with which to counter Iberian hostility and to secure for the Dutch that monopoly of the spice trade without which the burden of military expenditure could not be sustained." J. B. Harrison, "Europe and Asia," in *The New Cambridge Modern History*, vol. 4, *The Decline of Spain and the Thirty Years War, 1609–48/59*, ed. J. P. Cooper (Cambridge: Cambridge University Press, 1971), 647.

119. Jan de Vries and Ad van der Woude, *The First Modern Economy: Success, Failure, and Perseverance of the Dutch Economy, 1500–1815* (Cambridge: Cambridge University Press, 1997), 384.

120. Cox, *Foundations of Capitalism*, 232.

121. Boxer, *Dutch Seaborne Empire*, 49.

122. De Vries and der Woude, *First Modern Economy*, 385.

123. Boxer, *Dutch Seaborne Empire*, 26.

124. Ibid., 26.

125. "The Seventeen laid down only broad policies to be followed in the East." Cox, *Foundations of Capitalism*, 232.

126. See de Vries and der Woude, *First Modern Economy*, 386.

127. *The Foundations of Capitalism*, 232.

128. Ibid., 233.

129. K. N. Chaudhuri, *Trade and Civilisation in the Indian Ocean: An Economic History from the Rise of Islam to 1750* (Cambridge: Cambridge University Press, 1985), 87.

130. Ibid., 85.

131. Boxer, *Dutch Seaborne Empire*, 217.

132. Chaudhuri, *Trade and Civilisation in the Indian Ocean*, 88.

133. Ibid., 88.

134. The term is Wallerstein's. See *Modern World-System* 2:47.

135. Cox, *Foundations of Capitalism*, 239.

136. Ibid., 240, 239.

137. Ibid., 241.

138. Ibid., 244.

139. Boxer, *The Portuguese Seaborne Empire, 1415–1825* (New York: Knopf, 1969), 114.

140. Cox, *Foundations of Capitalism*, 244.

Chapter 5.   Capitalism from the English Revolution
to the Twentieth Century

1. Cox, *Foundations of Capitalism*, 288.

2. Ibid., 288.

3. Ibid., 327, 230.

4. Cox, *Capitalism as a System*, 18.

5. Charles Davenant, *An Essay Upon the Probable Methods of Making a People Gainers in the Balance of Trade*, 2 pts., (London, 1689), 308–9, as cited in Cox, *Foundations of Capitalism*, 348–49.

6. Cox, *Foundations of Capitalism*, 329.

7. Ibid., 215.

8. Cox, *Caste, Class, and Race*, 339.

9. Cox, *Foundations of Capitalism*, 222.

10. Ibid., 325.

11. Gustav Schmoller, *The Mercantile System* (New York; Macmillan, 1897), 50–51, as cited in Cox, *Caste, Class, and Race*, 338.

12. Cox, *Foundations of Capitalism*, 356.

13. Albert O. Hirschman, *The Passions and the Interests: Political Arguments for Capitalism Before Its Triumph* (Princeton: Princeton University Press, 1977).

14. Perry Anderson, *Lineages of the Absolutist State* (London: Verso, 1979), 61.

15. Goubert, *Louis XIV and Twenty Million Frenchmen*, 125.

16. Ibid., 126.

17. Eric Williams, *From Columbus to Castro: The History of the Caribbean* (New York: Vintage, 1984), 161, 163.

18. Cox, *Foundations of Capitalism*, 322.

19. Ibid., 293.

20. Ibid., 295, 292, 293.

21. See Brenner, *Merchants and Revolution*, 204.

22. Jack A. Goldstone, *Revolution and Rebellion in the Early Modern World* (Berkeley: University of California Press, 1991), 79.

23. Cox, *Foundations of Capitalism*, 298.

24. Ibid., 314, 299, 217.

25. Ibid., 438.

26. Eric Hobsbawm, *The Age of Revolution, 1789–1848* (New York: Vintage, 1996), 30.

27. Cox, *Foundations of Capitalism*, 406.

28. Ibid., 408, 421.

29. Hobsbawn, *Age of Revoltution*, 33, 37.

30. Cox, *Foundations of Capitalism*, 443.

31. Ibid., 308. Still, throughout the sixteenth century, the Merchant Adventurers continued to carry Dutch woolens that must have adversely affected England's wool industry.

32. Ibid., 308.

33. Ibid.

34. Ibid., 310–11.

35. Giovanni Arrighi, *The Long Twentieth Century: Money, Power, and the Origins of Our Times* (London: Verso, 1994), 177–78.

36. It is worth noting on this subject that in his recent survey of world economic leaders of the past 700 years, Charles Kindleberger devoted a mere page to the topic of national agricultural performance. See Charles P. Kindleberger, *World Economic Primacy, 1500 to 1990* (New York: Oxford University Press, 1996), 26–27.

37. Cox, *Foundations of Capitalism*, 313.

38. Stanley B. Greenberg, *Race and State in Capitalist Development: Comparative Perspectives* (New Haven, Conn.: Yale University Press, 1980), 54.

39. Cox, *Foundations of Capitalism*, 458. However, as far as the Dutch republic is concerned, Cox's claim is a gross exaggeration. According to B. H. Slicher Van Bath, in the mid-sixteenth century, Dutch grain imports were less than 15% of the nation's total consumption of grain. "The Rise of Intensive Husbandry in the Low Countries," in *Britain and the Netherlands*, ed. J. S Bromley and E. H. Kossman, (London: Chatto & Windus, 1960), 149.

40. Cox, *Foundations of Capitalism*, 72.

41. Ralph Davis, *The Rise of the Atlantic Economies* (Ithaca, N.Y.: Cornell University Press, 1973), 315.

42. E. M. Carus-Wilson, "Trends in the Export of English Woollens in the Fourteenth Century," in *Medieval Merchant Venturers: Collected Studies* (London: Methuen, 1967), 244, ff.1.

43. Cox, *Foundations of Capitalism*, 459, 461.

44. E. J. Hobsbawm, "The British Standard of Living, 1790–1850," in *Labouring Men: Studies in the History of Labour* (New York: Basic Books, 1964), 64–104, 65.

45. Cox, *Capitalism as a System*, 214.

46. Ibid., 218.

47. Cox, *Capitalism and American Leadership*, 128.

48. Ibid., 29, 4, 11.

49. Ibid., 10–11, 23.

50. On the subject of the possible role that American underconsumption of its products may have played in the Great Depression, John Kenneth Galbraith claims that the "high production of the twenties did not, as some have suggested, outrun the wants of the people. . . . [T]here is no evidence that their desire for automobiles, clothing, travel, recreation, or even food was sated" (p. 173). Yet the importance of expanding mass demand for the maintenance of capitalist profit cannot be dismissed by the mere affirmation that America still wanted to make purchases in the late 1920s; for it masks the fact that desires and abilities are separated by means and that the American "people" are divided into classes, one for which desires and abilities are customarily distinct, and another for which the two are bridged as a matter of course. Galbraith himself highlights two trends that illustrate the class dimension of American demand in the late 1920s: one, that while "output per worker in manufacturing industries increased by about 43 per cent . . . between 1919 and 1929 . . . [w]ages, salaries, and prices all remained comparatively stable, or in any case underwent no comparable increase" (p. 175); and two, that the "5 per cent of the population with the highest incomes in that year [1929] received approximately one third of all personal income" (p. 177). Both trends were related: the consequence of rising corporate earnings throughout the 1920s was that the average American could not purchase "durable consumers' goods such as cars, dwellings, home furnishings, and the like" (p. 175). The demand for these goods was largely provided by middle-class and wealthy Americans, the very people who, as Galbraith noted, pocketed an unprecedented portion of the nation's earned income in the 1920s. Given this quintessentially capitalist contradiction, it was only a matter of time before American demand for durable consumer goods would reach its limit, unless firms had the uncharacteristic foresight to lower the prices of their goods. Such was

not the case. Yet, as we all know, price reductions did come in the wake of the stock market crash, but by then, few were those with the funds to take advantage of the savings. See John Kenneth Galbraith, *The Great Crash, 1929* (Boston: Houghton Mifflin, 1988).

51. Galbraith, for example, puts the number of American investors at no higher than "one and a half million people." *Great Crash,* 78.

52. Cox, *Capitalism and American Leadership,* 32, 34, 29.

53. Ibid., 58.

54. Ibid., 41, 43, 79, 24.

55. Ibid., 88.

56. W. Arthur Lewis, *Economic Survey, 1919–1939* (Philadelphia: Blakiston, 1950), 57.

57. Cox, *Capitalism and American Leadership,* 46.

58. Lewis, *Economic Survey,* 58, 57.

59. Ibid., 56, 58.

60. Cox, *Capitalism and American Leadership,* 47.

61. Lewis, *Economic Survey,* 56.

62. Cox, *Capitalism and American Leadership,* 46.

63. Lewis, *Economic Survey,* 52.

64. Ibid., 59.

65. Cox, *Capitalism and American Leadership,* 51.

66. Ibid., 52.

67. Ibid., 100–101.

68. Paul A. Baran and Paul M. Sweezy, *Monopoly Capital: An Essay on the American Economic and Social Order* (New York: Monthly Review Press, 1966), 210.

69. Ibid., 153.

70. Cox, *Capitalism and American Leadership,* 121.

71. Ibid., 164.

72. Baran and Sweezy, *Monopoly Capital,* 192.

73. Ibid., 192. Cox made the same point in *Capitalism as a System,* 245.

74. Cox, *Capitalism and American Leadership,* 122.

75. Ibid., 133.

76. Ibid., 123.

77. Ibid., 146, 168.

78. Ibid., 121.

79. Paul Kennedy, *The Rise and Fall of the Great Powers: Economic Change and Military Conflict from 1500 to 2000* (New York: Vintage, 1989), 373.

80. Martin Bauml Duberman, *Paul Robeson* (New York: Ballantine, 1989), 189.

81. Cox, *Capitalism and American Leadership,* xix.

82. Philip S. Foner, *Organized Labor and the Black Worker* (New York: International Publishers, 1982), 309–10.

83. Cox, *Capitalism and American Leadership*, 231.

84. Ibid., 235.

85. Ibid., 242–43.

86. Ibid., 230, 253.

87. Ibid., 245–46.

88. Cox, *Capitalism as a System*, 195.

Chapter 6.   Black Nationalism and Socialism

1. The term "African-American" does not help matters for it implies that there is a unifying culture shared by all of those of some visible African descent. Many contest this assumption.

2. Cox, *Race Relations*, 196, 264.

3. Ibid., 194–95.

4. Ibid., 263.

5. Ibid., 197, 281.

6. Ibid., 238–41.

7. Another remark on Cox's use of the term "lower-class" is in order here. As I pointed out in an earlier footnote, it was/is generally understood in black communities that while all lower-class people are working-class people, all working-class people are not lower-class people. That is to say, frequently the label did not reflect one's *actual* economic condition, but rather one's moral and esthetic appearance. It is for this reason that the few black skilled workers, and not an insignificant number of those unskilled, consider themselves roughly the middle class equals of white collar workers and professionals. Drake and Cayton described the distinction that working-class Blacks made between middle class and lower class like this: "A part of the working class constitutes the backbone of Bronzeville's 'middle' *social* class, identified by its emphasis on the symbols of 'respectability' and 'success.' The largest part of this working class is in a 'lower' *social* position, however, characterized by less restraint and without a consuming drive for the symbols of higher social prestige. Desertion and illegitimacy, juvenile delinquency, and fighting and roistering are common in lower-class circles." *Black Metropolis*, 523. Today, we frequently hear working-class and middle-class Blacks refer to that behavior as "ghetto." Similarly, it is not uncommon to hear white working-class and middle-class people refer to some of their ranks as "poor white trash" or "trailer trash." It seems, then, that there are few self-labeled working-class Americans left. In any event, I believe that

Cox employed the term "lower-class" in the manner that we have just described, although he knew lower-class people to be members of the working-class as he defined it.

8. Perhaps the best-known (and most controversial) example of this type of thinking is found in Daniel Patrick Moynihan's *The Negro Family: The Case for National Action* (Washington, D.C.: Office of Planning and Research, United States Department of Labor, 1965). The full text and commentaries are included in *The Moynihan Report and the Politics of Controversy,* ed. Lee Rainwater and William L. Yancey, (Cambridge: MIT Press, 1967).

9. Cox, *Race Relations,* 171–72.

10. Cox's thinking about both the slave and "lower-class" black families is accurately described by Eugene Genovese: "Historians and sociologists, black and white, have been led astray in two ways. First, they have read the story of the twentieth-century black ghettos backward in time and have assumed a historical continuity with slavery days. Second, they have looked too closely at slave law and at the externals of family life and not closely enough at the actual temper of the quarters." *Roll, Jordan, Roll: The World the Slaves Made* (New York: Pantheon, 1974), 450–51.

11. The recognition of slave unions, slaveholders came to realize, could be effectively used for social control. "Although the slaveholders sometimes encouraged," remarked John W. Blassingame, "monogamous mating arrangements because of their religious views, they generally did it to make it easier to discipline their slaves. A black man, they reasoned, who loved his wife and children was less likely to be rebellious or to run away than would a 'single' slave. The simple threat of being separated from his family was generally sufficient to subdue the most rebellious 'married' slave." *The Slave Community: Plantation Life in the Antebellum South* (New York: Oxford University Press, 1972), 80. However, so as not to endure the sight of the abuse of their loved ones, many slaves preferred to seek "spouses" on other plantations. "So many slaves had 'broad" wives," comments Genovese, "that they may well have constituted the majority in some sections of the South." *Roll, Jordan, Roll,* 472. Of course, the drawback to such family arrangements was that it doubled the possibility of the sale of one of the slave partners, not to mention their children.

12. Manning Marable, *Race, Reform, and Rebellion: The Second Reconstruction in Black America, 1945–1990* (Jackson: University of Mississippi Press, 1991), 110–11.

13. Cox, *Race Relations,* 100, 141.

14. In light of the differences in political tone between the two halves of *Race Relations,* I am inclined to believe that Cox may have intended to write two works instead of one. Without documentary evidence, however, this statement is only speculation.

15. Cox, *Race Relations,* 142, 181, 177–80.

16. Ibid., 201. I obviously take the last sentence of this passage as an exaggeration on Cox's part. I believe that he intended it to deny the claim made by black nationalists and other skeptics of color that the American government and other American institutions did not take responsibility for their own racist beliefs and practices.

17. Ibid., 280

18. Oliver C. Cox, "The Program of Negro Civil Rights Organizations," *Journal of Negro Education* (summer 1951): 354–66.

19. Ibid., 360. Later in the same article (p. 365), Cox added: "Because the NAACP has now become largely burocratized [*sic*], rendering its important service in the struggle for civil liberties through respectable channels, it is in danger of becoming conservative and rightist."

20. See, among other such studies, Charles Murray, *Losing Ground: American Social Policy, 1950–1980* (New York: Basic Books, 1984).

21. Cox, "Programs of Negro Civil Rights Organizations," 363.

22. Cox, *Race Relations,* 211.

23. William K. Tabb, *The Political Economy of the Black Ghetto* (New York: W. W. Norton, 1970), 22–23. To this description, Tabb added two other criteria which must be present in a given relationship in order for it to be considered a colonial one: "There are two key relationships which must be proved to exist before the colonial analogy can be accepted: (1) economic control and exploitation, and (2) political dependence and subjugation. Both necessitate separation and inferior status. . . . An historical comparison of the forms colonialism has taken, and a description of the place of blacks in the American economy make clear that internal colonialism is an apt description of the place blacks have held and continue to hold in our society" (pp. 23, 24).

24. Cox, *Race Relations,* 274.

25. Cox, *Caste, Class, and Race,* 572.

26. Cox, *Race Relations,* 275, 278.

27. Ibid., 279.

28. James Boggs, *Racism and the Class Struggle: Further Pages from a Black Worker's Notebook* (New York: Monthly Review Press, 1970), 13.

29. Here is how Cox described the South African system of old: "The planned racial dichotomization of South Africa is revealing. Here the policy-making whites have sought to utilize even more basic means of keeping the races socially isolated. Their policy is to prevent the acculturation of the natives, a plan which is obviously expected to accomplish both the territorial and cultural segregation of the natives and thus ensure their continued exploitation. The policy is conducted under the anthropological euphemism 'that the natives should be allowed to develop along their own lines.' " *Caste, Class, and Race,* 369–70.

30. Cox, *Race Relations,* 218.

31. Ibid., 220–21. It should be noted that this remark seems to imply that capitalist society requires an unassimilated or out-group. In this case, Cox's use of the word, "unacculturated" rather than, "unassimilated," seems quite deliberate.

32. Stokely Carmichael (Kwame Toure) and Charles Hamilton, *Black Power: The Politics of Liberation in America* (New York: Vintage, 1967), 53.

33. This statement should not be taken to mean that people of color in ruling-class situation of race relations have enjoyed social mobility without political struggle. Anyone familiar with the history of the Caribbean, for example, knows that this was not the case. Still, in comparison to the intransigence of Whites in bipartite situations of race relations, the path of social mobility for people of color in ruling-class situations of race relations has been less rocky.

34. Cox, "Leadership Among Negroes in the United States," 263. However, as we noted earlier, Cox had greatly underestimated the racial appeal of Garvey's United Negro Improvement Association in the Caribbean.

35. Cox, *Race Relations,* 289, 301.

36. Cox, "Leadership Among Negroes in the United States, "233, 235.

37. Ibid., 229.

38. Cox, *Race Relations,* 294, 295.

39. Barbara Ehrenreich, *Fear of Falling: The Inner Life of the Middle Class* (New York: Harper Perennial, 1990), 78, 80.

40. Ibid., 15, 81.

41. Ellis Cose, *The Rage of a Privileged Class* (New York: Harper Perennial, 1993), 44, 38.

42. Andrew Hacker, *Two Nations: Black and White, Separate, Hostile, Unequal* (New York: Ballantine, 1992), 19.

43. Robin M. Williams Jr., "Prejudice and Society," in *The American Negro Reference Book,* ed. John P. Davis (Englewood Cliffs: Prentice-Hall, 1966), 728, as cited in Carmichael and Hamilton, *Black Power,* 8.

44. C. L. R. James, "Black Power," in *The C. L. R. James Reader,* ed. Anna Grimshaw (Oxford: Blackwell, 1992), 367.

45. Ibid., 372.

46. James told his comrades in the Trotskyist Socialist Workers Party that the "Negro must be won for socialism. There is no other way out for him in America or elsewhere. But he must be won on the basis of his own experience and his own activity. There is no other way for him to learn, nor for that matter, for any other group of toilers. . . . The Negro will have the satisfaction of supporting his own movement. The constant domination of whites, whether by the bourgeoisie or in workers' movements, more and more irks the Negro." He then admonished them: "What the Party must

avoid at all costs is looking upon such a movement as a recruiting ground for party members, something to be 'captured' or manipulated for the aims of the party, or something which it supports spasmodically at the time it needs something in return. The party should frankly and openly endorse such a movement, urge Negroes to join it, assist the movement in every way and, while pointing out the political differences and showing that revolutionary socialism is the ultimate road, work side by side to influence this movement by criticism and activity combined. It is in this way and on the basis of a common struggle, with the party always helping but never seeking to manipulate the movement, that the confidence of the Negro movement be gained by revolutionary socialism, without raising the impracticable slogan of self-determination." C. L. R. James, "Preliminary Notes on the Negro Question," in *C. L. R. James on the 'Negro Question,'* ed. Scott McLemee (Jackson: University of Mississippi Press, 1996), 8, 9–10.

47. C. L. R. James, "The Revolutionary Answer to the Negro Problem in the USA," in *The C. L. R. James Reader,* ed. Anna Grimshaw (Oxford: Blackwell, 1992), 183.

48. Cox, *Capitalism as a System,* 190, 195.

49. Ibid., 190–91, 195.

50. Ibid., 194. Elsewhere in the same work (p. 188), Cox made an even more provocative claim about a related theme: "Workers at the head of a capitalist state are in an absurd position: they almost always assume the very attitudes and behavior of the displaced ruling class. This is because the established attitudes and behavior of national leaders are essentially socioeconomic, and not merely political. The class system, therefore, cannot be changed without revolutionizing the societal pattern itself."

51. Ibid., 195, 198.

52. Ibid., 198–99.

53. Ibid., 199.

54. Ibid., 241.

55. Oliver C. Cox, "Marxism: Looking Backward and Forward," *Monthly Review* 26 (June 1974): 58. Incidentally, he offered the same advice to "smaller countries" a decade earlier in *Capitalism as a System,* 242, 57.

56. On this variable, W. Arthur Lewis remarked that the "bigger the population the greater are the opportunities for specialization, not only of persons, but also of firms and of industries." He also added that "most industries gain advantage from operating in a country which is large enough to support a range of other industries, even if the average factory is small, because of the extent to which industries depend on each other either as sources of materials, components, and services, or else as purchasers of intermediate output or of by-products." *The Theory of Economic Growth* (Homewood, Ill.: Richard D. Irwin, 1955), 323, 324.

57. Ibid., 334, 340.

58. Joseph V. Stalin, *Collected Works,* vol. 10 (Moscow, 1946–52), 305, as cited in Ulam, *Stalin: The Man and His Era* (New York: Viking Press, 1973), 291. Elsewhere Stalin described collectivization in less euphemistic terms. Here, for example, is Ulam's paraphrase of a portion of Stalin's address to his "colleagues" at the July 1928 Plenum of the Central Committee: "How did they think that the industrialization was going to be financed? Everyone was enthusiastic about such projects as the Dneprostroi dam and hydroelectric station, the railway lines in Central Asia. Where was the government getting the means for such huge investments? They were getting them out of the peasant: by taxing him heavily, by making him *over*pay for commercial products he needs, by *under*paying him for grain and other agricultural products." *Stalin,* 304–5.

59. Joseph Schumpeter described such a position in these terms: "Whoever is prepared to relax this requirement and to accept either frankly undemocratic procedure or some method of securing formally decision by undemocratic means, thereby proves conclusively that he values other things more highly than he values democracy." *Capitalism, Socialism, and Democracy* (New York: Harper & Row, 1950), 237.

60. Cox, *Race Relations,* 295.

61. For example, we read in *Capitalism as a System* (p. 242), the following cryptic remark: "Unlike capitalist nations, socialist countries cannot plan to exploit other peoples' resources; they must look only to their own land and manpower."

62. To illustrate this point, we need only compare Soviet attitudes toward the peasantry (particularly toward the intentionally ill-defined *kulak* or "better-off" peasant) and European attitudes toward their former colonial subjects. For the former, see Ulam, *Stalin,* 249, 295. Hannah Arendt suggested as much in her preface to "Imperialism," the second part of *The Origins of Totalitarianism,* when she wrote: "Scholarly inquiry [on totalitarianism] has almost exclusively concentrated on Hitler's Germany and Stalin's Russia at the expense of their less harmful predecessors. Imperialist rule, except for the purpose of name-calling, seems half-forgotten . . . [although it] proved to contain nearly all the elements necessary for the subsequent rise of totalitarian movements and governments." Hannah Arendt, *The Origins of Totalitarianism* (San Diego: Harcourt, Brace, and Jovanovich, 1968), xxi.

63. Compare *Caste, Class, and Race,* 222–96, with *Race Relations,* 292–96.

64. Schumpeter, *Capitalism, Socialism, and Democracy,* 237.

65. Alfred G. Meyer explained this form of payment like this: "The system developed in the 1930s and still prevalent today customarily provides for a basic salary which is paid for individual output conforming to a gen-

eral production norm for the particular job performed. Substantial increments are paid for output exceeding the norm, whereas wage deductions
or other penalties may threaten those whose work does not come up to the
production standards." *The Soviet Political System: An Interpretation* (New York:
Random House, 1965), 428.

66. "Owing to lack of precise information," remarked Meyer on the matter of ethnic stratification in the former Soviet Union, "it would be extremely
difficult to construct a scale of relative status for Soviet nationalities, but we
probably are safe in asserting that both the official regime and popular
opinion attribute to the Great Russians a status roughly similar to that enjoyed by white Anglo-Saxon Protestants in the United States." Ibid., 52–53.

67. Horace B. Davis put that figure at 55 percent. He went on to add
that when this figure is added to those for Ukranians and Belorussians, "the
eastern Slavs ma[d]e up 77 percent of the Soviet population." *Toward a
Marxist Theory of Nationalism* (New York: Monthly Review Press, 1978), 92.

Index

CHRISTOPHER A. McAULEY is associate professor in the department of Black Studies at the University of California, Santa Barbara.